GunDigest BOOK OF HUNTING REVOLVERS

MAX PRASAC

Copyright ©2016 F+W Media, Inc.

All rights reserved. No portion of this publication may be reproduced or transmitted in any form or by any means, electronic or mechanical, including photocopy, recording, or any information storage and retrieval system, without permission in writing from the publisher, except by a reviewer who may quote brief passages in a critical article or review to be printed in a magazine or newspaper, or electronically transmitted on radio, television, or the Internet.

Published by

Gun Digest® Books, an imprint of F+W Media, Inc.
Krause Publications • 700 East State Street • Iola, WI 54990-0001
715-445-2214 • 888-457-2873
www.krausebooks.com

To order books or other products call toll-free 1-800-258-0929
or visit us online at www.gundigeststore.com

Cover photo by Max Prasac.
All photos by author except where noted.

ISBN-13: 978-1-4402-4607-4
ISBN-10: 1-4402-4607-6

Cover Design by Sandi Carpenter
Edited by Corey Graff

Printed in China

10 9 8 7 6 5 4 3 2 1

CONTENTS

About the Author	4
Acknowledgements	5
Dedication	6
Foreword	7
Handgun Hunting Today	8
No Stunt Hunting	16
Handgun Hunting Mechanics	22
Revolver Care and Feeding	28
.44 Magnum vs. .45 Colt	72
Sighting Systems	92
Revolver Holsters for the Field	102
Big-Game Hunting Revolvers	108
The .35s	152
The .40s	160
The .44s	168
The .45s	180
The .475s	196
The .50s	212
The Handgun Hunters	234

ABOUT THE AUTHOR

Max Prasac was born and raised in once-normal, sunny Southern California, spending most of his time in a local gun shop, the now-defunct Lock, Stock 'n Barrel of San Gabriel. But the real blame for his career trajectory can be laid squarely on the shoulders of his parents for giving him his first Daisy BB gun for his eighth Christmas, back in the early 1970s.

However, his handgun fixation began with the purchase of a Smith & Wesson C02 pellet pistol, followed soon by his first revolver, a gift from his father when he was barely in high school.

Prasac joined the National Rifle Association (NRA) as a junior member in the early 1980s and enlisted in the U.S. Marine Corps at the age of 17, where he served as a rifleman until being honorably discharged in the summer of 1986. He holds a bachelor's degree from George Washington University and has been writing professionally since the mid-'90s. Formerly, he spent a number of years as a contractor performing disaster relief work overseas, work that included de-mining and ordnance disposal, reconstruction, and running food relief convoys in war zones. Later, he contracted in the security sector.

Beginning his professional writing career on the automotive side of the publishing industry, Prasac later made the leap to outdoor writing. His professional affiliations include membership in North American Hunt Club, NRA and a board member of the Ruger Collectors' Association. He is a regular contributor to the NRA publications, including *American Hunter* magazine, as well as *Gun Digest the Magazine* and the author of *Big-Bore Revolvers* and *The Gun Digest Book of Ruger Revolvers*.

Max Prasac hunts whenever possible, making frequent trips to North Carolina to test firearms and loads on wild hogs. In the winter, he hunts deer and black bear and is almost exclusively a handgun hunter. He resides in northern Virginia with his wife, daughter, dogs, turtle and numerous large-caliber hunting revolvers.

ACKNOWLEDGMENTS

I would like to take this opportunity to thank the following people for making this book possible: my rock, Katica — who again put up with the ravings of a lunatic, Lana, Buddy and Fiona, Jack Huntington, Jason Menefee, John Parker, Vincent Ricardel, David Bradshaw, Bud Rummel, Larry Weishuhn, Ken Jorgensen, Mark Gurney, Kurt Hindle, the Ruger Collectors' Association, John Dougan, Larry Welch, the Lee Martins, John Linebaugh, Hamilton Bowen, Dick Casull, Scott Olmsted, Bill Vaznis, John Taffin, Bryce Towsley, Dr. Mark Key, Mike Rintoul and the whole cast of characters at Rintoul Enterprises, Mike and Rhett McNett and Double Tap Ammunition, Gary Smith, Tom Roach of Ultradot, Milt Turnage and the crew at Hog Heaven Outfitters, Craig Copeland, Rob Millette, Jim Schlender, Corey Graff, Wes Daems of 7x Leather, Sitka Gear, Dur Thomason, Kim Ralston, Mike Barranti of the Barranti Leather Company, Ken O'Neill, Veral Smith of LBT, Michael McCourry, Jim Tertin and Joby Goerges of Magnum Research, Ernest Holloway, Greg Wilburn, G. Needleman, Greg Wagner, Ashley Emerson of Garrett Cartridges of Texas, Dr. Larry Rogers, #9 Lake Outfitters, Lynn Thompson and Andy Smith of Cold Steel, "James from Jersey" Swidryk, Rich Pasquarello, Darrell Harper, Mike Giboney, Ross Seyfried, Mike Distin, Dan Smitchko of CEB Bullets, JJ Reich, Tim Sundles of Buffalo Bore Ammunition, Richard Muennink and the crew at Action Outdoor Adventures, and lastly Chad Kearny and Dr. Don Heath may you both Rest In Peace.

DEDICATION

To the inimitable Lana — life began with you.

FOREWORD

"Son, I shot him with what I had at the time ..."

Several years ago, I interviewed an old-time deputy sheriff from South Texas for an article I was writing about hunting with big-bore handguns. Years earlier, he had taken a Boone and Crockett white-tailed buck with his .45 Colt Peacemaker.

The way his story unfolded was, two prisoners had escaped from a local jail and run off into the nearby Brush Country. It was the middle of December, and the Texas deer hunting season and the local whitetail rut were in full swing. The deputy knew well the dense thorn and cactus thickets where the prisoners had supposedly disappeared. He frequently hunted deer on the ranch.

As he was walking through a rugged piece of brush country looking for tracks of the escaped prisoners, a huge buck jumped up right in front of him. The deputy, almost without thinking, pulled the .45 Colt revolver from its holster and shot the monster deer. As soon as he did, he realized he had given away his presence and position. Fast thinking, he immediately hollered, "Take that you dirty no count escapee!"

No sooner had he shouted than one of the prisoners raised up from behind a clump of prickly pear, hands held high in submission. Almost immediately the other escapee appeared from behind a gnarly, ancient mesquite tree, his hands reaching for the sky. Later, the sheriff learned both escaped prisoners thought the deputy had shot the other one and the survivor had best give himself up before he, too, got shot.

"What did you do after they surrendered?" I asked.

"Made them gut and load my deer, and then I took them back to jail. Always loved that old thumb-buster," he said, as he handed me the nickel-plated, stag-gripped big-bore handgun.

When it comes to big-bore handguns we've come a long way, not only in terms of great ammo but also the guns themselves. Today, we have the best possible handguns, as well as commercially available ammo, bullets and powders for those who prefer to load their own.

My first big-bore handgun was a World War I Remington Model 1911 in .45 Auto. Not what I would consider these days an ideal hunting handgun, but at the time it was all I had — just like the old deputy. That old semi-auto was soon replaced by a succession of various revolvers I personally consider true hunting guns — revolvers in such calibers as .44 Mag, .454 Casull, .45 Colt, .460 S&W Mag, .480 Ruger, .500 S&W Mag and others in between and even beyond.

With mine, particularly my longtime favorite, a Ruger Super Blackhawk Hunter in .44 Mag, I've taken numerous big-game species in North America and Africa, from elk and African antelope down to the Southwest's unique javelina. With other calibers and rounds I've taken Alaskan brown bear and monstrous American bison. Hunting with larger-caliber revolvers, I've never felt over- or under-gunned.

The words that follow were written by "someone who has been there and done that" and who'll do "to ride the river with." Max Prasac has the technical knowledge and experience of shooting and hunting with big-bore handguns, but more importantly, he is passionate about them.

The first time I met Prasac was at a NRA Convention where we were introduced by our mutual friend, Gary Smith, another big-bore "practitioner." I knew immediately I was going to like this guy. Talk turned quickly to hunting revolvers, comparing experiences, and discussing bullet choices and loads. Later that evening we shared tales of great stags pursued, those we bested and those that bested us.

The information within this book is accurate and honest. It is based on science, but it is also practical and tempered by personal experience. Enjoy and learn.

— *Larry Weishuhn*

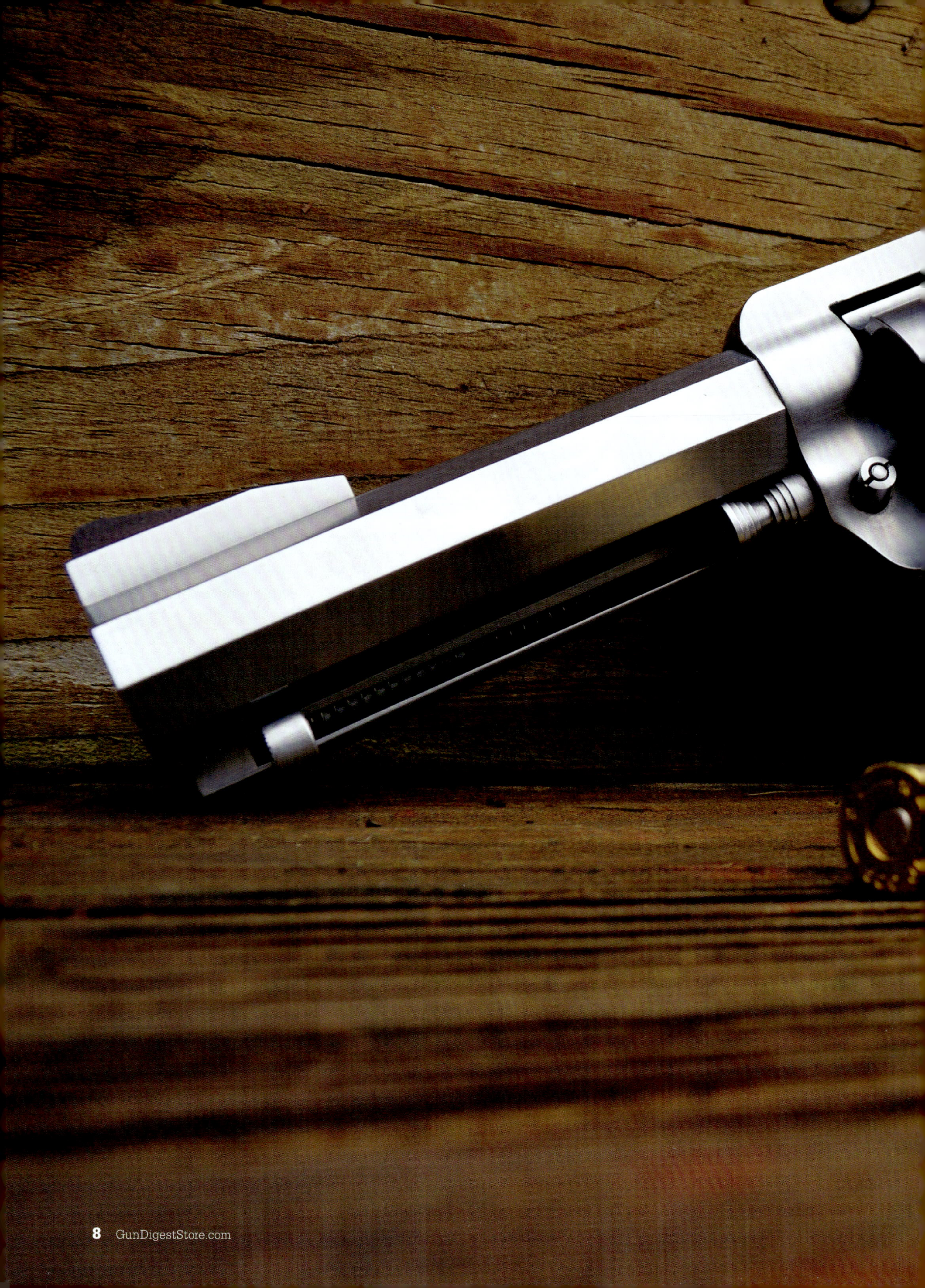

CHAPTER 1

handgun hunting today

The day I began writing this book, I was motivated to put ideas I have been carrying around for years on paper for you to use and enjoy. This book has been a long time in coming, and is frankly overdue for this niche we call big-game handgun hunting. It is a book I have been contemplating and creating in my mind for years. It needed to be written, rain or shine.

While there have been books written on the topic over the last few decades, they are, in a word, dated. This is not a criticism but an acknowledgement that we need to take our sport, our way of life, into the 21st century. And it's not to slight the pioneers of handgun hunting such as Al Goerg, Larry Kelly and Lee Jurras, to name but a few. Rest assured, you will see some of these names mentioned in these pages, and some rather frequently, as their contributions cannot be ignored by anyone truly interested in the topic at hand.

You will notice that some of the handgun-hunting luminaries are not only discussed, but I have also interviewed them. As a result, their words, thoughts and insights grace the following pages.

In my two previous books, I set aside a number of pages dedicated to the topic of handgun hunting. I've done that here, too, and like before it will be limited to hunting with revolvers and not include the single-shot specialty pistols. In my humble opinion, the revolver, in both single- and double-action form, personifies the very term "handgun," as it is truly a handheld tool that is not saddled with an overly long barrel requiring a bipod or chambered in a bottleneck rifle cartridge. Perhaps I'm a bit prejudiced.

The author took this wild hog with the .454 version of the new Super Blackhawk, stoked with Garrett Cartridge's new 365-grain .45 Colt +P load.

Handgun hunting for me is singularly challenging, exceedingly rewarding and absolutely exciting. While I practice at what some would consider longer ranges with a wheelgun, for me getting close — real close — captures the essence of handgun hunting. I want to smell the bad breath of my quarry.

My own handgun exploits began long ago in a sleepy suburb of Los Angeles called Pasadena, California. The house my parents bought when they migrated west from the bitter cold of Milwaukee, Wisconsin, was a typical California ranch style home, sitting on a rather large half-acre lot. The large number of trees and shrubbery fueled my imagination, and with my CO2 pellet pistol I turned that backyard into Alaska, the deepest, darkest recesses of Africa, the Western plains, the Southeastern swamps. Little did I know that what started in the '70s in my parents' backyard would become my lifelong passion and obsession.

The first revolver I would come to call my own was handed down to me by my late father. It was a Smith & Wesson Model 36-1 in .38 Special. My imagination made up for its lack of bore size.

Immediately following high school, the Marine Corps distracted me from the early to mid-1980s, but when I got out, the big-bore revolver bug bit me, and hard. A few .44 Magnums passed through my hands from a number of manufacturers in those days, as did my first foray into handloading.

In college, I dreamed of owning one of the berserk wildcats that a gentleman in Cody, Wyoming, was producing on Ruger frames. That man was John Linebaugh, and he was creating previously unthinkable power levels in a handheld package. Freedom Arms' Model 83 in .454 Casull, the brainchild of none other than Dick Casull, also had my adrenaline pumping. I remember thinking I would someday be able to afford some of these revolvers. (I have them now, but still can't afford them.)

Then one day, back from an overseas stint as an aid worker in an unfriendly corner of the world, I stopped into my local childhood gun store, the Lock, Stock 'n Barrel, to see how the guys were doing and to see if there was anything interesting in their display case. And that's when I found it—the all-new .480 Ruger Super Redhawk! I was drawn to that thing as if under a spell. Such a big cartridge! But could a handgun really harness all that power? I would soon find out as I purchased it on the spot. Not long afterward, the Super Redhawk spilled its first blood, a couple of Florida wild hogs. There was no turning back as I sought more and more power.

So deep are the misconceptions about power minimums to cleanly take large game, that I am often faced with defending my choice in hunting firearms. The term "stunt" is often bandied about in conjunction with the notion of hunting dangerous game with a handgun, from staunch doubters citing minimum energy levels as if the calculated figures somehow had some magical influence on the effectiveness of any given cartridge. My frequent arguments with these people have made me a rather serious student and layman of terminal ballistics, a topic near and dear to me. I find myself defending my hunting firearm choices not only among my peers, but also in print. However, that reality has never deterred me. I will humbly keep fighting.

In these pages I delve into that oft-misunderstood topic of terminal ballistics. Having said that, I am not going to reinvent the wheel. I have written extensively on this topic in my first book, *Big-Bore Revolvers*. Of course, I have updated and added more material in the ensuing years.

Dur Thomason took this beautiful buck with his Freedom Arms 353 in .357 Magnum loaded with 140-grain XPBs. The shot was 145 yards!

We will look at bullet design, conduct penetration tests and, most importantly, relay exciting big-game kills. I will again pit the .44 Magnum against the .45 Colt, as apparently there are still those out there who doubt the .45 Colt's superiority.

This time around, I used an independent lab to conduct my testing, and had two identical revolvers built to eliminate any perceived or unfair advantages one might have over the other. Same platform, barrel length (and brand), twist rate, cylinder length, etc. I want to put this topic to bed, even though there will always be skeptics irrespective of the preponderance of evidence to the contrary. But such is human nature, and on we march.

Also covered in this book are practice techniques, field positions and how to graduate to actual fieldcraft. When you choose to hunt with a handgun, you choose to really hunt, in the literal sense of the word. Fieldcraft is a missing art among many hunters, but not the handgun hunter. He chooses a difficult platform to master and has to get close to his game. With the advent of better technology, we as a society are becoming lazy and addicted to convenience. I consider the handgun hunt to be a more "pure" practice of the art of pursuing game.

Throughout the book you will be treated to vignettes about some of your favorite industry leaders, handgun hunters and innovators. I will highlight the more popular calibers and platforms and some of my personal favorites. My focus will be contemporary revolvers, with the occasional examination of revolvers that are no longer produced but remain significant in their influence on our sport, hobby and life.

I'll introduce you to some of the new handgun-hunting leaders of our time, and you'll hear tales of their more interesting hunts. Many are friends I've made over the years who share my passion for doing things the hard way.

You'll see some of the finest hunting handguns ever made. You will also get a whole slew of photographic proof that a big-bore revolver, loaded correctly and in the right hands, is a formidable killer of even the largest and most dangerous game this planet has to offer.

I'll examine the revolver as a backup for animal protection. You will note that many stories of bear attacks in the wild involve a hunter skinning out an animal when a bear moved in to reap the benefits of the hunter's marksmanship, only to find that the hunter's rifle was propped up against a tree, conveniently out of reach. At times like these, it's nice to have a big-bore hanging from your belt — a leather-wrapped insurance policy, if you will.

When I head into the game fields with a big revolver strapped on, I never feel under-gunned or at some sort of disadvantage. In fact, I've felt downright awkward the few times I've actually ventured out with a rifle. Fortunately, this doesn't happen very often.

Yes, it is hard to master a hard-recoiling revolver. Yes, it is harder to become proficient with a firearm that doesn't give you the advantage of a buttstock. Indeed, handgun hunting is more difficult than with a scoped rifle. So why do it? The thrill and challenge have no equal as far I am concerned, and I know you, the reader, are more than well aware of what I speak. You get it. That is why you are reading this.

Through this book I challenge you to go afield with a handgun this coming deer season instead of a long gun. At the very least, if you've tried handgun hunting but haven't yet succeeded, you can expect to gain insights here to take your hunting to that next level.

I watched a video clip some years ago of a well-known professional hunter (PH) in Africa who was facing a charging Cape buffalo. The PH was armed with a large English double rifle chambered in .600 Nitro Express, a cartridge that dimensionally resembles a rather large cigar. Well, this cool customer took a careful bead on the hell-bent bovine that was quickly closing the distance. The PH let the right barrel rip, a solid body shot resulting.

When a "dead" animal of this size reanimates, you had better be on your game. The author was forced to put the animal down with his .500 Maximum.

Despite the thousands upon thousands of foot-pounds of muzzle energy (energy that is calculated and not measured) being administered by the 900-grain bullet, the buffalo didn't even miss a beat and it continued its beeline of destruction. And despite this mythical level of horsepower, the buffalo required a solid central nervous system (CNS aka brain) hit from the second barrel to stop the onslaught. So close was that buff to the PH that the rifleman had to sidestep the crashing creature as it plowed terra firma, stopping cold at the hunter's feet. What does it all mean? Well, one incident is statistically insignificant; however, maybe this muzzle energy thing is meaningless.

This whitetail buck was shot at 60 yards by Kim Ralston, using a Field Grade Freedom Arms M83 in .44 Mag. The gun sports a 7.5-inch barrel and custom mesquite burl grips. It's topped with a FX II 4x Leupold scope, TSOB mount and Weigand mag rings. He was shooting a Hornady 240 XTP over 24.5 grains of H110. Photo by K. Ralston

On the opposite end of the spectrum, I was witness to a rather large bison — much larger in stature than the aforementioned Cape buffalo — shot by a friend with a revolver. The bison reacted to the shot as if a large truck had just run into it at 80 mph. The revolver was a .500 Linebaugh, slinging 525-grain bullets at a scorching 1,150 fps from the muzzle. That calculates out to somewhere around 1,400 foot-pounds of muzzle energy, which is rather anemic by dangerous-game hunting standards.

Despite the bison's CNS remaining intact, one shot brought the one-ton beast down rather quickly. While that's also statistically insignificant, it's interesting nonetheless. You see, it's another example of how muzzle energy can be misleading.

Many myths abound that have been perpetuated by the gun press over the decades to the point that they have become convention. It's time to debunk some of those myths as they apply to handgun hunting. I will show you in no uncertain terms that as long as you do your part, a properly loaded big-bore revolver is more than up to the task of taking the biggest and baddest animal that Mother Nature has to offer.

It won't be easy to master, but if you dedicate yourself to the disciplined practice necessary to become truly proficient, your handgun will serve you well. It's not a discipline that will allow you to blow the dust off of your firearm the day before the season opener and expect success. No, you will need to practice year round, but you will enjoy the practice and gain much satisfaction.

So, pull up a chair, put your feet up and settle in. This ride will take you to places you thought impossible. You may even catch a whiff of burnt smokeless powder, a slight ringing in your ears and the bellow of a large bovine drawing its last breath.

Welcome to big-game handgun hunting in the 21st Century!

This 1,400-pound water buffalo cow was no match for the JRH-built Ruger .500 Maximum slinging 525-grain Cast Performance WFNs.

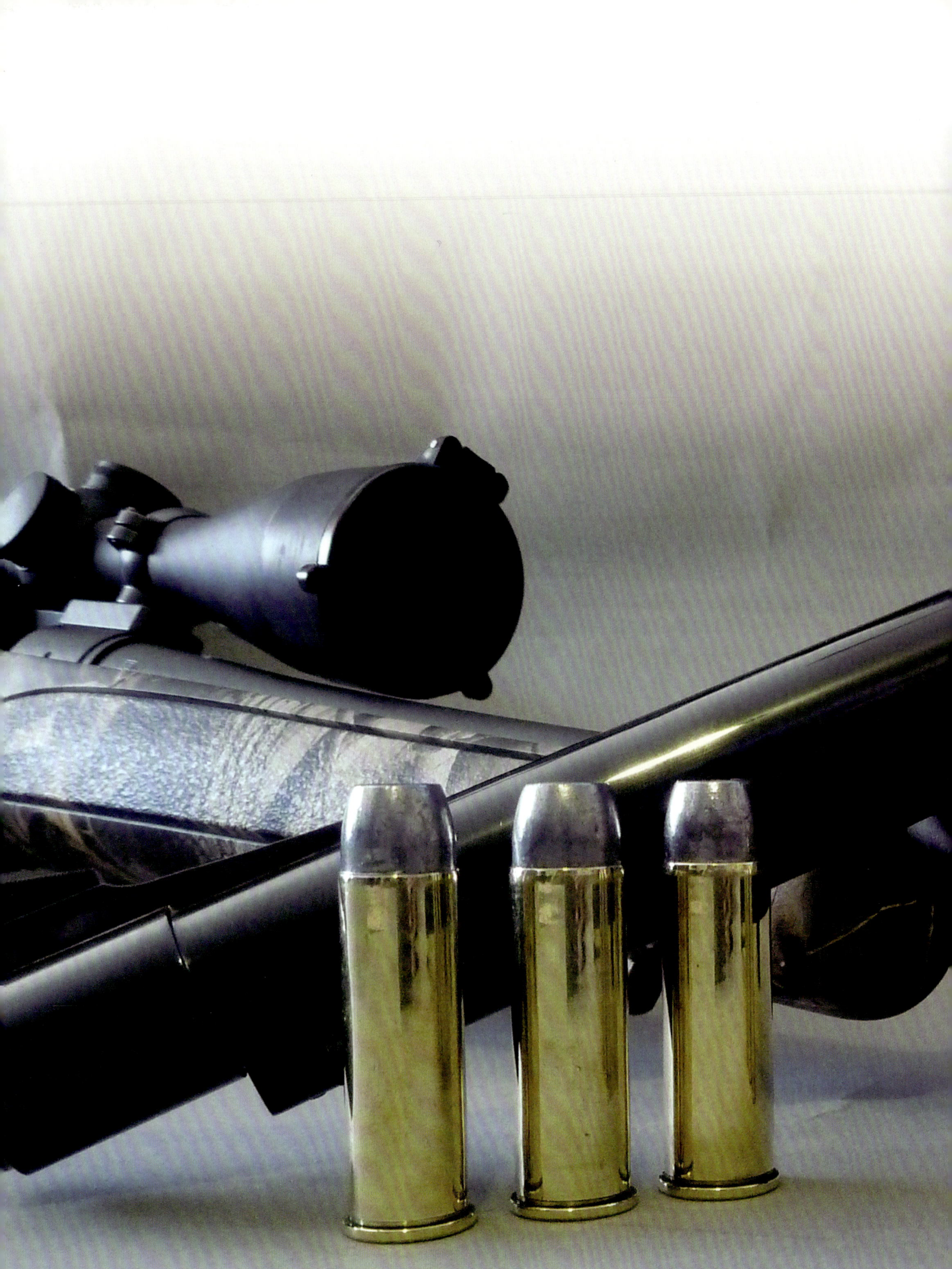

CHAPTER 2

no stunt hunting

There are few things in life that I allow to upset me (aside from traffic and bad weather). Life is too short, and most times it's just not worth it. However, I recently read a post on an Internet gun and hunting site by a man whose opinion I have always accepted and respected. This gentleman declared that the .45-70 Government makes for a poor dangerous-game cartridge. He went on to ask, "How many PHs in Africa are using the .45-70 for client hunter backup duty?"

As an experienced big-game handgun hunter, that question struck me as particularly offensive. That's because revolver caliber, bullet and load combinations that I would consider more than adequate for big and dangerous game in many cases actually mimic the .45-70 loads of old. This doesn't even take into consideration the advances we have made in the realm of bullets and powders that make the .45-70 a lot more capable than when it was an old black-powder round. So, by deductive reasoning, if the .45-70 is inadequate, that means the big-bore revolvers we now use are woefully inadequate, as well.

This rationale brings my blood to a boil. I can accept ignorance to a degree, but when there is a topic I am not well versed in, I default to silence, observation and research, steering clear of making declarative statements on the Internet. However, it's a brave, new online world, where accessibility and anonymity has created a new and unique culture where unsubstantiated statements are made and the veracity of such claims are largely unverifiable. There is no big- or dangerous-game animal on the face of this earth that revolvers have not taken cleanly — not barely, not by the skin of the teeth, not merely adequately, but cleanly and decisively. Hunting big game with a revolver is no stunt.

In his seminal piece, "The Ultimate Sport, Handgunning Cape Buffalo!" from the April 1986 issue of *Guns & Ammo* magazine, Ross Seyfried stated: "I am offended by the argument that this was a crazy stunt, or that I was obsessed with some death wish. I hadn't the slightest intention of getting scratched. As a cattle rancher, I have had barehanded wars with more cattle than most people have eaten, watched the bovines move, react and try to kill. I had hunted buffalo for several years before, studied their ways and their anatomy."

Seyfried's article should have opened a lot of eyes to the feasibility of a revolver as a big- and dangerous-game hunting tool. I also have trouble accepting the conventional attitudes toward big-game handgun hunters. Myths permeate what can only be called "conventional wisdom," but who decided long ago that muzzle energy was somehow a determinant of terminal effectiveness? We may never know, and I suspect it doesn't really matter at this point.

I have heard handgun hunting called a stunt on many occasions, particularly when large and dangerous game is in question. I go out of my way to correct these perceptions at every opportunity. I feel it is one of my duties as an ambassador of the sport. The problem is that so-called conventional wisdom is often rife with misperceptions, myths and a healthy dose of bovine excrement.

The one myth that is routinely repeated and regurgitated is muzzle energy as a determinant of lethality. I cannot overstate with enough enthusiasm just how irrelevant muzzle energy is to putting down game. Muzzle energy is not measurable. Muzzle energy is calculated. Muzzle energy sells ammunition. There, I said it. It's a good marketing ploy as more efficiency, more horsepower, more miles per gallon, more watts, and more fill-in-the-blank sells products. That is human nature, and anyone in marketing will tell you this with a straight face. If some is good, more is better — More's Law.

Well, I'm here to tell you this is hogwash. Being unprepared, irrespective of weapon choice, might qualify as a stunt. Or making a bad shot — like putting a 500-grain bullet from a .458 Lott into the belly of a Cape buffalo, resulting in one hell of a rodeo — that could be called a stunt.

However, loaded properly — you will hear this caveat frequently from me in these pages — your big-bore revolver is more than up to the task of taking down any game animal you choose. Penetration is your greatest ally, and penetration is something revolvers can deliver in spades, particularly when using good bullets (as in, non-expanding types). Ignoring the perceived shortcomings of the big-bore revolver, and keeping an open mind and equally open eyes, you can see for yourself that a properly loaded big-bore handgun is not a minimum standard for big-game hunting, but a viable alternative to a high-powered rifle.

Lynn Thompson of Cold Steel fame took this bull elephant with a Freedom Arms .454 Casull. Was it a stunt? Absolutely not!
Photo by L. Thompson

Greg Wilburn shot this buck with his Ruger .41 Magnum Hunter using one 250-grain hardcast bullet at 50 yards. Photo by G. Wilburn

Really, big game is a showcase for the capability of a cartridge. When going up against an animal weighing 1,000 pounds or more, you'd better have a capable bullet and load combination. I've taken a number of bovines and have been witness to even more being killed and have come to some conclusions based on my observations.

A properly loaded .44 Magnum, .45 Colt or .454 Casull are more than enough to kill a Cape buffalo, water buffalo or other bovine. With the right load, your bullets may pass all the way through the animal and, by default, produce a large wound channel. Remember that expanding rifle bullets rely on expansion to make a large wound channel, but the act of expanding arrests a bullet's forward motion much like a parachute.

A .45 Colt already makes a big hole without the need to expand and without the penetration limitation caused by expansion. That said, the .50 calibers (and the .475s to a lesser extent) offer even more terminal "ability," for lack of a better term. I have seen water buffalo run off without missing a beat after being hit perfectly by a .44 Magnum, but there is a physical reaction when similarly hit with the .500 JRH, .500 Linebaugh, .500 Maximum or .500 Smith & Wesson. In some cases it was obvious something of significance had hit them. This is where you can clearly see the virtues of the .50 calibers, when the game gets really large and really tough.

However, the same can't be said for smaller game where .50 calibers simply aren't required. I often hear sentiments about .50 calibers not killing deer any better than a properly loaded .44 Magnum. I tend to agree, but add 1,000 pounds to that animal and tell me how similarly they kill. This is where the .50s really shine.

Those who assail big-game hunting with a revolver as being some sort of stunt have undoubtedly never used or witnessed one used on large game. Also, if one is incapable of shooting a big-bore revolver well, which is often the case, they should not impose their limitations on others. I simply ask you to approach this topic with an open mind.

HE CHAMPIONED THE BIG BORES:
DR. DONALD HEATH

The late Dr. Donald "Ganyana" Heath led a life of intrigue and adventure. He also had the distinction of having demonstrated the viability of handgun hunting to the government officials of his native Zimbabwe (Rhodesia) who were responsible for deciding the hunting laws of that nation. He advanced the case for big-bore revolvers with panache, and for that we are grateful.

In his own words:

I was born at a small gold mine in rural Rhodesia, and hunting was the normal way my Dad put meat on the table. By the time I was 8 years old, attacks on isolated homesteads by communist guerillas were becoming increasingly common, and dad had acquired a lightweight F.N. .22 rifle and a High Standard "Double 9" revolver for me to carry whenever we went anywhere.

I was already popular with many of the Bushmen who crossed the border near us making their way to the mission clinic or school. My air rifle kept them well supplied with doves. With a .22 LR I could now take bigger birds like Guinea fowl and Francolin. We were not an affluent family, but I got a box of 50 .22 LR cartridges per week to practice with in both the rifle and revolver. (When traveling I put the .22 Magnum cylinder into the revolver). As I got older and the war got worse I put in ever-increasing amounts of practice with a Webley air pistol and the revolver as it would almost certainly be the handgun I would have to use riding to school.

One war ended and nine months later the next one began. The provincial police chief approached me with an offer: if I would quit school early and join the Police Anti-Terrorist Tracking Platoon (the trackers were Bushmen and needed an officer who could speak their language), he would guarantee me a scholarship to a university. I didn't last long before I was severely injured and completed my school studies from a hospital bed. The promise of the scholarship was kept, and I was transferred from Police to National Parks. For bush work, I bought a Smith & Wesson Model 58 in .41 Magnum. Our issue handguns were old Webley .38 revolvers, and I didn't have much faith in them stopping anything.

Over the span of my career with National Parks I got to use it on a lot of impala and baboons, a hyena that was trying to bite its way through the mosquito net, and a couple of really unpleasant people. Then the question of handgun and black powder came up. Under the Rhodesian regime both had been legal, but as soon as Robert Mugabe became president there was a massive clamp down on firearms in general. A clerical error aimed at banning people from using an AK-47 for hunting stipulated the minimum barrel length of 20 inches — which of course banned handguns. The white officers were pushed out from senior management at parks, and the new political appointees had, for the most part, never fired a gun, let alone shot anything with one.

The new director claimed it was impossible to kill big game with a handgun. Since the departments setting hunting quotas came under me, I organized a demonstration to prove how effective handguns could be. The top brass came down to Matusadona National Park where, from the safety of a tree stand, they watched me sneak out across the flood plain and shoot a bull elephant and, a couple of hours later, a Cape buffalo. Both were easy shots. The elephant gave me a perfect side brain shot at 10 paces, and the buffalo a slightly quartering-away angle so I could put the bullet behind the elbow and through the heart. As a result, handgun hunting was allowed on 'special' permit.

Author's Note: Dr. Heath used hardcast bullets that weighed in at 225 grains, which he pushed to just over 1,400 fps.

Photo by C. Magera

CHAPTER 3

handgun hunting mechanics

Much like renewing your vows, getting back to basics can serve even the veteran handgun hunter well. My goal is to introduce the uninitiated, drill the experienced and reflect on my own handgun-hunting regimen. I'll focus on the mechanics and not the fieldcraft of handgun hunting — that is a topic for another book.

Choosing a Platform

Finding a platform that suits you well is critical. Comfort goes a long way to building confidence. Should you choose a single- or double-action? .357 Mag. or .44 Mag? .454 Casull? Long barrel? Short barrel? Scope? Open sights? What configuration will fulfill your needs? There are a number of questions you need to answer honestly to zero in on what will best serve your big-game hunting aspirations. If at all possible, you should try a number of different revolvers. Recoil characteristics vary greatly between the different types and makes, and let's face the facts, large-caliber revolvers deliver sizable recoil.

Double-action revolvers tend to concentrate recoil force straight back into the web of your hand, while single-actions tend to twist upward, sparing the shooter some of the unpleasantness. The two configurations are worlds apart in how they transfer recoil to the shooter.

I could go into the various single-action grip-frame profiles, but we don't have room for that here. My personal favorite is Ruger's take on the Bisley grip frame, as it is optimal for control in my hands because it has more of a double-action-like recoil dynamic. Freedom Arms' Model 83 grip is another that I really like.

I would again recommend testing out a few of the different makes, models and calibers before you make this decision. If you don't know anyone with a variety of revolvers to try, I would suggest joining any number of websites that are dedicated to revolvers and handgun hunting. You may find someone local who is willing to let you shoot some of their guns.

Everyone has different preferences, so there are no hard and fast rules when it comes to picking a platform. For me, single-action revolvers point more intuitively than double actions. They are almost an extension of the hand. Gunslingers of the Old West were undoubtedly well aware of this handling characteristic, relying on point shooting for survival. On the other hand, we are not gunslingers but handgun hunters, and the double action may offer some advantages when quick follow-up shots are needed to dispatch a departing animal.

This is as good as any time to briefly discuss calibers. While the .357 Magnum is not my first choice, it can be effective. Remember that shot placement is key, and a half-inch hole won't make up for lousy marksmanship. Loaded with a quality bullet, I wouldn't hesitate to use the .357 Mag. on deer. However, I still prefer erring on the larger side with regard to calibers. The .41 Magnum is a good starting point and compromise, though factory ammunition is somewhat scarce. The champion of all big-revolver rounds from an ammunition availability standpoint is the ubiquitous .44 Magnum. No other caliber can boast the sheer variety and quantity of available ammunition, and it is fully up to the task of taking any and every game animal that has ever walked the face of this earth.

One of my personal favorites is the .45 Colt — yeah, that old black-powder cartridge from the late 1800s. It can be loaded considerably hotter than its original configuration (limited to 14,000 psi). I'm not suggesting turning your .45 Colt into a .454 Casull, but revolvers like Ruger's Blackhawk in .45 Colt are considerably stronger than a Colt Single Action Army or the many facsimiles available on the market and are able to safely handle considerably hotter loads than the 14,000-psi maximum imposed upon the smaller and more fragile revolvers. Adhere to published load data, and do not exceed the maximums recommended by the manufacturer, as there is no need to turn your favorite revolver into a hand grenade.

There are quite a few big calibers that are fairly brutal to shoot, and I don't recommend them to the neophyte. There are some, such as the .480 Ruger, that offer a fine compromise between power and recoil. However, you can load the big calibers down to "soft" levels and they still offer a sizable advantage over their smaller siblings. They don't need to be pushed hard to be terminally effective. Keep this in mind when you are deciding on a caliber for a hunting revolver.

You need to be honest with yourself as far as your limitations. There is no shame in a low tolerance for recoil. These big-bore revolvers can be very difficult to shoot, as you generally have only 3 pounds to contain the considerable recoil generated by some cartridges. Take pride in being able to shoot your chosen revolver well and effectively. Let someone else's ego dictate their caliber choices. Confidence and competence will go a long way to filling the freezer with game meat. Confidence follows competence, and consistent competence is the offspring of practice, which we'll discuss later.

Let's briefly talk about bullets. We live in what I consider the Golden Age of handgun bullets. There are bonded, jacketed, controlled expansion, violently expanding, deep penetrating, soft-point, flat-point, hollow-point, monometal and hardcast, to name just the big players. It's important to match your bullet to your game. Soft, thin-skinned game respond well to violently expanding bullets where deep penetration isn't needed. When hunting thick-skinned, heavy-boned animals, an expanding bullet of tougher construction, such as Hornady's Magnum XTP or the Swift A-frame, or a minimally expanding bullet, such as a flat-nosed hardcast, are preferable. Expansion is more critical in smaller calibers, but when your bullet is starting out at or nearly a half-inch in diameter, expansion isn't all that important. All that said, I always prefer two holes to one and put a premium on penetration.

Learning to Shoot

Now that you have chosen your revolver, it is time to learn how to shoot it well. Simply stated, shooting a handgun accurately is more difficult than a rifle. You won't have the luxury of using your body to stabilize the firearm by bracing the buttstock firmly into your shoulder.

Consistency is the name of the game here — of grip pressure and trigger control. Changing your grip tension will change the point of impact of your bullets. This is why it is so important to shoot in the same manner each and every time, and repetition is habit forming. If fatigue begins to rear its head as you practice, either rest or stop for the day. Bad habits can form quickly when pushing your own limits, and if your grip begins weakening during a shooting session your marksmanship will suffer.

Limit your time on the range so you end each range session on a high

Practice shouldn't be limited to the range. TV time can double as dry fire practice time. This is a great way to practice trigger control. Of course, make sure your revolver is unloaded and the cylinder stuffed with snap caps or you will have some explaining to do!

Handgun Hunting Mechanics **25**

note. This will allow your muscles to retain the memory of doing things correctly. It won't serve you well to shoot until you develop a flinch. Undoing a flinch can be frustrating and time consuming. You will know when you reach your limit and, when you do, hang it up until the next practice session.

Range time should be spent practicing the various field positions, while the bench should be visited sparingly — to sight in and to check zero. Field positions include offhand practice, which I find to be very useful. In fact, I spend most of my practice time shooting offhand.

The two reigning offhand shooting stances are the Isosceles and the Weaver stances. The Isosceles puts both of your feet on line (actually, the latest trend is to drop the strong side foot back a bit but not as severely as with the Weaver stance), while you face nearly flat toward the target with both arms parallel and straight out or slightly bent. Equal pressure is applied to the gun in a 360-degree fashion. It's great for defensive shooting, but not so good with a heavy revolver that generates a lot of recoil.

The Weaver pulls the revolver with the weak hand, pushes with the strong. I use a modified Weaver stance with my weak-side forward and my supporting arm's elbow tucked to my side for support. The Weaver, at least for me, is more logical and comfortable. I boxed for a couple of decades, and a fighting stance, leading with the weak side, is natural for me.

Shooting sticks should also be part of your practice regimen. I have a tripod from Stoney Point I am quite fond of. I'll use support systems at the range and out in the field. Sticks aren't burdensome to carry and are quickly and easily deployed. They provide a solid rest. In fact, any kind of rest should always be considered where available, as it can increase your success rate immensely.

Also, you can practice without breaking the bank or your wrists. Sessions don't have to be long on time and ammunition. Focus on your first shot, as this is always the most critical when hunting. You don't need to be able to put strings of shots together in one hole at 100 yards, but you should be able to put one bullet in your intended target the first try.

Practice should not be limited to the range. If you are like me and have a life that is chaotic, short on time and long on work, making frequent trips to the range isn't really an option. Burning powder is good, but dry firing is also a great way to get in shape for the hunt.

Keep in mind that some revolvers will require snap caps to perform this practice regimen (contact the manufacturer for their recommendations). A snap cap is a plastic or aluminum dummy round with a spring-loaded primer that allows the firing pin to fall safely on a surface with good resistance — preventing potential damage to your firing pin and fire control mechanism. Trigger squeeze and control is the name of the game here. A jerked trigger will throw shots way off target. Muscle memory requires time on the trigger, and there is no way around this if you want to be a successful handgun hunter. Much to the chagrin of my wife, I get in front of the TV and practice my trigger squeeze by dry firing. Even the dogs look at me like I am crazy — they are very intuitive. Perform so many repetitions that your shots become mechanical and devoid of emotion. This will help you when you have the buck of a lifetime in your sights.

One more thing: small-caliber revolvers are good for practice. There's no need to assault your senses and abuse your body all of the time. Low recoil will allow you to perform and analyze your fundamentals, as well as practice that all critical trigger squeeze. Similarly sized revolvers chambered in .22LR are a great choice here.

Sighting Options

I want to lightly touch upon sighting options here, but there is a chapter dedicated to sighting systems later on in the book. Your eyes and, most likely, your age will play a large role in helping you choose a revolver sighting system.

I am not a big fan of scopes on revolvers. The eye relief is just too great for me and the wobble all shooters exhibit is greatly exaggerated when peering through a scope with some magnification. I understand the appeal — a good rest and a variable-power scope make those long shots doable — but that's not why I got into handgun hunting. I like to get close. It's just a personal preference. I really like red-dot sights, as they are very hard to beat in low light. The downside is, they rely on batteries to function and could leave you high and dry out in the field. I carry spares in case of a failing battery, though I am happy to report that I have never experienced such a failure on a hunt.

For the purist, open iron sights are the only way to fly. Some of my revolvers will never be fitted with an optic. This is purely aesthetic for me, but I also love that an iron-sighted revolver can sit in a holster, not be intrusive in any way and be pressed into action quickly.

For now, I would like you to go back and re-examine your regimen. Remember that practice is absolutely critical and that a dry-fire routine can be performed in the comfort of your home. Trigger control is of absolute importance to making first shots on game. What are you waiting for? Practice. You will be better for it and reap the rewards, knowing that you successfully chose the harder path to hunting prosperity.

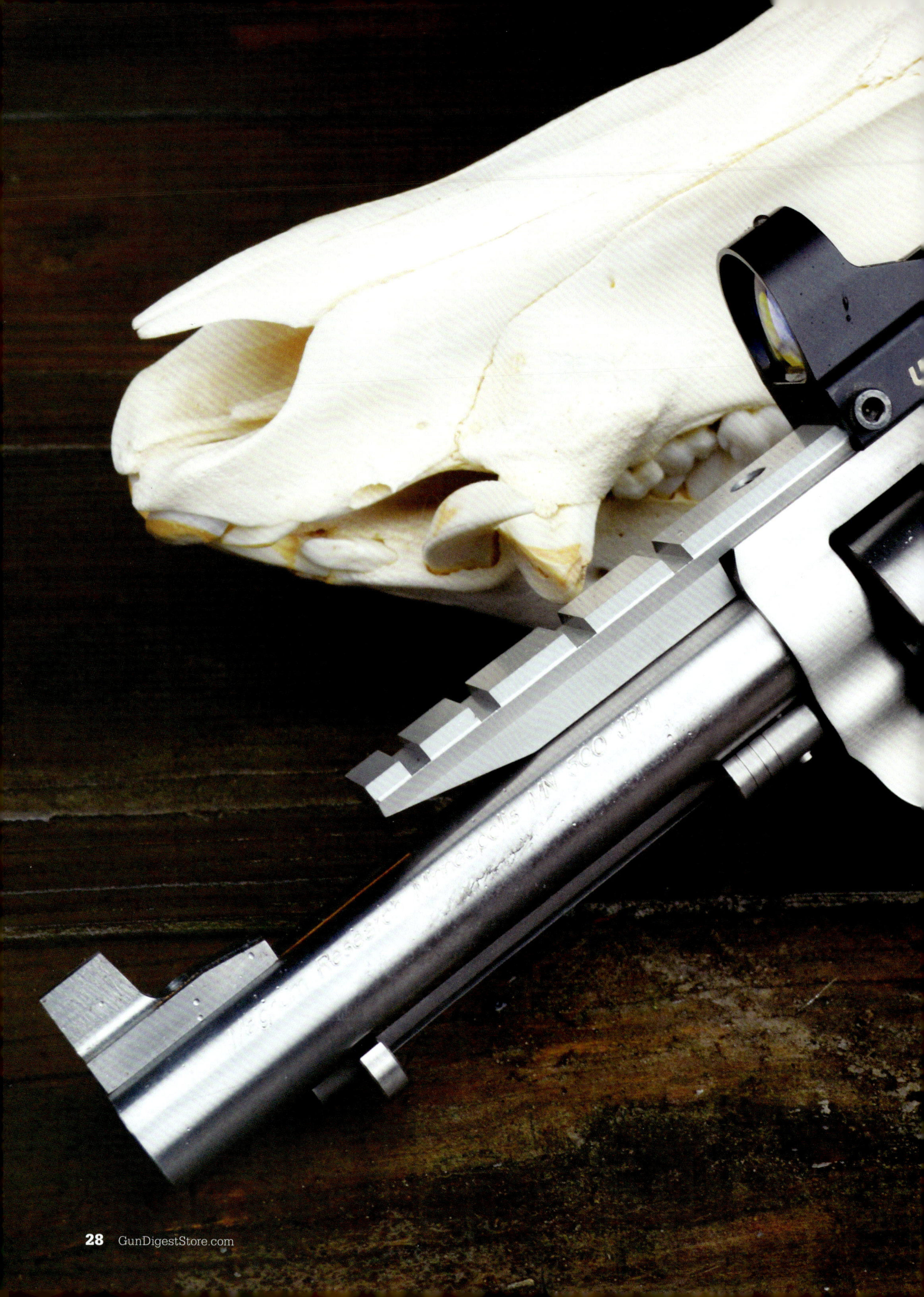

CHAPTER 4

revolver care and feeding

Terminal Ballistics

Since the very first critter I killed way back when, I have been interested in the mechanics of terminal ballistics. Of course, my approach back in those days wasn't scientific, but that would change later on. As I stated in my first book, Big-Bore Revolvers, I believe this is an underdeveloped topic particularly within the limited parameters of revolver ballistics. I believe this can of worms needs to be opened, regardless of what fire is drawn from those on the other side of the terminal performance divide.

I don't claim that this will be the final word on terminal performance, but I can clarify some common misconceptions and question some of what has become conventional wisdom. Maybe I can change the minds of some of the jaded who believe all that they read in the common gun media. However, at the end of the day, if the words, testing and anecdotal evidence don't convince you, maybe the real-life photos of big-game animals taken cleanly with revolvers will.

But what is terminal ballistics? Terminal Ballistics is a subfield of ballistics and the study of the behavior of a projectile when it hits a target. In this case, a live game animal is mainly what we are concerned with.

Getting Started

Now that you've taken delivery of your hunting revolver, you need to decide how you will feed it. Obviously, proficiency and accuracy with your new handgun will require extensive shooting, as you grow accustomed to the recoil. How you plan to use the revolver will dictate your chosen loads. If you're just punching paper, then the nod goes to accuracy over terminal potential. If pressing your revolver into service as a defensive piece, accuracy will likewise be at the forefront of your ammunition needs. But, for the purposes of this book, we will only concern ourselves with the realm of hunting.

Factory ammo is an option, but to really extract the full potential from your chosen sidearm I recommend handloading. Reloading will save you a bundle of money — excluding the initial cash outlay for the tools — and you will get the opportunity to tailor your load to your particular revolver, something that is not possible with one-size-fits-all factory ammunition. I'm not denigrating the factory stuff, as it is a true engineering feat to manufacture ammunition for the masses that works as well as it does.

Reloading will enable you to extract the maximum performance from your chosen caliber and you can design a load that is comfortable to shoot. I often start with factory loads when I acquire a new firearm until I build a sufficient inventory of once-fired brass, and then I purchase loading dies, powder, primers, etc. before beginning the load-development process. It is well worth the initial expense and effort to make your own ammunition, particularly if you plan on shooting a lot.

Another important issue is loading for accuracy. No matter how you plan on using your revolver, it will provide a lot more fun if accurate. All else is moot if you cannot hit what you are aiming at. I tend to load for accuracy, and then, as an afterthought and bow to curiosity, I break out the chronograph, which in my case is an Oehler 35P. What does it tell me? The chronograph provides a good indication of acceptable pressures when compared to published load data using the same components and velocity.

If reloading isn't an option, there are a number of specialty ammunition manufacturers that can supply you with quality ammunition for your big bore, including Grizzly Cartridge, CorBon, Hornady, Garrett Cartridge Company, Double Tap Ammunition, Federal, Underwood and Buffalo Bore Ammunition. These companies offer dedicated loads for large-caliber handguns. Here's a closer look at these top ammo choices.

The Grizzly Cartridge Company

Grizzly Cartridge front man Mike Rintoul is a mechanical engineer by trade whose approach to ammunition manufacturing is scientific, precise and methodical — what you would expect from ... an engineer. Having retired from the oil fields of Alaska, he needed something to do with his abundant free time, and on a whim he created the Grizzly Cartridge Company in 2003.

In the early days of the company, Rintoul used Cast Performance bullets exclusively, as he felt they were the best product of their kind on the market. When Cast Performance became available in 2005, Rintoul jumped on it and brought it under the wing of Rintoul Enterprises.

A handgun hunter himself, Rintoul began his new endeavor by offering ammunition for revolver and lever-action hunters, but he has expanded the line to include 350 different loads in calibers ranging from .32 all the way to .500 Nitro Express and just about everything in between. In particular, Grizzly Cartridge offers everything the discriminating big-bore revolver owner could ever want, particularly with top-shelf ammunition for more obscure calibers such as the .475 Linebaugh, .500 Wyoming Express and even the .357 Maximum.

Prior to retirement, Rintoul was hunting feral hogs with a .44 Magnum stoked with his own handloads and topped off with Cast Performance bullets. He shot a 650-pound slab of bacon at a measured 12 yards, killing the animal in impressive fashion. A necropsy revealed the bullet lodged between vertebrae in the neck. Rintoul was a bit underwhelmed by the .44's penetration, which provided him with the motivation to step up to something bigger and more decisive. After thorough and exhaustive research, Rintoul settled on the .500 Linebaugh and commissioned Hamilton Bowen to build him one on a Ruger Super Blackhawk frame. Rintoul reports that his .500 Linebaugh has no trouble in the penetration department.

In 2011, Rintoul acquired Punch Bullets from Belt Mountain when they became available for purchase. Many, including Rintoul, believe the Punch Bullet is the best choice for maximum penetration and performance on dangerous game. A dedicated devotee to the sport of handgun hunting, the man behind this company has a unique insight into the needs of handgun hunters. He takes the development of loads and the manufacture of ammunition very seriously. One day, he shot a full 300 rounds of full-house .500 S&W Magnum loads during a development session. He couldn't even pick up a pencil for two weeks following the testing. Now that's dedication to the craft.

DoubleTap Ammunition

Owner and CEO of DoubleTap Ammunition, Mike McNett grew up handloading with his dad and earned a degree from Gonzaga University in Spokane, Wash. A career in advertising followed his college years, and it was in the year 2000 that McNett realized he wanted to start his own business and do something he truly enjoyed.

Manufacturing ammunition was a logical direction for him, and the research began. Prior to this, McNett discovered and developed an immediate crush on a then-new offering called the 10mm. McNett's father brought home a Colt Delta Elite in 1987, started handloading and his infatuation blossomed into a full-time love affair with this high-performance cartridge.

In the early '90s, he bought his first Glock 20 in 10mm, and after sending more than 150,000 rounds through it, retired the old workhorse. When the FBI adopted the 10mm as its caliber in 1988, it was soon found to be too hot for agents of smaller stature, and it was steadily emasculated to the point that it morphed into the .40 S&W.

The straw that broke the camel's back and solidified McNett's resolve to get into ammunition manufacturing was when CorBon dropped velocities in its line of 10mm ammo. They were the last full-power 10mm ammunition producer left standing. DoubleTap Ammunition sprung to life out of a perceived need. McNett developed four full-power 10mm loads in his garage for a year before he officially opened his doors, and in 2002 DoubleTap was born.

After six months, the fledgling company had sold enough ammo so McNett could make a full-time go of it. In 2005, after twice outgrowing its manufacturing facilities, DoubleTap relocated to Cedar City, Utah, at the base of the Rocky Mountains. In 2007, the company providing hardcast bullets for

DoubleTap was bought, bringing hardcast manufacturing ability in-house.

DoubleTap has grown leaps and bounds, and, as of this writing, is celebrating its 14th year in business. They offer a very wide range of calibers (59 to be exact) and nearly 300 loads for all occasions. The standard big-bore revolver cartridges are well represented, with some of my favorites being the 320-grain .44 Magnum load and the 360-grain .45 Colt load.

Buffalo Bore Ammunition —
"Strictly Big Bore, Strictly Business"

Tim Sundles, of Boise, Idaho, is the proprietor of Buffalo Bore Ammunition. An enthusiastic handgun hunter, Sundles turned a hobby into his life by bringing the fabulous .475 and .500 Linebaugh to legitimacy with the very first factory ammunition ever offered. It didn't start out that way, though, as he was a contractor in Northern California before making the move to the ammunition manufacturing industry.

Sundles credits Ross Seyfried with the patience and willingness to pass down the finer points in load development in theory and practical application to him. Sundles is quick to remember Seyfried's graciousness when he starts getting impatient.

The entrepreneur started out in 1983 when the Freedom Arms 83 in .454 Casull was released. He immediately bought six of them and began experimenting with a variety of loads. Prior to the release of the FA 83, he'd been playing with heavy .44 Magnum and .45 Colt loads and got to know John Linebaugh, and was introduced to the .500 Linebaugh. In those days, brass and bullets were hard to come by, but Sundles commissioned Linebaugh to build him a number of .475 and .500 Linebaugh revolvers. Following intensive load development for these cartridges, Linebaugh regularly sent his customers to Sundles for loaded ammunition.

The writing was on the wall, and one day Linebaugh asked Sundles to go into the business of manufacturing specialty ammunition, particularly for Linebaugh's signature cartridges, the .475 and .500 Linebaugh. Starline was contacted to make brass, and in 1997 the doors of Buffalo Bore Ammunition swung open. The company started out by making the Linebaugh offerings, but soon added the popular .44 Magnum, .45 Colt and .454 Casull. Eventually, Sundles contacted Bob Baker of Freedom Arms and pestered him to build a revolver in .475 Linebaugh. By the time Freedom Arms offered the Model 83 in .475, Buffalo Bore had ammo on its shelves ready to supply the masses.

Today, the firm offers quality ammunition in 50 or so calibers and more than 160 different loads.

The Garrett Cartridge Company

The Garrett Cartridge Company, which earned a deep reputation for serious .44 Magnum and .45-70 loads, also earned owner Randy Garrett derision for his penetration claims. In my personal opinion, the criticisms have been unfounded and likely generated by those who are uncomfortable with firearms of lower status and mild paper ballistics that happen to challenge conventional wisdom. It's just a theory.

Ashley Emerson purchased the company from Garrett. And while new ownership can bring a modicum of skepticism, rest assured that Garrett Cartridge is in great and capable hands.

"I often bugged Randy Garrett about how Hammerhead loads optimized for the Blackhawk, the Redhawk and the Freedom Arms 83 would be really useful in .45 Colt and .454 Casull," says Emerson. "I envisioned the gas-checked 330/.44 bullet grown up to .45 caliber and begged him for it. Randy's answer: 'When you own and run Garrett, knock yourself out! I am not interested.'

Eventually, the stars aligned and Emerson took over the company. "My first order of business," recalls Emerson, "was to focus all I had learned to build the ultimate Hammerheads for three classes of .45 Colt and two levels of .454 Casull. For a modern Colt single action and clones, as well as the M29 series S&W (great in Marlin's, too, though not by design), there is now a 265 HH at 1,000 fps (7.5-inch barrel) and less than 23,000 psi. For the full-sized Blackhawk based guns, there is a 365-grain LFR load, 365 HH at 1,250 fps (7.5-inch barrel) under 35,000 psi (1.735 o.a.l., won't fit in a Colt or S&W). For the .45 Colt-chambered Redhawk, to take full advantage of its long, heavy cylinder and its 1:16 rate of twist, there is the 405 RHO (Redhawk Only) load consisting of a 405 HH at 1,250 fps (7.5-inch barrel) at 45,000 psi, (1.785 o.a.l., won't fit in Colt, S&W or large frame Blackhawk). The .454 has two loads, both featuring 365 HH bullets, and they are safe in any factory chambered .454. The .454 Hammerheads go 1,350 fps from my 7.5-inch FA 83 and the H454 loads go 1,500 fps."

As a side note, Emerson's new loads are every bit the high quality of the .44 Magnum and .45-70 Government loads that Garrett carefully developed years ago. The tradition thankfully continues.

Underwood Ammo

A family owned business started by Kevin Underwood in Charleston, W.V., Underwood Ammunition is quickly establishing a reputation for really fine ammunition. A lifelong shooting enthusiast, Underwood reloaded ammunition in his spare time like many shooters and hunters, but unlike all but the most dedicated, one reloading press turned into an operation set up for more than 40 calibers! The company's growth could not be stopped. Underwood Ammunition relocated and built a brand new ammunition manufacturing facility in Sparta, Ill., enabling them to better serve their growing customer base.

Using nothing but the highest quality components, assembled with absolute precision, each and every loaded round is individually sight inspected before packaging. If you use Underwood Ammunition for hunting, target shooting, plinking or personal defense, you can rest assured the ammo is safe, reliable and of the highest quality. All of Underwood's loads are field-tested using real firearms that hunters would likely own and use.

A variety of loads for all popular revolver calibers, as well as pistol and rifle ammo, are available from .357 Magnum up to .500 S&W Magnum (even a 700-grain hardcast load) loaded with expanding or hardcast bullets for all types of hunting situations.

Bullet Selection

Let me put this up front. Attempts to turn revolvers into rifles by loading light bullets on top of max powder charges usually fall short on big game — not a situation you want to find yourself in when hunting bear or any animal capable of bringing a fight to you. Handguns do not have the necessary physical attributes of a rifle to achieve rifle-like velocities, and, therefore, they cannot be loaded similarly to a rifle. Note I am talking about revolvers and not the single-shot specialty pistols chambered in rifle calibers. We need to approach terminal ballistics a bit differently in wheelguns. In order to cover this topic completely, we would need quite a few more pages, but let's start with an overview.

We are now talking about hunting, for which bullet selection is crucial. There are basically two types of bullets that are in use by handgun hunters: those that expand dramatically and those that expand minimally, if at all. When we talk about expanding bullets, we are usually referring to jacketed soft-nose, hollow-point or monometal hollow points. Minimal expanders are represented by the hardcast lead bullets, as well as a number of high-quality jacketed bullets designed for uncompromised deep penetration, as well as some monometal solids. These jacketed deep penetrators are more resistant to deformation than even a hardened lead bullet and are better able to withstand high velocities and impacts with hard surfaces. Hardcast bullets derive their name from their alloy composition as well as the hardening process to which they are subjected (water quenching or heat treating) after casting — processes that enable them to maintain their shape even when striking hard objects such as bones. Limiting their impact velocity is the key to their success, as upsetting the shape of the nose will affect penetration and wound-channel production.

There are many factory-loaded, expanding jacketed bullets available in popular handgun calibers. The preference is a stoutly constructed jacketed bullet that will not over expand upon striking a game animal. While violent expansion works well on thin-skinned game such as deer, you don't want a bullet that expands at the expense of penetration. The net effect is like a parachute that will rapidly slow the bullet and inhibit penetration.

There is a very fine line between sufficient expansion and adequate penetration. Fortunately, there are very good offerings from the likes of Hornady that provide a limited yet significant amount of expansion, ensuring penetration.

Lynn Thompson, of Cold Steel fame, took a number of large wild hogs and Asian water buffalo with a Ruger .44 Magnum stoked with Hornady's 300-grain XTP hollow-point load. The minimal expansion enabled the bullets to penetrate deeply and perform impressively against the large bovines. Of course, it doesn't hurt that Thompson is one hell of a shot! However, I have to take issue with using a hollow point that doesn't reliably expand, as it will end up performing a poor imitation of a good flat-nosed hardcast bullet.

The most reliable performers are flat-nosed hardcast bullets, monometal solids, such as Cutting Edge Bullets (CEB) and North Fork offerings, and their jacketed counterparts like the Punch Bullet, Barnes's Buster, and CorBon's Penetrator line. We will discuss the Punch, Penetrator, Buster and CEB handgun solids in more detail later. The LBT-style (Lead Bullets Technology) of hardcast bullet features a wide meplat (pronounced, Mee-Plat — the flat nose of the bullet). The blunt nose crushes and tears tissue creating a much bigger wound channel than the original diameter of the bullet. Flat-nosed hardcast bullets are popular with savvy handgun hunters and offer an economical alternative with unparalleled penetrative ability, due in part to a resistance to big expansion. Also keep in mind that a true big-bore revolver — .45-caliber plus — do not require much expansion as they start off "pre-expanded," as Ross Seyfried so succinctly stated.

But, not all flat-nosed bullets are created equally. Many feature a rather narrow meplat. A wide meplat not only creates a larger wound channel, but it also helps the bullet stabilize in flesh and, thereby, penetrate in a straight line.

What is a large meplat? In independent testing, I've found that between 75 and 80 percent of the overall diameter seems to be optimal. Below 70 percent, and wound-channel size is compromised, as is stability. A small or narrow meplat will sometimes tumble like a round nose in flesh or veer off course, not only inhibiting penetration but also decreasing the likelihood of the projectile going straight through to the vitals. For straight-line, deep penetration, a large meplat is recommended.

When choosing a bullet or factory load, bullet weight must be taken into consideration. Light-for-caliber bullets, while able to achieve impressive velocities, do not possess the momentum or penetrative ability of a heavy-for-caliber bullet, all else being equal.

A well-known handgun hunter, the late Larry Kelly, once had a grizzly bear break into his cabin in Alaska. Kelly emptied his .44 magnum revolver into the offending bear, but the 240-grain bullets failed to even slow the bear down before his hunting partner and guide took a rifle to the bear, ending the burglary. The lack of penetration offered by the 240-grain bullets made him a convert to heavier slugs. Consider heavy-for-caliber bullets as being heavier than the normally accepted standard loads.

- .357 Magnum: 180 to 200 grains
- .41 Magnum: 230 to 265 grains
- .44 Magnum 265 to 340 grains
- .45 Colt/.454 Casull/.460 S&W: 300 to 400 grains
- .475 Linebaugh/.480 Ruger: 400 grains plus
- 500 S&W/.500 Linebaugh/.500 JRH/.500 WE: 440 grains plus

Simply put, there are standardized bullet weights for calibers that are probably attributable to the bullet weights that were commercially offered upon the introduction of that firearm and caliber. In all fairness, these tended to be the weights that were utilized during cartridge and load development. But today's handgun hunters are seeking to increase the terminal performance of their big-bore revolvers by moving considerably up in weight over the standard loadings of the past. "The importance of selecting a heavy bullet is twofold," states Randy Garrett, of Garrett Cartridges. "First, heavier bullets penetrate deeper than lighter bullets. Second, because heavier bullets cannot be driven as fast as lighter bullets, they experience less impact stress and are therefore less likely to fracture on impact." Of course, Garrett is referring to cast bullets and considers them the only option for defensive purposes in dangerous animal encounters. This is important to keep in mind, particularly when loading your big-bore revolver to protect against large, scary beasts. The Punch and Barnes Buster series bullets are even less likely to lose their nose shape on impact with heavy bone.

In a hunting situation, if using a bullet designed to expand, you may have to pass on certain shots. That is a problem if the trophy bear, elk or deer of a lifetime makes an appearance. I personally choose bullets that can kill a large animal from any and every angle presented. Hardcast, flat-nosed bullets allow you to engage the animal no matter the angle offered.

Expansion is not a bad thing, per se, as long as it's not at the expense of adequate penetration. You need to reach and destroy the vitals in order to kill an animal — any animal. Penetration is the single most important factor in terminal ballistics (assuming correct shot placement, of course). Granted, smaller animals typically offer less resistance and don't necessarily require maximum penetration, but if really big game is on the menu, you shouldn't skimp on penetration.

No matter what type of bullet or load you ultimately choose, accuracy is paramount. No amount of horsepower or terminal bullet performance will make a lick of difference if you can't hit your intended target. When you find that perfect load, you owe it to yourself and the animal you are hunting to be as proficient as possible with your revolver of choice. No one I know wants to follow a wounded bear into the briar. Your first shot must be well placed, and that requires an accurate load and a practiced shooter. There is still no replacement for shot placement.

Stopping Angry Four-Legged Adversaries

Don't overlook defensive duty — in this case, defense against a four-legged adversary — as a potential field use of your revolver. You can choose a dedicated wheelgun for this role, or press your main hunting sidearm into double duty. Either way, how you load your back-up revolver is important.

There are two ways you can do it: expanding bullets, or minimally expanding bullets. Many folks think that expansion is a plus when trying to stop an angry animal, but penetration is far more important, in my opinion. Expanding bullets may slow too much, hindering the bullet's ability to reach the vitals. Keep in mind that the calibers we are discussing are already starting out at a large diameter, largely negating the need for expansion.

Don't look at paper ballistics when choosing your load. Even the mildest rifle loads make revolver cartridges look meek. Muzzle energy is a poor measure of a cartridge's ability to kill. A heavy-for-caliber bullet with a large meplat at a moderate velocity will penetrate adequately from any angle, ensuring that the vitals can be reached when placed properly. Again, shot placement is vital, which leads to the issue of reliability.

Note: We have referred to hardcast bullets as "minimally expanding" bullets, which may be raising a red flag in your mind. The reason we use this term is that, technically, all handgun bullets sold in the United States are "expanding bullets" — by law. Hence, you have expanding and minimally expanding bullets. I think you get my drift.

Ultra Reliability

Let's say you've decided to carry a revolver in the field as protection against dangerous animals. You've settled on the platform and caliber and have started experimenting with loads. You must test your chosen combination thoroughly to expose any potential problems that could lead to you getting maimed or, in a worst-case scenario, stomped or mauled to death.

For example, the story of Alaskan fishing guide Greg Brush and his close call with a hungry grizzly bear. Brush actually experienced ammunition failure in his revolver — but was successful in ending a very precarious situation nonetheless. After one of the shots, his revolver tied up, meaning he could not advance the cylinder to the next round. This would have presented a big problem had he needed the next round. The failure he experienced was from a bullet becoming uncrimped from its case, pulling out enough to put a halt to using the revolver. The stubborn bullet had to be pushed back down into the case to open the cylinder and remove the offending round.

We sometimes witness and experience this phenomenon with heavy-recoiling revolver rounds. The recoil is so severe that the bullets manage to pull themselves out of the case. The .454 Casull has been guilty of this more than most, as it utilizes heavily compressed loads of powder to attain impressive velocities, but this puts additional strain on the crimp before recoil even comes into play, not to mention that the recoil is rather violent. In all fairness, any high-powered revolver cartridge can experience this phenomenon, but we tend to see this more frequently in the .454 with heavily compressed loads and heavy bullets.

I had two batches of commercially loaded .454 Casull ammunition from two different manufacturers both pull crimp in testing. I was on the range shooting for accuracy and measuring velocity. The test revolver (a single action) only allowed for one or two shots before becoming tied up and rendered inoperable. It generally doesn't take much to tie a revolver up when a bullet pulls crimp.

My good friend John Parker used to carry a small wooden dowel or screwdriver in his back pocket whenever he went out in the field with his .475 Linebaugh. It just wasn't that uncommon with the heavy kickers in older brass (keep in mind the early .475 Linebaughs used cut down .45-70 brass and not the dedicated cases we have today) to pull crimp, locking the gun up. It was also conventional wisdom at that time that the .475 Linebaugh should be loaded to maximum velocities with heavy bullets for maximum effectiveness on game. Parker would simply push the bullet back down enough to open the cylinder and remove the offending round.

Carrying a field-handy tool of some sort to address this issue is still a good idea. You need to be prepared for the worst at all times. I used these same two batches of ammo in another test, this time in a Ruger Redhawk (it has been fitted with the cylinder out of a Super Redhawk in .454 Casull), and in the case of both types of ammo, it took four or five shots before the bullets pulled out enough to jam the gun. Undoubtedly, the bullets began pulling immediately, but due to greater clearances between the front of the cylinder and the frame, I was able to fire it a number of times before the inevitable jam. The greater clearance bought me a little time.

The issue would have been obvious had I been shooting over a chronograph, as the rounds that had experienced crimp pull would have lost velocity over those that hadn't. I believe this is what happened with Greg

Brush. There is obviously an advantage to having a longer cylinder and/ or a little more clearance in the unfortunate instance when ammunition pulls crimp, as these factors might buy you a little time before lock-up occurs. Even better is ammunition that doesn't pull crimp.

When bullets pull crimp, as this photo demonstrates, the revolver will tie up, leaving it inoperable. Not a good thing when being mauled by an angry animal.

Keep in mind that this is an ammunition issue and not a problem with the firearms we tested. The ammunition should not pull crimp. Further investigation revealed the culprit to be a bad batch of soft brass. In subsequent testing, with new batches of the same stuff, we were not able to duplicate the incident — testimony to the integrity of the respective producers of the ammunition.

Due to the .454's propensity for pulling crimp with heavily compressed, heavy-bullet loads, Buffalo Bore Ammunition loads 360-grain .454 Casull to lower velocity and pressure levels as a nod to reliability as they know folks carry the .454 for protection against dangerous animals. Why else would someone put up with the .454's recoil? Lord knows they aren't plinking with this caliber. The company recognizes that people will shoot their .454 better and more accurately if they're not afraid of its punishing recoil.

Buffalo Bore also uses a proprietary crimp as a double insurance policy. "We could have run these bullets faster but have found that at 1,400 to 1,500 fps they'll penetrate lengthwise through any bear," said owner Tim Sundles when asked about the subdued velocities of the company's 360-grain .454 loads. "When you drive the .454's speeds up, it becomes unruly and unreliable."

Buffalo Bore actually redesigned the crimp groove area of their .454 bullets. Typically, hardcast bullets have a gently sloping, angled crimp groove or edge. Buffalo Bore cut the crimp grooves with a square bottom edge so that when the crimp is applied, it has an edge onto which to grab.

The ammo manufacturers recommended in this book take great care in the details, as any mistake or carelessness in the assembly process could lead to crimp pull, which could result in serious injury. All the power in

Revolver Care and Feeding **41**

the world will do you no good if you can only get the one shot off before another round pulls crimp. This is why it is so important to test your equipment in the field. When a bear or mountain lion is closing the distance on you at a high rate of speed, it is a poor time to find out that your rig isn't reliable. Reliability rules the roost. There is no excuse for not testing extensively for reliability, and the consequences may be grave for not having a rock-solid combination. Test ahead of time, and spare no expense. Your life is worth the time, cost and inconvenience.

Bullet Types

The two major types of bullets for big-bore revolvers are jacketed or monometal expanding, and cast or lead-alloy bullets. Both designs operate well within the parameters for which they were designed. Obviously, there are varying qualities of each bullet type, but we'll focus on premium bullets.

Jacketed Expanding Bullets

Today, there are a number of very good jacketed expanding bullets available to the revolver hunter. In the past, bullets of this type tended to be entirely too frangible for reliable use on big game, yet they were perfectly adequate for anti-personnel use. They also tended to be of a lighter weight than may be needed in a big-game killing scenario.

The newest iterations of these bullets are trending toward heavier weights and much tougher construction than in the past. This is actually a double-edged sword. The tougher jacket ensures the bullet will stay together even with high impact velocities, but it may also hinder the bullet's ability to expand. Limited expansion is good for penetration, as violent expansion absolutely hurts penetration at revolver velocities. A bullet that fails to expand but still penetrates well will not deliver the wound channel that a good, wide-meplat cast bullet is capable of delivering. This is why I stated previously that expanding bullets that fail to expand do a poor cast flat-nosed bullet impersonation. Ultimately, controlled minimal expansion is the perfect scenario for the jacketed expanding bullet.

Hornady's XTP line of jacketed expanding bullets (flat nosed and hollow point) has come a long way over the years. Criticized for over expansion in its original form, the XTP has evolved into an outstanding jacketed expanding bullet. I've rather extensively tested the 300-grain .44 Magnum XTP load from Hornady, and have found that the secret to its significant penetration is the limited expansion it provides. Hornady has definitely engineered this particular load very well, as they have kept the velocity to a moderate level — ensuring minimal expansion, almost guaranteeing deep penetration. One only has to watch Cold Steel Owner Lynn Thompson's video, Handgun Hunting Down Under, to see just how lethal Hornady's 300-grain XTP .44 Magnum load actually is on large game. Thompson puts a number of water buffalo down with a combination of great bullet performance and expert shot placement.

Sierra produces what I consider one of the finest jacketed expanding bullets for handguns. Their bullets feature a tough, thick jacket and a higher antimony lead alloy in the rear, nonexpanding portion of the bullet. This ensures adequate expansion up front, while the hardened rear remains intact for deep penetration.

Swift's A-frames are some of the best jacketed expanding bullets available to the handgun hunter. They can be had as reloading components or as loaded ammunition from Federal. These bullets are tough and up to the task of high impact velocities.

Monometal Expanding and Nonexpanding Bullets

Barnes Bullets

Barnes' monometal XPB line of hollow-point bullets are perfect if you hunt in some of the lead-free zones of California or elsewhere. These bullets are exceedingly tough and will stay together even when pushed to relatively high velocities. They will also hold together when they make contact with bone. Two perfect candidates for the XPB are the .454 Casull, and Smith & Wesson's velocity champ, the .460 S&W Magnum.

Cutting Edge Bullets (CEB)

I'm always fascinated when new products hit the market claiming bigger, better and more efficient performance topped off with less recoil, more energy and better accuracy. They also claim their ideal for all of your needs — long range, short range, medium range, spitting range, target shooting, plinking, hunting, etc. It's exhausting. Occasionally, a product does deliver on multiple fronts, but this is a rare bird indeed.

Relative newcomer, Cutting Edge Bullets, is manufacturing premium solid copper and brass projectiles for many different applications. CEB's stated goal is to produce a single projectile that can perform equally well in a variety of circumstances. This no-compromise mantra has led to bullet designs that not only shoot flat and accurate, but are also terminally effective on game. CEB's products are precision machined to very tight tolerances and held to the highest standards of manufacture.

CEB's solid-copper bullets feature a unique and patented SealTite ™ band that eliminates the possibility of "fliers" that are sometimes associated with other solid-copper bullets. This makes them ideal for long-range competition and hunting. This band design also significantly reduces copper fouling.

Big-game hunting is where I believe CEB really shines. Their designs have been thoroughly vetted and independently tested for terminal effectiveness in both the lab and, more importantly, the field. The big-game rifle hunter is well-served by CEB's extensive line of bullets in all popular and some not-so-popular calibers.

As a handgun hunter, I'm always looking for a better mousetrap. I've performed a significant amount of load development on the .480 Ruger. For this caliber, CEB offers three different bullet weights, including a 220-grain hollow-point Raptor, a 280-grain Raptor and a 340-grain flat-nosed solid.

The concept behind the Raptor design is not something new, but CEB's bullets perform consistently and reliably. The four petals are designed to break off in animal tissue, wreaking havoc in four directions, while the solid shank continues on its forward path, penetrating deeply. I've tried them all on a number of animals of varying stature and found the lighter-weight bullets to be ideal for medium-sized, thin-skinned game. The accuracy delivered by these bullets out of my Ruger Super Redhawk was astounding, with regular ¾-inch five-shot 50-yard groups.

The big test came when I killed a water buffalo in Argentina with 340-grain CEB solids. The 1,500-pound bovine didn't offer enough resistance to stop the bullets from exiting, proving their worth as viable big-game bullets. I have always been a believer in flat-nosed hardcast bullets for the uncompromisingly deep penetration they offer on large game animals, but when costly trophy fees are on the line, and the animal possesses enough physical attributes to do you irreparable harm, the idea of a solid bullet that can neither deform nor break apart is a good piece of insurance for the discerning hunter.

While there are less expensive bullets available, you will be hard pressed to find a better one that actually delivers on marketing material promises. My only complaints are the smallish 67 percent meplat and the inability to use slow magnum powders like my favorite H110/296. Some report good performance with these powders, but my own experience has been erratic. That said, there are other powders that work with this bullet design and, as we go to print, I have taken delivery of some prototype CEB solids with 80 percent meplats. Now we're cooking with gas!

All of the bullets mentioned here are ideal for deer and other thin-skinned game animals. They will work on larger and tougher game as well, but more care must be taken to choose your shot, avoiding heavy bone.

Cast Bullets

As the name suggests, cast bullets are cast from lead or, more accurately, lead alloy. The term that is most associated with big-bore handguns in this category is hardcast — a term you have read about here on numerous occasions, as well as in the handgun media. I don't want to delve too deeply into semantics, but there are certain aspects of these bullets that anyone seriously considering their use should know.

There is much misinformation floating about that has achieved dogma status. The term hardcast has come about to draw a distinction between high-performance cast bullets capable of handling even the largest of game, and soft, malleable lead bullets. While "hard" is a rather vague concept to define, there are some industry- and community-wide accepted levels of hardness to help you determine whether or not an adequate bullet has been chosen for the intended purpose. The most commonly utilized measurement for a bullet's hardness is the Brinnell Hardness Number (BHN), long used in the machining trade and made popular by Veral Smith of Lead Bullets technology (LBT). LBT sells BHN testers you can use to evaluate the hardness of your home creations.

Obviously, the alloy used will determine the characteristics of the bullet — malleability, hardness, brittleness, etc. For a complete guide to casting, as well as the technology around the process and the designs of cast bullets, I recommend Veral Smith's book, Jacketed Performance with Cast Bullets. Smith goes to a depth and level beyond my capacity, and you cannot go wrong following the advice offered in this book.

In this case, a hardcast bullet with a Brinnell hardness of 20 or so (20 is considered hard), with a wide meplat at a modest velocity, will exit even the largest of game in most cases, even when or if the bullet encounters bone in its path. The large, flat point ensures deep, straight-line penetration, allowing you to be less choosy with shot placement.

"Keith-Style": A Case of Mistaken Identity

In the realm of handgun bullets, no term is misused and misapplied more often than "Keith-style." The reference is to the late Elmer Keith's great contribution to handgunning (actually, Phil Sharp experimented with this design in the 1930s in .38 and .357 calibers), with the design of a number of semi-wadcutter profiles that were known for their great accuracy potential. The Keith bullet brought to light the penetration potential of a flat-nosed bullet profile, and as a gun writer he had a wide audience with which to share his observations and adventures.

Oddly enough, big- and dangerous-game rifle hunters are now embracing the flat-nosed solid for its straight-line penetrative abilities and tissue damage — something handgun hunters embraced decades ago. Better late than never, I say, a trend I place squarely on the shoulders of Elmer Keith. There are a couple of Keith-profile bullet molds available that are true to his original design parameters, but for every "real" Keith bullet, there are a hundred facsimiles of wildly differing qualities and variations on the theme. One of the most important attributes of Keith's bullet was its great accuracy. I realize that it is heretical for me to declare the Keith-style bullet as being way past its prime, but I feel there are a number of much better designs available today that overshadow the old cowpoke's great contribution.

But how is it better? Generally, they're more terminally effective. Let me qualify my statement with the fact that every revolver is a law unto itself, and some bullet designs work better in some guns than in others. If you find a favorite load, by all means stick with it. I am not suggesting that you should change or replace a perfectly working design to something else, because you read it here. But how are some newer bullets better with regard to terminal performance? The answer is a larger meplat potential without the diameter-reducing step in the semi-wadcutter design. It's an indisputable fact that a larger meplat will produce a larger wound channel than a smaller one.

The "Keith-style" bullet remains popular with many shooters and hunters because it still proves to be an accurate bullet. Accuracy, in and of itself, goes a very long way to leaping over one of the biggest hurdles to harvesting game. If you are able to place the bullet where it belongs, and the bullet exhibits enough penetration potential, a dead animal will be the result.

We've come a long way since the great Elmer Keith was dabbling in bullet design, and some notable examples have taken center stage. SSK Industries, headed by J.D. Jones, was one of the first to offer truly heavy-for-caliber cast bullets, most notably for the .44 Magnum. Probably the greatest examples from a design standpoint are the bullets that come from Lead Bullets Technology, or LBT, the second-most misused nomenclature in the industry.

Designed by LBT proprietor, Veral Smith, there are many copies on the market today. They say that imitation is the greatest form of flattery, and Smith should be proud his designs are so often reproduced. However, it is the name that is more often reproduced and not necessarily the design. LBT coined a whole new nomenclature in bullet design such as LFN, WFN and WLN, meaning long flat nose, wide flat nose and wide long nose, respectively. You will see any of the above three letters attached to many bullet descriptions, but they must be true to Veral Smith and LBT's design parameters to actually use this terminology accurately and honestly.

Master Gunsmith Jason Menefee built this Ruger Blackhawk in .41 Magnum with an oversized six-shot cylinder and a PacNor barrel. Photo by Author

Revolver Care and Feeding **47**

Nose Profile

I've talked about some popular and prevailing bullet designs with distinct nose shapes that are in use and available commercially. We revolver wonks tend to make a lot of references to the term "nose profile," but what is nose profile, exactly? Simply put, it is the shape of the bullet's nose — the killing end of the bullet.

There are many different nose profiles that have been used over the years, including round nose, flat nose, hollow point and pointed (spitzer). Most common commercial loadings for big-bore revolvers feature a jacketed expanding bullet of some type or a flat-nosed hardcast design. Round-nosed bullets should be avoided for all activities, save for plinking. You can use them to target shoot, but if hunting is on your list of activities, it's better to leave your round-nosed bullets at home. That's because they tend not to track straight in media, making them less than ideal for hunting. The round nose also limits the potential for creating a large wound channel. Consequently, we will not spend much time on round-nosed bullets.

By far the most preferred and effective nose profile is the flat nose. But isn't expansion a good thing? Yes, if you are starting off small. We, however, are not. Large diameter, by virtue of big caliber, is built into our chosen big-bore firearms. This is the single biggest advantage that we can boast — a sizeable diameter. Big-bores sport diameters any expanding .30-06 bullet would be ecstatic to own, and this is where Lead Bullets Technology, or LBT, enters the conversation in full force.

Lead Bullets Technology: LBT — More Mistaken Identity

Cast-bullet guru Veral Smith, opened Lead Bullets Technology back in 1984, but began experimenting with cast-bullet design in 1980. This was when he acquired a mold lathe that allowed him to make variations in his bullet designs. He made identical molds with one change in design at a time, enabling him to thoroughly vet his designs.

Through design trial and error and exhaustive testing, Smith introduced a whole new vernacular to the handgun-hunting world with a series of acronyms that would change the way we load our revolvers with cast bullets. LBT is the second-most misused term in commercial lead-pistol bullet making. Unless the molds came from Smith and LBT, or are dimensionally true to Smith's designs, they cannot truly be called LBT.

The acronyms of which I speak are the aforementioned LFN, WFN and WLN. These are the three basic flat-nosed-bullet designs that have superseded all that have come before, including the vaunted Keith bullet, a semi-wadcutter design with a flat nose and a distinct shoulder. Smith determined that certain meplat sizes were ultimately better than others with regard to penetration and terminal performance on game.

There are many imitators, but only one true LBT.

He was largely concerned with meplat area multiplied by velocity at impact, as well as the weight of the projectile. While he never set out to create a percentage factor regarding meplat size, a formula nevertheless emerged. The true specification of the LFN is a meplat that is .125 inches under the bore diameter of the bullet, or roughly 74.5 percent of the bore's diameter. The WFN features a meplat that is .90 inches under the bore diameter, or 81 percent. A WLN is simply a WFN with a longer nose that retains the 81 percent meplat. With his designs, Smith sought to maximize powder capacity, bearing surface, bullet alignment at takeoff and meplat size, which is critical if used on live targets.

There is a common misperception that flat-nosed, non-expanding — actually, minimally expanding — hardcast bullets will produce a caliber-sized hole in game. This is simply not true. A large meplat from an LFN or WFN will produce a wound channel out of proportion to the bore size of the bullet. In Smith's excellent primer on cast bullets, Jacketed Performance with Cast Bullets, he states:

"All tissue displacement is determined by flat to nearly flat frontal area of the bullet. All wounding larger than bullet frontal area is created by displaced tissue spray. Violence of spray determines wound diameter, and spray violence is determined by volume of tissue displaced and speed at which it is displaced. The key to good kills with solids is enough displacement velocity to create rapid blood flow and enough bullet weight to hold bullet velocity up to good wounding speed during the full depth of penetration."

Because of "displaced tissue spray" created by the meplat of the bullet, the spray misses the shoulder of a Keith or semi-wadcutter (SWC) design. Smith found through much experimentation that the meplat does all of the work upon impact with live tissue and that the shoulder never gets "wet" or makes contact with anything inside of the animal until the bullet's velocity nearly slows to a stop. He goes on to say that the "only utility of the SWC shoulder is to cut paper!" The shoulder limits the size of the meplat, which is largely responsible for the size of the wound channel. In other words, there are better ways to skin a cat when it comes to bullet design.

Building a Better Mousetrap

Belt Mountain produced one of the finest flat-nosed bullet offerings for absolutely uncompromising performance on the largest and heaviest-boned animals on earth. Dubbed the "Punch" bullet, it featured a brass construction with a lead core. The Punch is essentially a harder hardcast bullet. This is the ultimate bullet choice if you're going after elephant or other large, heavy-boned game.

Mimicking a flat-nosed hardcast bullet with respect to nose profile and terminal

The Punch bullet left, and the CEB HG Solid ™ right.

Revolver Care and Feeding 49

performance, its advantage is material hardness that maintains the nose integrity even when pushed to high velocities and/or when encountering hard obstacles such as heavy bone. Whereas the hardcast bullet has velocity limitations to maintain integrity, the Punch can be driven to faster speeds with no negative effects. Punch bullets are now owned and produced by Rintoul Enterprises of Cast Performance and Grizzly Cartridge fame.

Cutting Edge Bullets offers a full line of copper flat-nosed solids for handguns in calibers up to .510 bore. These precision-made bullets provide unparalleled accuracy and deep straight-line penetration. I had an opportunity to utilize these premium bullets on a water buffalo hunt in Argentina. My firearm on this hunt was a Ruger Super Redhawk in .480 Ruger. I developed loads for CEB's 340-grain solid, utilizing a stiff charge of Power Pistol powder. The bullets delivered as promised, with all but one exiting the 1,500-pound animal. If large, dangerous game is on the menu, CEB is definitely worth looking at. As I mentioned before, the meplat could be larger for even greater effect.

Barnes produces a good line of solids called the "Buster," replete with tough construction and a flat-nose. Though best known for lead-free projectiles, the Buster line consists of a nearly pure copper jacket covering a hard lead core. Featuring a cannelure to enable you to crimp the bullet in a meaningful way, Barnes offers a good alternative to hardcast bullets.

My one criticism is the meplat. I would like to see a larger one; the smaller size is a concession to those who may use these bullets in a rifle where a large meplat could hinder feeding.

The Norma Triclad bullet had a tough jacket and a very hard core that wasn't designed to expand much and featured a fairly large meplat. Great design, but unfortunately at 240 grains, this .44 Magnum bullet was on the light side.

Too Much of a Good Thing

Is it possible to have too much of a good thing? In many instances, I think so. There are good weight ranges for optimum penetration, assuming the nose profile is also optimized, but there is definitely a tipping point — both literally and figuratively. When the bullet is too heavy for the caliber it can be subsequently too long for the twist rate, compromising the case capacity of the cartridge, thereby limiting the velocity potential for stability and creating a whole chain of issues.

Arguments about optimal weights abound, so let's put some commonly held beliefs to the test. If heavy is good, heavier must be better, right? Not exactly. I've performed a number of tests involving heavy-for-caliber bullets in two popular calibers: the .44 Magnum and the .500 S&W Magnum — both ends of the big-bore revolver spectrum.

The first test subject was the ubiquitous .44 Remington Magnum. The chosen extreme was a 405-grain hardcast lead bullet with a WFN-like (in meplat diameter) nose profile, designed for use in a .444 Marlin rifle (same bore diameter, think of it as a .44 Magnum on steroids) and Ruger Redhawk and Super Redhawk .44 Magnum revolvers. I also shot a number of commercially loaded 300- to 320-grain loads into the same wetpack, as well as a couple of handloads with homemade and designed cast bullets.

The commercially loaded ammunition came from DoubleTap Ammunition, who provided the 320-grain WFN loads at an advertised 1,325 fps, and I acquired bullets from Cast Performance who provided 320-grain WLN samples to load. I also tested a 330- and a 290-grain bullet, both designed by Jim Miner. Lastly, for grins and giggles I tested an old standby, a 240-grain "Keith-style" load at a scorching advertised 1,500 fps from DoubleTap Ammunition.

The 405-grain bullet is seen here next to a loaded 320-grain .44 Magnum round. The extreme length of the 405-grain bullet necessitates seating to the second crimp groove to make enough room for the powder payload.

Revolver Care and Feeding

The 405-grain load is on the far left. The challengers, from that cartridge's left to right, included Jim Miner's 330-grain load, Grizzly Cartridge's 320-grain WLN, and DoubleTap's 320-grain WFN.

The Test

Bundles of newspaper and phone books were soaked for two days prior to the actual test. While wet newsprint doesn't precisely mimic animal flesh, it provides a good idea of how loads will perform on game. If a bullet performs well in wet pack, it will surely work well in flesh, and probably better.

All of the bullets were fired into the same media to prevent any variations in the consistency of the media. I lined up 60 inches of wetpack, and if any of the tested bullets would traverse the full length it would be surprising. See chart below for test results.

Penetration Test 1 - .44 Magnum

BULLET/LOAD	VELOCITY (FPS)	PENETRATION (INCHES)	NOTES
405/.44 Mag.	960.6	22	exited box (turned)
405/.44 Mag.	950.5	31	exited box (turned)
405/.44 Mag.	944.7	28	began ascending (turned)
320 CP/.44 Mag.	1,247	29	straight line
320 DT/.44 Mag.	1,353	30	straight line
330 JM/.44 Mag.	1,264	34	straight line
240 DT/.44 Mag.	1,398	30	straight line
290 JM/.44 Mag.	1,285	36	straight line
405/.44 Mag.	938	34	straight line
405/.44 Mag.	947	28	straight line
330 JM/.44 Mag.	1,243	26	straight line
405/.44 Mag.	966	28	straight line

*CP = Cast Performance; DT = DoubleTap; JM = Jim Miner design

Left: The first 700-grain bullet fired changed course in the wetpack by angling sharply upward, ending up on the outside of the penetration "box."

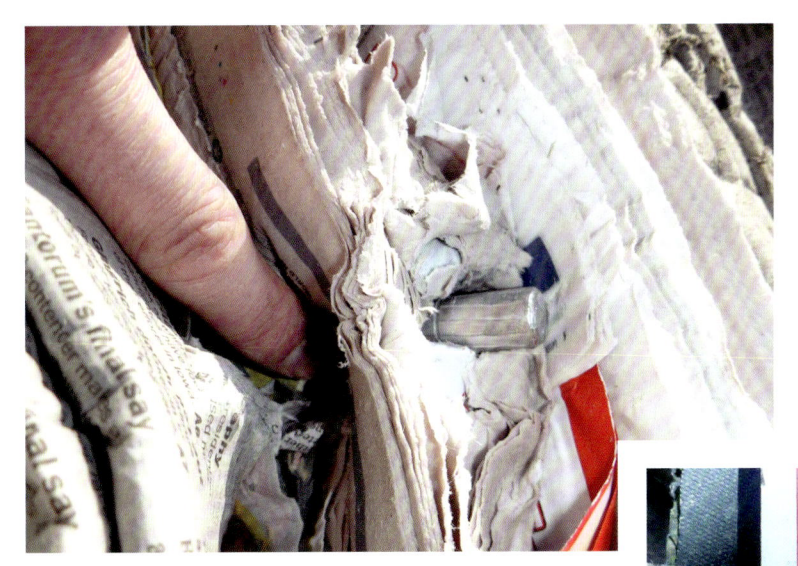

The next heavyweight bullet test was conducted in the same manner as the first. Newspaper and a number of phone books were soaked for one day prior to the actual test, resulting in media measuring 40 inches and set up on a private range for the session. This time the test subject was the heavyweight champ, the .500 S&W Magnum.

This cartridge has received a lot of hoopla in the gun press since its introduction in 2003. As a result, there is no shortage of commercial ammunition and loading supplies for the big .50. Since this test was all about finding the tipping point with regard to bullet weight, I assembled a number of commercial hardcast loadings, including CorBon's 440-grain at a scorching 1,625 fps of advertised velocity, Grizzly Cartridge's 500-grain LFN at 1,550 fps, and DoubleTap's 400-grain WFN load at a whopping 1,805 fps (8 3/8-inch barrel). The excessively heavy load consisted of a 700-grain flat-nosed bullet over a stiff charge of 296 powder. This is a max-effort load according to load data from John Ross for use with this bullet and was quite compressed. It is a good thing that production .500 Smith & Wesson

The 405-grain .44 Magnum bullets clearly exhibited instability in flight, as these two passed through the target sideways.

The 700-grain bullet (left) next to a loaded round with the same topper. Others tested from left to right were the 400-grain WFN from DoubleTap, CorBon's 440-grainer, and Grizzly Cartridge's 500-grain load.

Revolver Care and Feeding 53

revolvers feature a lengthy cylinder as the 700-grain load has a very long overall length (OAL) as the photo below clearly indicates. The test gun was a Smith & Wesson X-frame with a 6.5-inch barrel. All loads were shot over a chronograph and velocities were recorded.

The chart below shows the results, but this test confirmed our suspicions about exceeding the point of diminishing returns.

Penetration Test 2 - .500 S&W Magnum

BULLET/LOAD	VELOCITY (FPS)	PENETRATION (INCHES)	NOTES
700/.500 S&W	994	25	ascended; almost exited
700/.500 S&W	985	30	ascended; exited box
400 DT/.500 S&W	1,564	22	straight line
400 DT/.500 S&W	1,574	26	straight line
440 Cor/.500 S&W	1,513	27.5	straight line
500 Griz/.500 S&W	1,179	40	straight line with exit
500 Griz/.500 S&W	1,196	33	straight line

*Cor = CorBon; DT = DoubleTap Ammunition; Griz = Grizzly Cartridge Company

In summary, too much of a good thing really does exist. "More's Law" (more is always better) is nearly always pressed into action when the limits of something, anything, are being tested. It's how you find the upper limits of any and every performance envelope, and it's also a necessity if a theory is going to be fully explored.

I had to see what the upper limit of bullet weight was for these popular calibers, saving you the time, trouble, agony and resources necessary to come to the same conclusions. In many cases you really can do more with less. As a general rule, if you would like to move up significantly in weight in any given caliber, look at the next larger calibers and see where the heavy-weight bullets start. In many cases you will see greater terminal performance with an increase in diameter and weight over simply using heavier bullets when the diameter remains the same.

The maximum overall length with the 700-grain .500 S&W bullet exceeds the author's comfort level, as even a slight crimp pull would tie the revolver up.

More Heavyweights

There are a couple of honorable mentions in the possibly too-heavy-weight category, but these are offered in loaded factory ammunition. DoubleTap Ammunition has a 400-grain WFN load in .454 Casull, and Garrett Cartridge a 405-grain .45 Colt Redhawk Only (RHO) load in .45 Colt (a +P loading that runs around 45,000 PSI). Both of these loads appear a bit excessive on paper in regard to their respective bullet weights.

Having said that, I believe putting faith in paper ballistics is an exercise in futility. While I haven't performed any formal penetration testing with either of these loads, I have used them on game, which is a more credible test as far as I am concerned. While this evidence is anecdotal, it is telling.

Nearly a decade ago, I had the opportunity to use the 400-grain DoubleTap load on a wild hog hunt in central Florida. I was shooting this load from an open-sighted Ruger Super Redhawk with a 7.5-inch barrel. The target was a mature boar that weighed a touch over 200 pounds. The animal was going away from me, and I made a hard quartering-away shot that entered behind the onside shoulder, exiting through the offside shoulder. Even though no CNS was hit, the boar dropped at the shot, expired and never even twitched a muscle.

The other "overweight" load, the 405-grain Garrett .45 Colt, was shot from a .454 Super Blackhawk. Keep in mind that this load was designed for use in the .45 Colt Ruger Redhawk as a last ditch option. The Redhawk (and Super Redhawk) features a cylinder that's significantly longer than that of the Blackhawk/Super Blackhawk revolvers, enabling the use of a load with such a long bullet and a long overall length. However, it fits in the new .454 Super Blackhawk but leaves little wiggle room for crimp pull. That said, I shot a lot of this ammo in testing and never once experienced crimp pull. Keep in mind that Garrett ammunition is of a very high quality and carefully assembled with first-rate components. Garrett's bullets are cast from a proprietary lead alloy that is extremely hard, yet exhibits no brittleness.

I have to say I was a bit concerned how these extra-long bullets would stabilize with the slow 1:24 twist rate of the .454 Super Blackhawk. They stabilize well in the Redhawk, for which they were designed, but the Redhawk has a fast 1:16 twist rate. Theories be damned, though, as this load shoots very accurately out of the Super Blackhawk even at 50 yards, delivering five-shot groups right around an inch.

Revolver Care and Feeding **55**

Sierra 350-grain jacketed hollow points in the .500 JRH round, as loaded by Grizzly Cartridge Company.

Garrett's loads passed the accuracy test with high marks, but how would they do on animal flesh? We would find out in Hondo, Texas, with Action Outdoor Adventures, in October of 2015. Elsewhere in this book I have detailed this particular hunt, but to summarize, I shot a rather large water buffalo with three of Garrett's heavyweights, all in the shoulder area. The necropsy revealed that two of the three bullets were actually poking through the skin on the offside shoulder, and bullet No. 3 exited to parts unknown. The recovered bullets traveled straight and did not tumble, indicating that they stabilize fine. Impressive internal damage was also what I have come to expect from a good flat-nosed hardcast bullet.

Lesson learned? Both of these loads have proved effective, but I'm not sure they are better from a terminal standpoint then their slightly lighter brethren. However, I wouldn't hesitate to use either of these heavyweights in the future.

Two of the three .45 Colt bullets were recovered poking through the skin of the offside shoulder of the big water buffalo. The third bullet exited.

The author shot this 2,000-pound water buffalo in Hondo, Texas, with a .454 Super Blackhawk loaded with Garrett's 405-grain .45 Colt +P "Redhawk Only" loads.

This is a .41 Magnum Winchester Platinum Tip bullet recovered from a good-sized hog. It shows excellent expansion and was lodged in the hog's gristle plate on the offside. An unfired cartridge is shown for comparison. Photo by G. Smith

Point: The Case for Jacketed Bullets

By Gary Smith

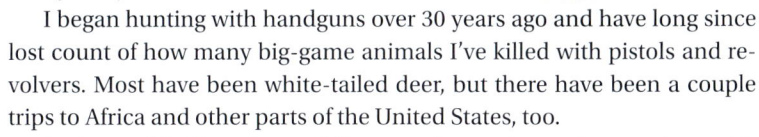

I began hunting with handguns over 30 years ago and have long since lost count of how many big-game animals I've killed with pistols and revolvers. Most have been white-tailed deer, but there have been a couple trips to Africa and other parts of the United States, too.

In the world of hunting and firearms, few topics evoke emotions with such religious zeal like the debate between cast and jacketed bullets in big-bore handguns. I have witnessed otherwise rational men nearly come to blows arguing about the merits of bullet types. It's just one of those debates that no one can quite settle once and for all.

I've used hardcast bullets on a number of occasions to take some very nice trophies; however, when it comes to big-bore, straight-walled cartridges, I prefer a jacketed expanding bullet when hunting all but the very largest game. And even then, unless it is my misfortune to try and stop a charge with a handgun, I would choose a jacketed bullet first.

My first handgun was a T/C Contender chambered in .44 Remington Magnum, and after several months of practice I felt I was ready to tackle deer hunting. My opportunity came one December morning when a fat Virginia doe came within 50 yards. I can't recall whether the bullet was a Sierra or Hornady, but it was a handloaded 180-grain JHP. The shot was placed perfectly on the point of her shoulder as she quartered toward me, and she made it only another 30 yards before going down.

I have since decided that a little heavier bullet in the .44 is more to my liking. However, if the 180s shoot well in your gun they are certainly up to the task of taking deer-sized game. Some of those early, jacketed-bullet designs were good, and some are still around. One in particular is the Remington 240-grain semi-jacketed hollow point. Back in the days when there was such a thing as a cheap box of handgun ammo, the Remingtons were always available, and after changing to a 240-grain load in the .44, I shot quite a few of them down the pipe.

I had largely forgotten about the Remingtons until a couple of years ago when I found myself very pressed for time leading up to a hunt using the Ruger Super Blackhawk Hunter .44 Mag. I started out intending to shoot a deer but found myself in the position to shoot a cow elk, and, of course, the bullets I had with me were factory Remington 240-grain semi-jacketed hollow points. That bullet has a lot of soft lead at the tip, and I was a little cautious about shooting that large of an animal with a soft-lead hollow point bullet. But that was all I had with me, and the gun was dead on at 100 yards, which meant I had complete confidence in the gun and my ability if I could get the right shot.

This is a 250-grain Winchester .454 bullet recovered from a white-tailed deer. Winchester has loaded some of its rounds with Hornady XTP bullets. Photo by G. Smith

We had spotted a herd of cows, and after a short stalk I was in position to take a shot from about 65 yards. It really worked out perfectly, as several of them started to move off when they realized something wasn't quite right. I took a quartering-away shot, and she went about 50 yards and dropped. The Remington retained 75 percent of its original weight and mushroomed perfectly. The bullet didn't exit, but I did get 24-26 inches of penetration before the bullet lodged in the offside shoulder. If you asked me, I probably wouldn't recommend a hollow-point bullet for elk because there are better choices in the .44, but it will work if you recognize the limitations. The quartering-away angle allowed me to avoid the heavy shoulder bones until significant damage had been done to the vital organs.

One of the favorite rationalizations for using cast bullets is that you don't need to worry about matching the bullet to the game, and that a suitable hardcast bullet could be used for taking anything from moose to mice. This is certainly true enough, but there are a few problems.

While on my first trip to Africa, I used a .44 Magnum to take several animals, including zebra and wildebeest with a 310-grain hardcast bullet. The wildebeest was broadside and hit on the shoulder at 50 yards, and that bullet whistled right through him. This was my first experience with relatively large, thick-skinned game and cast bullets, and the issue I had in those situations was a lack of blood trail. Neither the zebra nor wildebeest bled enough to follow the spoor even though they were very well shot.

The wildebeest traveled about 150 yards in a straight line, and fortunately the cover was open enough to make recovery possible by following the tracks. The exit wound in the skin was small, about 44 caliber, and simply didn't allow enough blood to flow out for easy tracking. I nearly lost a good warthog with a high double-lung hit had it not been for a tracking dog that found the hog still very much alive about an hour later. I am certain an expanding bullet would have done more damage to the lungs and that hog would have bled out within 100 yards. Regardless of what it has been shot with, finding even a fatally hit animal in all but the most open cover can be a big problem unless there is a sufficient blood trail to follow. Throw in heavy brush and ground cover or soil that's not conducive to seeing blood, and finding your game can become impossible until the buzzards start circling. Mark Hampton, a good friend and fellow handgun hunter with vast experience notes in his book, "... big cast bullets in revolvers essentially leave a half-inch-diameter hole but most cases they do not kill quickly ... Unless the shoulder or spine is broken, or a brain shot is made, the chase will be on." I agree. If I ever hunt grizzly, rhino or cape buffalo with a revolver I'll choose a large caliber gun in .475 or .500 and pick a heavy, bonded soft-point bullet for the first couple of rounds and then perhaps have a couple of cast bullets in the remaining chambers in case I need the penetration they offer. Even on elephant a hardcast bullet would not be my first choice for a frontal brain shot — the Punch bullet and similar designs are superior choices in my opinion because there is no risk of the projectiles coming apart.

Cast bullets provide several advantages; the ability to mold your own is perhaps the greatest for the active shooter. A custom-molded bullet can be very accurate, but even the best are no more so than premium jacketed alternatives. The downside to molding bullets is the time involved and finding and preparing suitable lead. Tire shops no longer give you a bucket full just for the asking.

Cast bullets also used to be significantly cheaper than jacketed bullets even if you bought them already molded, but that is no longer true if you buy top-quality ones for hunting. If you're not a reloader, cast bullets offer even less in terms of savings and, in many cases, the jacketed bullets will be cheaper, a lot cheaper. For example, a box of 20 loaded rounds in .475 Linebaugh with the Hornady 400-grain jacketed XTP is just under $30 at a popular online store, while a box of 20 Buffalo Bore 400-grain hardcast bullets is just over $60. If I had the time to put into finding lead and molding bullets, or if I could achieve a significant savings over jacketed bullets, I would undoubtedly shoot cast bullets a lot more. Realistically though, how many times a year do you shoot something that requires the penetration offered by a 300- to 400-grain hardcast bullet?

Winchester has a mildly loaded .454 Casull round that is excellent for deer and other medium-sized game, minus the punishing recoil of full-house loads. Photo by G. Smith

Having shot game up to the size of elk with revolvers, using both jacketed and cast bullets, I will choose a jacketed bullet every time. To be the most effective at killing an animal, the bullet needs to expand and penetrate to the vital organs. If either of those two conditions is not met, then you're making a trade-off.

Regardless of a bullet's design or material, there is a trade-off between penetration and expansion. The more it expands, the less it penetrates. Ideally, a bullet would fully penetrate on a broadside shot, but if it hits large bones and stops in the offside shoulder or just under the hide, I'll take that over a bullet that doesn't expand at all but penetrates fully. Jacketed bullet technology has come such a long way in the last 15 or 20 years and it continues to evolve. Many bullets offer excellent controlled expansion and enough penetration to bring down the largest game.

Although it's now discontinued, the Nosler Partition HG has been a mainstay in my revolvers for quite some time. They were available in .357, .44 and .45 caliber in a couple of different weights, and about the only thing in North America I wouldn't shoot with the 300-grain .45 bullet would be a grizzly in close cover — but that's a situation I would rather not find myself in, period. The Swift A-Frame is a very similar bullet to the Nosler in design, and unless something better comes along, it will be my first choice once my stockpile of Noslers is exhausted.

One company delivering advanced bullet technology and design is Winchester. They provide a number of great bullets for handgunners, and their latest achievement is a dual-jacketed, dual-bonded bullet called the Supreme Elite Dual Bond. The Dual Bond is a very unique design that consists of an inner jacket that is chemically bonded to an inner lead core and an outer jacket that is mechanically bonded, or crimped, to the inner jacket. It's designed to open at a controlled rate into 12 segments or petals, six on each jacket, with expansion of up to twice the original bullet diameter while retaining nearly 100 percent of its original weight. This provides a combination of knockdown power, solid penetration and significant tissue damage.

Most handgun hunters will end up using this bullet on game under 250 pounds, but I wanted to try it on something a good deal larger — elk. During one such hunt, after a few hours of spot and stalk, and an attempted ambush that went sideways, I finally got a shot at a spike bull from about 60 yards with my open-sighted, 4.75-inch .454. He stood at a slight quartering angle, and from the time I shot until the bull was down was just under 13 seconds. Impressive! The bullet penetrated the shoulder blade about 4 inches down from the top, took out two ribs and lodged next to the stomach on the offside of the body cavity. Penetration on the elk was approximately 28 inches and included some very significant damage to the soft tissue and bones.

Based on my observations on the elk, this bullet is a little light for large game because of its expansion characteristics unless you limit your shots to broadside encounters and try to avoid heavy shoulder bones in the largest animals. I'm certain this bullet will fully penetrate deer and other medium-sized game from all but very oblique angles and will likely fully penetrate larger game on broadside shots with proper shot placement. To perform as designed, the Dual Bond should not expand below the cannelure or crimp groove. If it does, it can separate, which makes me hesitate in recommending it for really large game. However, it's a great deer bullet in the .454 Casull.

Bonded bullets have become popular in recent years and show great promise for a handgunner who chooses a jacketed bullet. A bonded bullet has an inner core that is chemically bonded to the jacket to control expansion and, theoretically, prevent the dreaded core-jacket separation.

I have tried the bonded Speer Deep Curl in the .475 Linebaugh, specifically the 325-grain bullet on several animals including a huge cow elk. That shot was a sharp quartering-to angle, and it crushed her. I was unable to recover the bullet when it became lost in the paunch, even though a couple of us looked for about 30 minutes. Her shoulder was broken, the lungs were ripped open from the bullet traversing them, the liver was punctured and torn and she went 50 yards and piled up. I've also shot a few whitetail and several hogs with the Deep Curl but have yet to recover a bullet to see how it expanded. I can report that the exit wounds have been what I would expect from an expanding bullet that starts out at nearly a half-inch in diameter. I can find no justification for moving up to the 400-grain bullet unless I'm after grizzly or other large, dangerous animals.

For medium-sized game up to about 250 pounds, choose a quality jacketed hollow-point bullet. If black bear or larger animals are on the agenda, use a soft-point bullet in the middle to heavy end of the scale for the caliber and select a bonded bullet if available.

If you're already convinced that a cast bullet has some extraordinary ability to kill game, then nothing I can say will likely convince you otherwise. Like I said, it's just one of those debates. However, if you're open minded and honest about the size of the game you'll encounter, then a quality jacketed bullet may be all you'll ever need. They will kill quicker if the cartridge and bullet construction is appropriate for the size of the animal and will generally cause more internal damage. Most importantly, they will leave a good blood trail when a cast bullet often will not.

If you do choose a cast bullet you should make every attempt to shoot the shoulder of the animal — preferably both shoulders. The additional damage caused by bone fragmentation will impede mobility of the game and go a long way toward making a quick kill and recovering your animal.

Above: This cow elk was taken by Gary Smith using a Freedom Arms .475 Linebaugh. The animal was taken with a handloaded 325-grain Speer bullet at a muzzle velocity of 1,500 fps. The shot into the shoulder was from 60 yards, and she went about that far before piling up. Photo by G. Smith

Left: This warthog was taken with a 310-grain hardcast bullet out of a Ruger Super Blackhawk Hunter in .44 Magnum. Photo by G. Smith

Left: A jacketed expanding bullet may or may not do what it was designed to do — expand. This 240-grain Remington JHP expanded quite nicely.

Right: Inconsistency keeps the author away from using jacketed expanding bullets on large game, because they may not expand. When they don't, they do a poor impression of a flat-nosed hardcast bullet.

Counterpoint:
The Case for Hardcast Bullets

By Max Prasac

We are a society heaped in the tradition of convenience. Milk comes from a jug, food from the grocery store, money from a machine. Hell, we order products over the Internet that get delivered to our door, allowing us to never leave the comfort of home.

We also like to buy bullets in bulk at our convenience. But, a bullet is a precision tool and one must use the correct tool for the job. Many have based their opinions of cast bullets on cheap, mass produced, one size-fits-all bullets that are of questionable quality and design. And when results are less than spectacular, cast bullets are shunned as being ineffective and slow killing.

You will notice that I have displayed very few photographs of hardcast bullets I have recovered from game. The reason is quite simple in that I have rarely ever recovered one. They nearly always exit, a factor in using hardcast bullets that I find useful and comforting.

There is no doubt that big-game handgunners feel very passionate about their bullet choices, particularly with regard to hunting. One school believes that a violently expanding bullet at a high striking velocity is the best method to quickly bring down game. The other school of thought — the one we will refer to appropriately as "old school" — believes flat-nosed hardcast bullets are the choice for all seasons, all game and all reasons. Both schools offer solid reasoning, but in many cases those from the old-school camp didn't start out there but migrated there through a series of failures.

By that I mean that when many handgun hunters began pursuing game with a wheelgun, they chose hollow points or soft points at maximum velocity. The problem with that line of thinking is that such loads may kill one animal spectacularly one moment, and the next the hunter is tracking a wounded animal through the thickets. Why? There are a number of possible reasons, including impact velocity may not be high enough to induce expansion, and then you have a solid-type bullet with a big, open cavity at the nose that doesn't impart much damage.

Let's face the facts: a hollow point that does not expand is going to perform a poor imitation of a flat-nosed hardcast. A lot of thought has gone into the nose profile of LBT's WFN, WLN and LFN-type bullet. They not only penetrate deeply, but also create a wound channel proportionally larger than their diameter. There is a common misconception that flat-nosed hardcast bullets produce a bullet-diameter-sized wound channel. This is simply not the case.

I was one of those big-bore handgun hunters that started off in the jacketed expanding bullet camp and met with my fair share of successes in the game fields. But, a spectacular failure on a small wild hog in Florida got me thinking — and experimenting. Instead of packing it in, I used the same load the following day on a much larger animal and the bullet/load performed as advertised.

I was really confused and bewildered. I hate inconsistency. Inconsistency makes decisions difficult and conclusions difficult to draw. I don't want to wonder what will happen when my bullet strikes flesh, and that is not a good place to be if the animal in your sights can fight back.

A lengthy conversation with good friend and longtime handgun hunter John Parker convinced me to try something different. I started testing heavy-for-caliber hardcast bullets and found that they were very consistent. The cast bullets didn't necessarily produce the initial devastation that hollow-points are capable of, but more often than not they produced an exit hole, something the expanding bullet sometimes failed to do. Not only did the flat-nosed hardcasts provide more than adequate penetration every time, they would also penetrate from any angle presented. This advantage really helps because you do not have to be nearly as picky choosing your shot. Over the years I've revisited jacketed expanding bullets to see if I have drawn the wrong conclusions, but that old word keeps coming back to haunt me — inconsistency.

A fellow handgun hunter and hunting buddy of mine once killed a 700-pound bison, using a .500 S&W magnum stoked with 500-grain softpoint jacketed bullets. A full 30 minutes after the first shot behind the foreleg, the animal continued grazing. Stunned, he finished the animal with a rifle.

On any other day, this load may have worked like a charm. He reported that other large animals have succumbed to this load/bullet combination, but this one didn't. This is a tale of more inconsistency, but, again, it's not a case of bad ammo, only perhaps a poor choice for that type and size of animal. However, one would logically expect a 500-grain load to be in its element on large game animals.

There are a number of reasons for a bullet not to perform as designed, including the fact that hunting is done under less than ideal conditions and shot angles are rarely perfect. What's more, the animal may be alerted to your presence and adrenalized, the bullet may have clipped a bone just right to send it off its course by a millimeter, and the list of possibilities goes on. There are so many factors that can negatively affect terminal performance. This is exactly why I choose a more prudent route by going with the type of bullet and load that will likely work under most circumstances. It's a safer bet and not nearly as risky. While I would never consider myself particularly averse to risk, I feel I owe the animals I hunt the quickest and cleanest kill available.

Professional Hunter Bud Rummel enjoys hunting with a handgun when not guiding clients in Africa. Rummel also reported that upon purchasing his .500 Smith & Wesson Magnum in 2005, he had an opportunity to try out a bison hunt. At that time there were not many factory loads available for the big .500, so Bud chose what he thought to be a good load with a 500-grain jacketed flat-point bullet. He got a 32-yard broadside shot on a mature bull and, upon impact, the animal turned and began walking away. Then, it turned around and faced the perplexed Rummel, lowering its head and stomping the ground with its tail raised straight in the air.

Having hunted discontented bovines of the African variety in the past, Rummel prepared himself for the bull's imminent charge. Just then, a cow bison walked in front of the bull and the bull's attention was diverted momentarily. He sniffed the cow, began following her and then fell over dead. The bullet hit no bone, yet failed to exit.

Rummel hunted a year later using this same load chasing Asian water buffalo. He shot a 1,600-pound bull four times before it succumbed to its wounds. Fifty minutes passed from the first shot to the last, before the bull expired. No bullet exited and none were recovered. A conversation with Smith & Wesson's Tom Kelley pointed him to CorBon's 440-grain wide flat-nosed hardcast loads, and he has used it successfully ever since on all types of dangerous game, including African lion. He reports that this load performs consistently.

Tim Sundles of Buffalo Bore told me that for certain applications, particularly thin-skinned game such as deer, he prefers a bullet that mushrooms. He once had a customer call him and complain that he'd used Buffalo Bore's 420-grain LFN loads in his .475 Linebaugh for hunting deer. He placed the bullet through the shoulders of a trophy buck and killed two does behind the buck! This was clearly a case for an expanding jacketed bullet. The gentleman paid a hefty fine for his bullet choice in that particular application.

For large animals, Sundles prefers a hardcast bullet with a wide meplat but warns against overdriving the projectile. Just be sure to stay within its material limitations.

I have heard the claim that hardcast bullets fail to produce sufficient blood trails, but I would argue that an exit hole increases the likelihood of good sign by providing another escape route for blood. If the bullet stays in the animal, it can only bleed from the entrance hole. Thus, such claims seem implausible.

Once, when noted handgunner John Parker and his cousin were stalking Asian buffalo, they successfully killed a large buff with a Freedom Arms Model 83 in .500 JRH. That hand-cannon was loaded with 425-grain truncated cone flat-nosed hardcast bullets whizzing along at nearly 1,400 fps. They successfully put the animal down in less than one minute.

Preparing to leave and head back home, they decided to accompany a visiting hunter as he went after a mature bull bison with his .500 Magnum S&W. The hunter's choice in ammunition was a commercially loaded 400-grain hollow point at an advertised 1,675 fps — a stout load by anyone's standards. The first shot was true and nearly broadside at approximately 75 yards. The bull was obviously irritated, but relatively un-phased when it ran off. The hunter got another shot off that struck the bull behind the rib cage. This didn't slow the bison down, and the chase continued. The hunting party pursued, and once they caught up with the wounded bovine, one last shot was managed as the animal was quartering toward the hunter. After the shot, the bison finally dropped. The total time elapsed was 20 minutes — 20 full minutes! Once the bison was skinned and opened up, it was revealed that not one of the three bullets managed to exit, and the first broadside shot, which entered the onside shoulder, failed to reach the rib cage on the offside.

Many hardcast users have told me similar stories about starting in the shiny bullet camp and ending in the lead bullet camp. The other way around doesn't seem to hold true, and I have found that proponents of jacketed expanding bullets tend to have a very limited exposure to flat-nosed hardcast bullets and limited experience in their use. While this is simply anecdotal and not conclusive, ask around and you may see the same pattern.

I would argue that when your bullet exits a nearly half-inch diameter barrel or larger — keeping in mind the velocity will be rather anemic compared to a rifle of nearly any caliber — your main concern should be to actually reach the vitals of the animal. In other words, penetration is the most important action the bullet must take. Given the relatively limited velocities a revolver can deliver, the bullet can ill afford much expansion and the subsequent increase in frontal area, which will radically slow the forward motion down — if the bullet expands at all. If the bullet expands significantly and still has enough momentum to reach the vitals and destroy them, then you have a good situation on hand. If not, what you may have on your hands is a difficult tracking job. Not good enough for me.

There is also the very real risk of over-expansion that can hurt penetration. This can happen when the bullet's material is too soft, or it's being driven faster than it was designed to run, or it may be a combination of the two, which could result in a fragmenting bullet. This is why it is of the utmost importance to consult the bullet manufacturer to find out what the working parameters are for minimum and maximum velocities. While a

Over-expanded jacketed hollow points do not penetrate well. Photo by J. Parker

Revolver Care and Feeding **65**

The damage caused by a flat-nosed hardcast bullet with a large meplat can be deceptive from the outside looking in, but they typically produce a large swath of destruction in their travel path. This 200-pound Florida hog was shot at 80 yards with a .475 Linebaugh slinging 420-grain hardcast bullets.

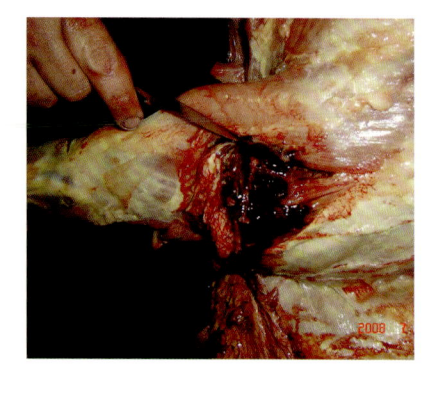

frangible bullet may exact much tissue damage, it may only create a shallow wound that does not reach the vitals of the animal. When bullets come apart, they often don't penetrate acceptably. A little expansion can be beneficial; too much is not good at all.

It sounds as if I am no fan of jacketed expanding bullets. That's not the case. When they work as intended and as designed, the results can be spectacular. I have witnessed this on a number of occasions. On the other hand, I have witnessed them not working as they should as many times, if not more. I have trouble accepting this ratio of success to failure. But I am not picking on the manufacturers of these fine bullets. However, I am picking on the concept and theory behind them and their use, and I am addressing those who choose to use the wrong type of bullet on the game being hunted.

We've come a very long way from a technological and material standpoint, and expanding jacketed bullets are better than ever — truly a far cry from what they were merely two decades ago. Yet you should not expect them to perform miracles under less-than-ideal conditions on game for which there are better bullet choices.

The author killed this 1,400-pound water buffalo cow with a custom .500 Maximum Ruger. The gun was loaded with 525-grain hardcast bullets from Cast Performance.

The author shot this cow moose using a .500 Linebaugh loaded with Grizzly Cartridge's 500-grain LFN loads at 1,200 fps. Damage from the big hardcast bullet was impressive.

It is especially critical to match the bullet to the game and application when hunting with jacketed expanding bullets. I would argue this is not the case with flat-nosed hardcast bullets. Small calibers can definitely benefit from an increase in diameter — no doubt this is a good thing from a terminal performance standpoint — but we large caliber handgunners don't suffer this inadequacy.

That is the beauty of big-bore revolvers. They perform their task easily. They don't have to be driven hard and they don't require high pressure, high velocity or big expansion. Again, I have seen cases that leave little doubt to the awesome effectiveness of jacketed expanding bullets, particularly the ones that are being produced today, but that same load on a similarly sized animal on another day may not perform in the same manner. If they performed spectacularly more frequently, you wouldn't see me using anything else. I am pragmatic enough to use what works and am not blindly loyal to one narrow train of thought. I simply use what works. Prove me wrong, I'm all ears.

Now, white-tailed deer are great candidates for the expanding bullet. They are narrowly constructed and really don't require maximum penetration. Even though they have an admirable and tremendous will to live, they aren't particularly hard to kill. I use both types of bullets on them successfully, depending on the caliber of revolver I am using on the hunt.

Cutting Edge Bullets also produces some great monometal bullets — designed to shed their petals on impact. But they offer a complete line of flat-nosed solids in many calibers for use when uncompromising penetration is necessary. If the need didn't exist, they wouldn't manufacture them.

Commercial hardcast bullets are fantastic and have their place, but casting your own offers you several options to tailor your bullets to the game you are hunting. You can cast your bullets hard by adding linotype, water quenching or heat-treating. You can also cast them soft for expansion, or you can cast a soft nose on a hard bullet, giving you the best of both worlds. Casting can be very versatile if you are willing to put in the time and effort.

Like all bullets, hardcast have limitations. Such bullets will not withstand very high velocities. High velocity and contact with a hard object such as bone can degrade the nose of the projectile, hindering its ability to penetrate deeply. If you feel that you need to push your .454 Casull or other high-velocity cartridge to maximum velocity, there are better choices. In this case, I defer to the Punch or similarly constructed bullets with flat-nosed profile that penetrate deeply and cause good wound trauma. But, to me at least, that is the beauty of the hardcast flat-nosed bullet. It doesn't need to be driven fast to be effective, meaning you can get away with lower velocity, pressure and recoil.

When chasing more densely constructed game, bullet requirements change. I have used both jacketed expanding and hardcast flat-nosed varieties successfully on wild hogs. Living in the southeast provides me with the opportunity to test guns, loads, bullets and theories on a year-round basis. No seasons on hogs, no limits.

Hog toughness can go either way. Sometimes they drop instantly, and other times it takes them some time and a whole lot of lead for the signal to reach the brain telling them they are indeed deceased. I am amazed at the amount of lead some wild hogs can absorb prior to conceding defeat. I once shot a smallish 100-pound boar in North Carolina with a Smith & Wesson .460 XVR stoked with CorBon 395-grain WFNs. Two shots from the big .460 in the lung area, and the hog still lead me on a wild goose chase through the swamps of Johnston County.

I emptied my Model 29 .44 Magnum into that tough little pig before he finally gave up the ghost. When I finally stopped him, I was underwhelmed by his size and overwhelmed by his toughness. A pig of that size would have been downed quicker with a good jacketed expanding bullet. Wild hogs can be very tough if not hit right, and I've had my share of them express their unhappiness to me. Wild hogs are built more densely than deer, and if you are facing a large boar, it may have a thick gristle plate — not to mention notoriously heavy bones — that can challenge the construction of your bullet. Again, it's hit or miss regarding wild hogs. They are not bullet proof, but they are much harder to poke holes through than deer.

Again, if thin-skinned game is on the menu, there is nothing wrong with expanding bullets. In fact, I've used expanding bullets in a .500 JRH BFR on a hog. But if you don't want to rely on perfect shot angle, then penetration is the premium you seek. And for that a genuine hardcast bullet can be the ticket to success.

On Velocity

Fact: Higher velocity produces a large "splash" and initial wound-channel size. However, higher velocity also produces greater resistance and has a propensity to slow the bullet down more than one traveling at a moderate or sedate speed.

There are other factors to consider such as bullet type. If a jacketed hollow point is being used, sufficient velocity will be needed to expand the bullet — the primary reason for a hollow-point design. It is possible to push a flat-nosed hardcast bullet too hard and experience poor performance. When you hear stories of hardcast bullets breaking apart or not penetrating well, it may simply be a case of too much speed. Breaking apart may also be a case of a bullet that's too brittle. If the nose shape is compromised by an excessive impact velocity, the ability to penetrate will also be diminished.

Moderate velocities seem to work better with hardcast bullets. With too much speed, you can exceed the material limitations of a lead bullet. But if your chosen bullet will plow lengthwise through a large, wild hog and cleanly exit given a modest muzzle velocity of 1,200 fps, you gain no advantage driving that same bullet to 1,500 fps. You will increase recoil and discomfort and may actually compromise the bullet's penetrative ability by exceeding the limitations of its material makeup.

I've spoken with a number of knowledgeable folks, most notably hunter Otto Candies, Jr. and John Linebaugh, who have noticed a veritable "dead zone" from approximately 1,400 fps to roughly 2,100 fps. There is seemingly no real gain in performance through that velocity range, so any attempt to push things over this will result in more recoil and noise and not necessarily an increase in performance (by performance, I mean depth of penetration). This is particularly evident when using cast bullets, as they do not stand up well to high velocities. I've seen this occur at the Linebaugh seminars during the penetration testing phase, where high velocity often did not equate to deeper penetration. Compound resistance is the term for this phenomenon, increasing speed does not equate to an increase in penetration — at least not linearly. In other words, the harder the hit, the greater the resistance will become, requiring even more force to overcome.

The Energy Myth

The fact that I am referring to energy as a myth flies in the face of conventional wisdom. Boxes of ammo are stamped with energy figures. Ammunition retail websites offer ballistic comparisons between cartridges, with muzzle energy as the comparative figure. Gun magazine articles talk about the energy of hunting cartridges. Threads on hunting and shooting websites discuss energy as it relates to killing power. Books about hunting are filled with references to energy as a determinant of effectiveness.

Energy has been utilized to rate the lethality of cartridges and loads for some time now, but what is energy? Is it definable? Is it measureable? Ask proponents of energy to define how it enables a bullet to kill game, and they will respond in vague terms. Really press them, and they will accuse you of having a poor understanding of terminal ballistics. Visit any web forum where arguments about energy erupt on a regular basis. Even many game laws call for muzzle-energy minimums for specified game. Seems like everyone is in on the sham! The terms energy, energy dump, kinetic energy, muzzle energy and more are tossed around by proponents with utter, complete and unfounded confidence until, that is, they're forced to explain.

A number of African big-game hunters I have been in contact with who have killed numerous elephants in their day often cite that a safe, effective cartridge for hunting elephant must have, at minimum, a 400-grain bullet and 5,000 ft-lbs of muzzle energy. I have not killed an elephant with a revolver or a rifle, so I defer to those with this experience. In their significant experience, this has held true as most of the cartridges utilized on elephant have met this minimum requirement. Yet, in the cases where they have not met this arbitrary minimum, it has been noted that the cartridges in question have not worked very well.

Having said all that, it's plausible to imagine taking an elephant with a frontal brain shot from a .475 Linebaugh revolver loaded with 420-grain bullets moving at 1,300 fps, assuming enough penetration to reach the brain and kill the elephant. Such a load would not meet the minimum velocity requirements, but surely that cartridge would be adequate despite the so-called inadequate muzzle energy. By the way, a 420-grain bullet at 1,300 fps "generates," or rather calculates, out to a whopping 1,576 ft-lbs of energy.

Energy, as such, cannot be measured. Muzzle energy figures are calculated. And once they are calculated, you can file them away in the useless information bin. Yup, muzzle energy has no reflection on the lethality of one round over another. Any .22-250 loaded to spec will create a higher muzzle energy than some loads for the .454 Casull. Which one would you rather have when facing down an angry grizzly bear? For me it wouldn't be the .22-caliber choice, despite the so-called advantage it would have over the revolver round.

Just about every centerfire rifle cartridge can boast better paper ballistics than a revolver. It doesn't require a doctorate in physics to see why, but big-bore revolvers don't rely upon velocity and rapidly expanding bullets to kill game. Big-bore revolver cartridges feature a large diameter and a relatively heavy bullet, which are constants, while velocity is ever diminishing.

Bullet wound trauma expert, Duncan MacPherson, has the following opinion:

"The assumption that bullet effectiveness (as measured by the damage that it causes) is proportional to energy is demonstrably not true in general, and all the evidence suggests that it is wrong for tissue damage. Kinetic energy absorption (i.e., the process of transformation of kinetic energy into heat energy) does not equate to damage in many physical processes ... The reason that kinetic energy and damage are not always correlated is that dynamic damage is not due to energy absorption, but to stress (force per area)."

In other words, energy proponents incorrectly attribute wound trauma to the mythical concept of energy. Kinetic energy does exist, but is mostly transformed to thermal energy, or heat, in layman's terms.

While perusing one of my favorite hunting and shooting Internet sites, I came across an uncivilized discussion about the ethics of using a so-called inadequate cartridge on large game at long distance. In this instance, an experienced long-range hunter wounded an antelope at 740 yards. His rifle of choice was chambered in .243 Winchester loaded with 105-grain bullets. Seems the shooter flubbed the shot, wounding the animal, but corrected the dope (settings) of his scope and followed up with an impressive, fatal head shot.

Immediately, the self-righteous Internet ethics police attacked the brutally honest author of the post about shooting game at that range. He was also taken to task and roundly criticized for utilizing a cartridge that was deemed minimal, inadequate and underpowered. Despite all of the evidence to the contrary with regard to the terminal effectiveness of the .243 cartridge in question, the naysayers unloaded in anger about optimal game weight for the cartridge's muzzle energy and threatened to form an

Internet lynch mob. This argument seems to crop up on these websites every few months now that everyone, qualified or not, is able to voice an online, rather anonymous opinion. Isn't the Internet wonderful?

Which brings me to the point: more often than not, so-called inadequate and underpowered cartridges can and do reach and destroy the vitals of an animal, yet some still consider them inadequate. Simply amazing. In my experience, energy, paper ballistics and conventional wisdom are often critically flawed in determining the lethality of a cartridge on game. You don't have to look any further than the black-powder cartridges of old, like the .45-70 Government that launched a 500-grain bullet at 1,200 fps (at the muzzle) and the terminal effects that load had downrange on game as large as bison. Bison populations out West were diminished with this inadequate cartridge. I guess they actually do work.

Proponents of muzzle energy tend to interpret the results of their observations in a manner that is not objective. I recall watching a hair-raising charge by a Cape buffalo in one of Mark Sullivan's African hunting videos, where the buffalo was zeroing in on Sullivan in high gear. A 900-grain solid from his .600 Nitro Express double rifle into the chest of the advancing beast failed to give the animal even minimal pause. Ultimately, Sullivan's second shot brained the buff, bringing the charge to an immediate halt, even though he still had to sidestep the crashing mountain of meat.

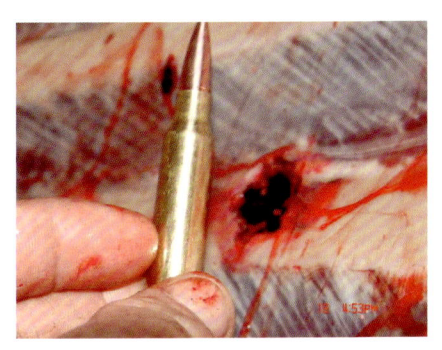

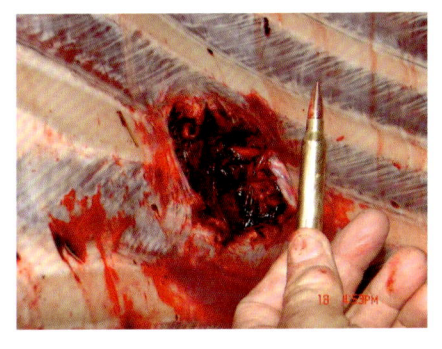

The hole in the ribcage of a bull elk was produced by a 180-grain TSX from a .300 Win Mag. Impact velocity was estimated to be 2,600 fps at the range the animal was shot, which calculates out to approximately 2,700 ft-lbs of muzzle energy. Photo by J. Parker

This hole (same bull elk), also an exit in the ribcage, was produced by a 440-grain wide, flat-nosed hardcast bullet in .500 JRH, loaded by Buffalo Bore at an advertised 950 fps at the muzzle. The muzzle energy is calculated to be approximately 888 ft-lbs. Muzzle energy alone, as a determinant of lethality, doesn't tell the whole story. Photo by J. Parker

Energy dump is a variation on the topic. Proponents of energy dump claim that if a bullet exits the animal, it has not deposited its full potential energy into the animal. But I ask, if the bullet stops in the animal, did it deposit all of its energy in the animal, or did it simply not have enough momentum and run out of steam to exit? The bullet may have over-expanded, at the expense of penetration.

In essence, big-bore revolvers mimic the ballistics delivered by the old black-powder cartridges, which were considerably more than adequate. Despite anemic power levels (think: muzzle-energy figures), these big revolvers, such as the .45 Colt, .500 Linebaugh, etc., when loaded correctly, are damn effective on even the largest of game. If the cartridge in question has enough penetrative ability to consistently reach and destroy the brain of a mature bull elephant, then, to me at least, the cartridge cuts the mustard. The deceased horse I keep beating here is that paper ballistics should be ignored when rating the lethality and effectiveness of any cartridge or load. Remember, holes kill, not energy.

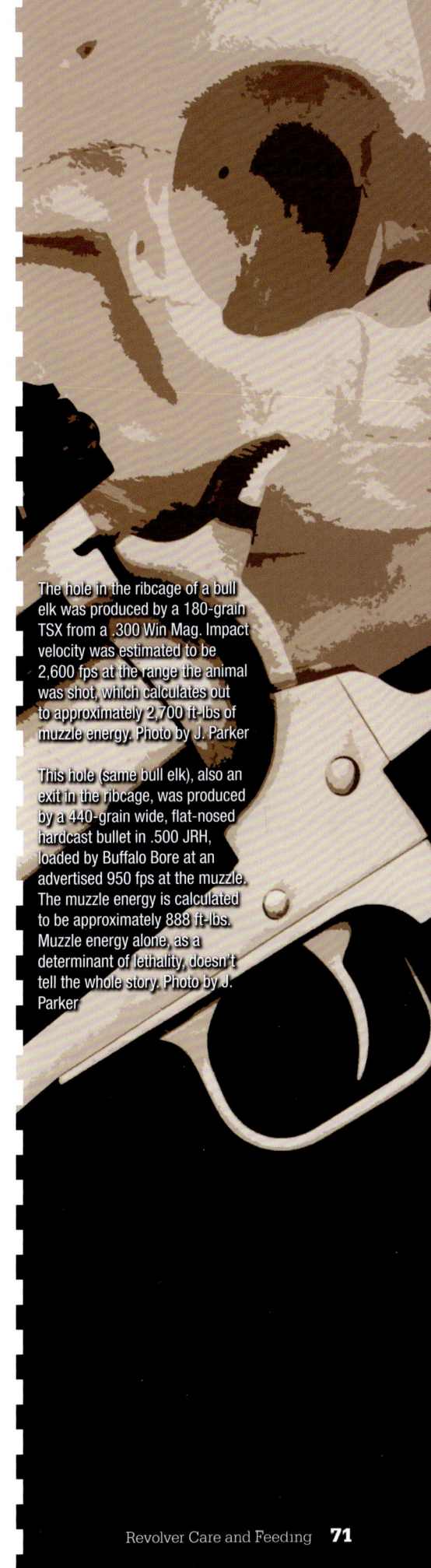

Revolver Care and Feeding   **71**

GRIZZLY
CARTRIDGE COMPANY
44 REM. MAG.
300gr. WFNGC
44 REM.MAG.
320 gr. WLNGC
45 COLT+P
300gr. LFNGC
45 Colt +P
335gr. WLNGC

CHAPTER 5

.44 magnum vs. .45 colt

Photo by W. Daems

The debate between the .44 Magnum and .45 Colt rears its head frequently among those who hunt big game with a revolver. Is there a difference? .44 and .45 are pretty close in size, correct? Not really. The .44 Magnum is actually .429 inches in diameter, while the .45 Colt is .452, a real difference of .023 inches. Proponents of the .44 Magnum are quick to point out how insignificant the size differential is between the two cartridges. Ironically, many of those same .44 proponents will readily acknowledge the significance of the bore-size differential between the various .45s and the .475s, despite the fact that the size difference is virtually identical.

While I have been a fan of the .44 Magnum for decades, I prefer the .45 Colt. Granted, not your grandfather's 14,000 psi .45 Colt, but the "Ruger-only" 30,000-plus-psi .45 Colt. I believe it to be a bigger hammer on big game, a conclusion I've reached through observation and the experience of others I trust in the field.

I've included the segment and testing I performed for my book, *Big-Bore Revolvers,* when I pitted the .44 Magnum against the .45 Colt. But I couldn't leave well enough alone and have performed another, even more comprehensive test, attempting to minimize factors that may give one opponent a leg up over the other. Immediately following the first segment is the expanded test I ran recently.

The Magnificent .45 Colt

This segment is dedicated to what I think is one of the finest revolver rounds to ever take a head of game — the magnificent .45 Colt. The .45 Colt was born in the 1870s as a black-powder round. In its original form it was no slouch, able to sling 250 grains of lead at nearly 1,000 fps. It accounted for many a human life in many a shootout. Times have changed, and so has the .45 Colt. No longer a black-powder-only proposition, the .45 Colt has matured into a powerful revolver cartridge able to take even the largest of game without breaking a sweat.

The .45 Colt is the Goldilocks of all revolver cartridges — not too big, not too small, just right. It will handily outperform the much vaunted .44 Magnum with bullets of similar weight, at considerably lower pressures, and leave it stepping on its tongue when loaded with heavy bullets the .44 is incapable of launching with any meaningful velocity. In this section I compare the modern .45 Colt to its younger progeny, the .454. I'm not advocating turning the .45 Colt into a .454 Casull, which is easy enough to do with a five-shot revolver in .45 Colt. With modern brass, the same pressures can be attained by the .45 Colt as the .454 Casull, but the .45 Colt doesn't need to mimic the Casull. The .45 Colt is lacking nothing loaded to the 30,000 psi range.

I ran a penetration test between the heavy-loaded .44 Magnum (300-grain bullets are the accepted heavy bullet weight), the .45 Colt and the .454 Casull. Does the extra speed of the .454 buy you more penetration? We will see.

For the penetration test, I again utilized wet newsprint that was soaked for 24 hours prior to the first shots fired in testing. The penetration "box" was positioned approximately 10 feet in front of the bench rest, with all shots fired over a chronograph to record velocities. Penetration was measured in inches (see chart below).

Only hardcast flat-nosed bullets were tested, as I was interested in maximum penetration. I chose factory-loaded ammunition from the Grizzly Cartridge Company for these tests, as the loads are all known commodities, with tested and confirmed pressure levels. There was no guesswork and no pitting one ammo manufacturer against another. Grizzly Cartridge Company stepped up with two .44 Magnum loads: 300-grain WFN at a claimed 1,325 fps, and a 320-grain WLN at a claimed velocity of 1,300 fps. The second load represents the upper reasonable limit in effective bullet weight for the .429 diameter and the twist rates of production .44 Magnum revolvers.

.45 Colt loads from Grizzly Cartridge consisted of a 300-grain LFN at a rated 1,250 fps, and a 335-grain WLN at 1,150 fps. None of the loads exceeded 30,000 psi in pressure. The .454 Casull was well represented by Grizzly's 300-grain LFN at an advertised 1,750 fps, 335-grain WLN at an advertised 1,600 fps and the 360-grain WLN at an advertised 1,500 fps.

As a side note, the .454 is a brutal cartridge, as you will hear me mention a number of times throughout this book. The high pressure, relatively high velocity (relative to rifle velocities), and violent recoil impulse all lead to unpleasant recoil. This aspect of the .454, in and of itself, will keep many away from this cartridge.

Three revolvers were used in this test. The .44 Magnum was represented by a Ruger Bisley Hunter equipped with a 7.5-inch barrel, a Ruger Vaquero in .45 Colt also equipped with a 7.5-inch barrel and, lastly, a Freedom Arms Model 83 in .454 Casull with a 7.5-inch tube.

CARTRIDGE	BULLET	ADVERTISED VELOCITY	ACTUAL VELOCITY	PRESSURE (PSI)
.44 Magnum	300 gr. WFN	1,325 fps	1,362.6	36,000
.44 Magnum	320 gr. WLN	1,300 fps	1,364.4	36,000
.45 Colt	300 gr. LFN	1,250 fps	1,326	30,000
.45 Colt	335 gr. WLN	1,150 fps	1,365	30,000
.454 Casull	300 gr. LFN	1,750 fps	1,539	59,000
.454 Casull	335 gr. WLN	1,550 fps	1,538	59,000
.454 Casull	360 gr. WLN	1,450 fps	1,467	59,000

Penetration Test
.44 Magnum vs. .45 Colt vs. .454 Casull

BULLET/LOAD	VELOCITY (FPS)	PENETRATION (INCHES)	NOTES
300/.44 Mag.	1,362.6	20.5	straight line
300/.44 Mag.	1,345.6	24	straight line
320/.44 Mag.	1,361	26	straight line
320/.44 Mag.	1,364.4	25	straight line
300/.45 Colt	1,326	26	straight line
300/.45 Colt	1,309	28	straight line
335/.45 Colt	1,365	27.5	straight line
335/.45 Colt	1,341.6	26	straight line
300/.454 Casull	1,525.8	25.5	straight line
300/.454 Casull	1,539	30.5	straight line
335/.454 Casull	1,538	29	straight line
335/.454 Casull	1,534.3	25	straight line
360/.454 Casull	1,456.6	32	straight line
360/.454 Casull	1,467	24	straight line

As you can see, all three cartridges performed well. The biggest disparity was clearly between the 300-grain .44 Magnum load and the 300-grain .45 Colt load. The .45 Colt demonstrated a significant step up in penetration — surely not a deal-breaking gain, but keep in mind the .45 Colt load penetrated deeper, with less pressure and less velocity, even though the velocity was close.

Despite the popular belief that sectional density plays a significant role in determining which bullet will penetrate deeper, my testing shows that this is not the case in many instances. The lower sectional density number of the 300-grain .45 Colt bullet compared to the 300-grain .44 Magnum bullet seems to play no role in the deeper penetration. Recoil was about the same, and the .45 Colt makes a discernibly larger hole. Yes, some will say we are splitting fine frog hairs here, yet most will acknowledge the greater diameter of the .475 over the .45, even though the size difference is roughly the same as the .44 Magnum to the .45 Colt. The 335-grain load also outperformed the 320-grain .44 load, but not by much.

The .454 showed some gains, but keep in mind I'm using bullets that are better suited to lower velocities in order to maintain nose shape. When the nose degrades, penetration suffers. In cartridges with faster velocity potential, a hardcast bullet may not be the best choice, particularly when engaging a lot of bone. That said, if you keep the velocity in a particular range, they are very hard to beat. If you're using hardcast bullets, the higher velocities of the .454 really aren't necessary and all you gain is recoil, muzzle blast and the possibility of a reduced level of penetration due to the limitations of the bullet material.

In conclusion, there is little about the .45 Colt not to like, and I can say the only real criticism one can objectively level at the old warhorse is commercial ammunition availability. The .44, and to a lesser extent, the .454, have the .45 Colt beat in spades. But, as you can readily see, there are a few manufacturers of really fine, high-performance .45 Colt ammunition.

Hot-Rodding the .45 Colt

The discussion of hunting revolvers wouldn't be complete without a look back at John Linebaugh's work building "Super .45s" on Seville revolvers (U.S. Sporting Arms — see sidebar) in the early '80s. Hot-rodding the .45 Colt cartridge was nothing new, but it wasn't widespread either. Remember that Dick Casull had been doing just that since the 1950s. The .45 Colt wasn't really looked at as a contender, particularly with all of the old Single Action Army models that were in the hands of shooters. Instead, it was viewed more as a has-been that had seen its glory days a long time ago. Linebaugh and Casull were visionaries in that they could see the potential the old Colt had to offer, if housed in an adequate revolver where the .45 could stretch its legs a bit. Casull's exploits are legendary, but Linebaugh's work with the .45 cannot be ignored and deserves to be examined.

Let me step off to the side of this conversation for a moment and introduce another player in this tale, a man by the name of Ross Seyfried.

If anyone has led an unusual and interesting life — including ranching, writing, guiding in the States and Africa, and trail blazing — that would be Seyfried. We have cited a number of his seminal works throughout this book, and for a good reason. If he wrote about it, it was thoroughly vetted and tested, and you could take his conclusions to the bank. Without his contributions to handgunning, the likes of John Linebaugh may never have been known, which would have been tragic to say the very least.

Growing up on a ranch in eastern Colorado, Seyfried got his first revolver, a Smith & Wesson Model 19 in .357 Magnum, when he was only a freshman in high school. He tried every commercial load available, including those with the highest velocity and lightest bullets, and reports that they didn't live up to his expectations.

An avid reader of Elmer Keith, the young Seyfried sat down with a pen and paper and wrote Keith of his test results. Keith promptly replied back that the .357 was useless and that Seyfried should acquire a .44 Magnum, and that is exactly what he did. Seyfried even carried a 4-inch Model 29 in Africa, loaded with the requisite 250-grain Keith loads and found it left him wanting more, having used it on many wounded game animals.

Then, John Linebaugh entered his life, and the game changed. Linebaugh convinced Seyfried of an alternative, a perfect revolver for hunting big game that was a sizable step up, over and beyond the vaunted .44 Magnum. An incredulous and skeptical Seyfried invited Linebaugh to his ranch to give him a demonstration from a good, safe distance away. Not only was he impressed with this display of power, but he was also determined to find out for himself how this rejuvenated .45 Colt would perform in Africa, a wonderful "laboratory" for testing his new pet caliber. The results spoke for themselves and culminated in Seyfried killing a Cape buffalo with a .45 Colt — with no big double rifle backing him up.

As a gunwriter with *Guns & Ammo* magazine, he had a platform on which to float new ideas to a weary and skeptical audience. But unlike many, Seyfried walked the walk and was in a position to talk about it. Seyfried stoked the fires of our imaginations with tales of slaying the wild beasts of Africa with only a revolver, introducing us mere mortals to such exotic and unknown calibers like the .475 and .500 Linebaughs, and the mythically powerful Maximums. He showed us that not only could the biggest and most ferocious animals be conquered with revolvers, but that their effectiveness was no fluke, with repeatable results. Seyfried didn't just talk about it, he went out and backed his theories with quantifiable and tangible results from the field.

His contributions to big-bore revolver development, shooting and hunting cannot be understated. He was a seriously competitive shooter, having won the 1981 World Practical Pistol Championships. A licensed professional hunter in Tanzania and Zambia, he spoke from a place of authority. Until recently, he served as a guide and outfitter in Oregon.

Seyfried reports that he has come full circle and that after many rodeos with some truly big and nasty calibers, he is back to the .45 Colt. He claims to have crossed that line of old age and practicality. We spoke at length, and in a candid and unguarded moment, he mentioned that his greatest regret in life was "not being able to hand Elmer Keith a five-shot .45 Colt. Not only would he have loved it, he was a man who would have been able to use it for all it was worth."

The smiling Richie Bochenek took this 42-inch Cape buffalo with his JRH-built .500 Maximum Ruger. The revolver features an 8 3/8-inch barrel with muzzle brake, topped with a Burris 2.5-7 scope. It was stoked with 525-grain Cast Performance hardcast bullets over a heavy charge of WW680. The bovine took three shots to earn mortality — all bullets exited.
Photo by J. Huntington

.44 Magnum vs. .45 Colt

This is an early John Linebaugh custom Seville in .454 Casull with a six-shot oversized cylinder. Photo by L. Martin

WHO IS JOHN LINEBAUGH?

This segment would be incomplete without acknowledging the contributions, influences and impressions John Linebaugh has left on our hobby.

The one word invoked by the name John Linebaugh is humble. He could also be said to be persistent. Missouri born and bred, Linebaugh was a full-time cowboy in the early '80s who drove a concrete truck during the winter. When the sun went down, he built revolvers. It was the ubiquitous .45 Colt that provided him with the inspiration he needed to eventually develop such iconic cartridges as the .475 and .500 Linebaugh. Armed with an old Uberti revolver in .45 Colt, he soon realized that the old .45 was capable of doing things the .44 Magnum wouldn't, even at significantly lower pressures. In his words, the .45 Colt would "do more work with less pressure." Soon enough, Linebaugh and his posse were riding the .45 Colt for all it was worth with modern brass and oversized six-shot cylinders.

In the early '80s, Linebaugh used nothing but Sevilles and El Dorados as foundations for custom six-guns, believing Rugers were of shoddy quality. All of this changed in the mid-'80s when El Dorado and Seville inventories dried up and were no longer produced. Linebaugh realized that the Ruger Bisley was everything he could hope for as a platform, offering strength and a grip frame well suited to heavy recoil. But his new foundation was also predicated by a supply of Sevilles and El Dorados that by then was rapidly dwindling. But it worked out for the better as he discovered that the Ruger's grip frame was even better suited to the recoil that was on the horizon. The writing was on the wall.

Linebaugh's big break came when he convinced Ross Seyfried to shoot one of his hot-rod .45 Colt creations — that is after he demonstrated that it was safe to push his custom Seville to before unseen levels. Seyfried was so taken aback by the .45 Colt's newfound performance that he commissioned Linebaugh into building a Seville in .45 Colt with an oversized six-shot cylinder. Seyfried eventually took this Linebaugh creation to Africa where he killed a Cape buffalo without the safety net of a PH backing him up. Actually, he had a PH with him, but his backup weapon was a camera! All was recorded and immortalized on the pages of *Guns & Ammo* magazine. John Linebaugh had arrived.

SEYFRIED'S CAPE BUFFALO REVOLVER

I have mentioned Ross Seyfried's Cape buffalo hunt with a .45 Colt on a couple of occasions in these pages, as it has been well documented and stands as a milestone event in the development of the sport of handgun hunting. The tool he successfully pressed into service bears a closer look, particularly in a book dedicated to hunting revolvers.

In John Linebaugh's early days, his foundation of choice for serious big-game hunting revolver conversions was the Seville by U.S. Sporting Arms (see segment on United Sporting Arms). At that time, these revolvers were the only revolver Linebaugh would consider. They were strong, reliable and of consistent quality. It is important to note that this predates the release of Ruger's Bisley, which would be a game changer later on.

Back in the early to mid-1980s, Linebaugh was fitting the Seville frame (after opening the cylinder window) with an oversized six-shot cylinder of heat-treated 4310 steel in .45 Colt. He also re-barreled it and tuned the action. In this configuration the .45 Colt could really flex its newfound muscle, and flex it did, as it was able to handle loads that were easily more than three times the SAAMI maximum pressure for the .45 Colt. Very hot, and terminally effective.

In the April 1986 issue of *Guns & Ammo* magazine, Seyfried stated: "I worked with John Linebaugh from Cody, Wyoming, designing what I felt was the most efficient, powerful, hunting handgun/ammunition combination on the earth. We used an early Seville action, capable of taking an oversize cylinder to handle my turbocharged loads, and fitted a 5.5-inch barrel. The 5.5-inch barrel was the perfect compromise between sight radius, overall length, balance, speed and the ability to carry the gun all day, unnoticed, in a belt holster."

What the two men had created was the ultimate big- and dangerous-game hunting handgun for the time. This revolver left an indelible mark in my mind and an unforgettable impression on six-gun fanatics across the nation. It was a badass hot rod that delivered the goods.

As a tribute to Linebaugh's early .45 Colt conversions and Seyfried's famous "buffalo gun," I commissioned Jack Huntington of JRH Advanced Gunsmithing to perform a makeover on my Williams Shooters Supply dealer exclusive Ruger .45 Colt Bisley. The revolver was fitted with a Shilen 1:20 twist 5.5-inch banded barrel. The window was opened to accommodate an oversized six-shot cylinder made from heat-treated 17-4PH stainless steel, the action was tuned, and the grip frame was modified and fitted with beautiful Claro walnut custom grips made for my hand. The original five-shot cylinder was capable of handling higher pressures, but even in the new six-shot configuration you will run out of comfort long before you run out of capacity. Lastly, I would have had the revolver chambered in .454 Casull had I the desire to load to Casull pressure levels.

Here it is in all of its buffalo killing glory, the Linebaugh-built .45 Colt Seville belonging to Ross Seyfried. Photo by R. Seyfried

Above: My modern-day homage to the Seyfried Seville is this Ruger Bisley fitted with a six-shot oversized cylinder and a banded 5.5-inch barrel, built by JRH Advanced Gunsmithing.

Right: This is a Martin creation (with the Linebaugh .454 Seville) and faithful reproduction of the famous Seyfried "Buffalo Gun." Through painstaking research, the Martins were able to build this facsimile of the famous Seville. Photo by L. Martin

Another Man's Perspective

After years of arguing the merits of the .44 Magnum and the .45 Colt, in heated exchanges that bordered on the verbally violent, I approached my nemesis, a Mr. Craig Copeland, to produce a piece for this book about the superiority of the .44 Magnum over the bigger .45 Colt. I would write the counterpoint and then produce a penetration test, pitting the two cartridges against each other. I even went as far as to have two custom revolvers built (in the name of science, of course) with the same specifications, aside from caliber, to remove as many variables as possible. I then assembled a dozen different loads for each to put head to head, to include some of Copeland's pet giant-killer .44 Mag loads.

Internet blows aside, I stopped arguing, made contact and recruited Copeland to take part in this latest endeavor. You will recall in the first test, the .45 Colt edged out the .44 Magnum in penetration. But would the .45 reprise act one? We were about to find out. Well, Copeland one-upped me in that he performed his own penetration test that is included below, backing his blather quite convincingly. Things weren't looking so good for me, or the old .45 Colt.

The .44 Magnum versus .45 Colt: Part I

By Craig Copeland

The .44 Magnum has reigned supreme as the most powerful revolver cartridge commonly available for the better part of three decades. That is, until some industrious folks discovered that the Ruger .45 Colt Blackhawk, which was made on the same large frame of the Super Blackhawk, had a lot more potential than what was offered by the ammunition companies. Factory .45 Colt ammunition is typically loaded to no more than 14,000 psi in deference to the many old black-powder guns that chamber the ancient cartridge. John Linebaugh may not have been the first to explore the .45's potential, but he is probably due the most credit for making it a mainstream practice.

Through destructive testing, it was deduced that the .45 was about 80 percent as strong as the .44 Magnum. Thus, the accepted maximum pressure was set at 32,000 CUP, or 80 percent of the .44 Magnum's 40,000 CUP. What Linebaugh found was that the .45 Colt could meet or exceed .44 Magnum performance, despite the lower pressure threshold. He also found that the cartridge was most efficient with heavier bullets of 300 grains or more. Well respected gunwriter Ross Seyfried heard of Linebaugh's claims of exceeding .44 Magnum performance with the .45 Colt, and when the two met in the early 1980s, Seyfried was skeptical at best. They tested loads in the 55,000-CUP range using a Seville revolver with an oversized six-shot cylinder, and Seyfried was so impressed he used a similar revolver to take African Cape buffalo years later.

Let's get back to the 32,000-CUP loads appropriate for the factory six-shot guns. Touted loads are a 260-grain at 1,400 fps, a 310- to 320-grain at 1,300 fps, and a 350-grain at around 1,100 fps, all at less operating pressure, less felt recoil and less muzzle blast than the .44 Mag. Seyfried, along with other influential gunwriters, began writing about the subject, including John Taffin, Brian Pearce, Dave Scovill and our own Max Prasac. These loads quickly gained in popularity as more and more shooters discovered them. They eventually found their way into many reloading manuals as a special "Ruger only" section. Today, the practice of realizing the full potential of the .45 Colt is more popular than ever in stronger guns such as the large-frame Ruger single actions, the double-action Redhawk, Colt Anaconda, Dan Wesson revolvers, T/C Contender and many lever-action rifles.

I grew up reading the works of Keith, Skelton, Seyfried and Taffin in the 1980s. I pored over every six-gun article I could find and absorbed everything possible. Bought my first single action at age 12 and my first .44 Magnum at 16. I accepted what I'd read of the .45 Colt and what it was able to do and took it all to heart. Enough folks who knew better than myself claimed it, so it had to be true. It didn't matter; I was happy with my .44s.

Having always wanted to try those mystical "Ruger only" loads, I had to wait until a friend bought a Vaquero that I was able to load some up and try them. Having spent a good bit of time with a rambunctious 4-inch Super Blackhawk, I remember the first time I let go of a "Ruger only" load in the big 5.5-inch Vaquero. I was anxious to see if there really was less recoil and blast. It seemed to me like it stung just like the short .44 and was just as loud. We finished the box and went on about our business. It was a few years later that I procured my own large-frame Bisley Vaquero .45 Colt and was able to fully explore the world of "Ruger only." I tried several different bullet weights and took some game but found nothing extraordinary about it and went back to shooting the .44s.

One versus the Other

These days, when this discussion comes up, it almost always degrades into a heated battle, not unlike Ford vs. Chevy arguments, as though we are all required to choose a side and bitterly hate the other. The argument is always the same — the .45 Colt yields better performance at less pressure. It handles heavy bullets better. It handles heavier bullets. It penetrates better. It has history. It does this, it does that. Reading such exchanges, one might wonder why the .44 Magnum doesn't just crawl into a quiet place and kill itself. You'll get your dog spit on and your mother's reputation ruined if you find yourself in the wrong place, on the wrong side. It's as if no other cartridge exists, nor should it ever.

I honestly do not understand this need to choose one and forsake the other and take a different approach, because I do not choose a side. I love both cartridges for different reasons. I own several guns in each chambering and load for them in high quantity on a pair of Dillon 650s. I cannot be labeled a .45 Colt hater, but I do strive to maintain some objectivity when assessing them and the guns that chamber them.

The .45 Colt is a grand, old cartridge, but let's be honest, it's not perfect. A great many of the guns chambering the round are cut with unnecessarily large chambers and chamber mouths can be greatly undersized or greatly oversized, none of which is very conducive to accuracy. The best of .45s are either made from rechambered .41s and .44s, have brand-new, scratch-built cylinders or have Freedom Arms etched into the barrel. My own New

Frontier sports .457-inch chamber mouths but still manages to shoot well with .452-inch cast bullets. The above-mentioned Bisley Vaquero has been fully tuned and reamed by David Clements but is still no more than an average shooter. Oversized chambers lose pressure and velocity, not to mention overworking of the brass. I've sold .45 Colt guns because they blew too much debris in my face when shooting anything less than high-pressure loads, due to the oversized chambers. The .44s do not tend to suffer these maladies and shoot very well out of the box.

The .45 Colt has a cavernous case, and that works against it at standard pressures. It's big and impressive, but when loaded to 14,000 psi, there's a lot of empty room in there. At that level, the .44 Special and .45 ACP are much more efficient cartridges, getting the job done with less powder. It's not until loaded to at least "Ruger only" pressures that the big .45 comes into its own and seems to eclipse the .44 Magnum. At least that has always been repeated as gospel since the 1980s, but is it still true?

I discovered something one day that would make me question it. It wasn't a wild story of over-zealous handloading practices. It was Hodgdon's reloading manual. In it I found all manner of heavy bullet loading data for both the .44 Magnum and .45 Colt. I noticed that the .45 Colt data correlated handily with Linebaugh's own numbers. That's not what was interesting. What was downright fascinating was the data being reported for the .44 Magnum. With heavy bullets of 300 grains up to Beartooth's monstrous 355-grain WLN, the .44 Magnum delivered velocities exceeding those of the .45 Colt loads. Could it be true? Could it be that the .44 Magnum doesn't really lurk in the .45's shadow? I set out to discover the truth.

The test guns, nearly identical Ruger Bisley's built by David Clements. Photo by C. Copeland

The Guns

No test would be fair without eliminating as many variables as possible. In this case, both test guns sport their original chamberings. Both guns were worked over by the same gunsmith, David Clements. Both wear the same 4-inch factory barrels. The only advantage of one over the other is that the .45 Colt has had its chamber mouths reamed to a proper .4525 inches. The two guns are as close as they can be.

The .45 is a large-frame Bisley Vaquero that originally had a 5.5-inch barrel. Clements cut it back to 4 inches, tuned the action, freewheeled the cylinder, recut the forcing cone, removed any rotation slack in the cylinder, rounded and butted the grip frame, installed a Bowen lanyard ring, installed a custom front sight with a post blade, and milled the rear sight channel for his proprietary S&W-style adjustable rear sight. The .44 started life as a 4-inch Super Blackhawk that was converted to the Bisley configuration by yours truly. It was later sent to Clements for tuning, custom sights, round butting and another Bowen lanyard ring along with a Bowen rear sight.

The Loads

Orders were placed through several vendors to procure enough of these monster-masher bullets for testing. Bullets came from Cast Performance, Beartooth, Leadheads, Oregon Trail, Hornady and Dry Creek Bullet Works. Bullets came in ranging from 250-260-grain semi-wadcutters to the 360-grain Cast Performance WLN. The 360-grain .45 and 355-grain .44 were deemed as the heaviest practical bullets for these cartridges. Because this argument is primarily regarding heavy bullets, the lighter bullets and Hornady XTP's were only brought in for reference. Loading data was compiled from various sources, including Hodgdon, Speer, Grizzly Cartridge and LoadData.com. Virgin Starline brass was used to work up to the published maximum for each bullet used, and then enough of each load was assembled for both penetration and chronograph testing. All loads comprised of Hodgdon H110 powder from the same container and CCI 350 magnum primers from the same box of 5,000. All reloading equipment used was RCBS, including the turret press, dies, shellholders and electronic scale.

The .44 Magnum bullets and loads tested. From left to right, 250-grain from Leadheads, 300-grain Hornady XTP, 310-grain Oregon Trail WNFP, 320-grain Cast Performance WLN, 330-grain Beartooth LFN, 355-grain Beartooth WLN. Photo by C. Copeland

The .45 Colt bullets and loads tested. From left to right, 265-grain from Dry Creek, 300-grain Hornady XTP, 300-grain Cast Performance LFN, 325-grain Cast Performance LFN, 335-grain Cast Performance WLN, 360-grain Cast Performance WLN. Photo by C. Copeland

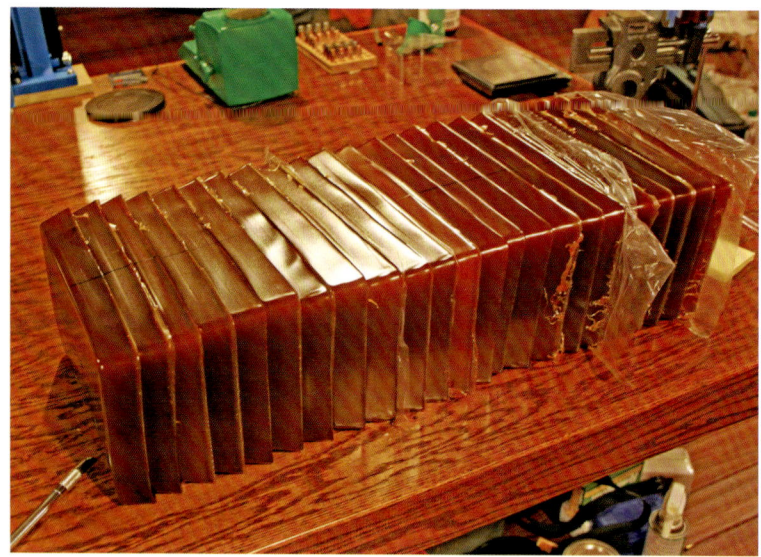

The test media, 120 pounds of Sim-Test, cast in 11 x 7 blocks approximately 1- to 1.5 inches thick and a total length of 30 inches. Photo by C. Copeland

The author shot this West Virginia doe with a BFR in .500 JRH loaded with a 440-grain flat-nosed hardcast bullet at 1,300 fps.

The Test

Testing was comprised of a penetration test, through Sim-Test ballistic testing media, and chronograph testing using a Shooting Chrony Gamma Master chronograph. An order was placed for two 60-pound cartons of Sim-Test ballistic media from Corbin. This material is made from animal protein and is designed to simulate muscle, adipose or brain tissue. It was chosen because it is more consistent than wet newsprint and can be melted down, recast and reused many times.

The entire 120 pounds of material was melted down and cast into 11x7-inch cake pans yielding approximately 30, 1- to 1.5-inch thick blocks to be stacked into a frame made of scrap oak lumber. This size gave me enough room to test several loads in each session and enough depth to ensure we recovered all loads fired. The plan was to test equivalent loads against each other so the results would be as consistent as possible. It is impossible to use the results to calculate how each load would penetrate on a live animal. Unfortunately, this material tells us very little about wound channels. All we can assume is that larger meplats create larger ones.

The Results

No matter which side you find yourself rooting for, the results are interesting. There was no cherry picking or retesting involved. The results were in no way manipulated to reflect a desired result.

CARTRIDGE	WEIGHT	MAKER	STYLE	MEPLAT DIA. (IN.)	VELOCITY (FPS)	PENETRATION DEPTH (IN.)	NOTES
.44 Mag.	355	Beartooth	WLN	0.340	1,130	24	Penetrated straight
.44 Mag.	330	Beartooth	LFN	0.300	1,226	25	Penetrated straight
.44 Mag.	320	CPBC	WLN	0.340	1,282	21.5	Penetrated straight
.44 Mag.	310	Oregon Trail	WFN	0.370	1,314	17.75	Nose flattened slightly
.44 Mag.	300	Hornady	XTP	n/a	1,156	9.75	Expanded to 0.64"
.44 Mag.	250	Leadheads	Keith	0.280	1,296	16	Nose flattened slightly
.45 Colt	360	CPBC	WLN	0.355	1,060	23	Penetrated straight
.45 Colt	335	CPBC	WLN	0.345	1,225	19	Penetrated straight
.45 Colt	325	CPBC	LFN	0.300	1,241	23	Penetrated straight
.45 Colt	300	CPBC	LFN	0.310	1,176	23.25	Penetrated straight
.45 Colt	300	Hornady	XTP	n/a	1,267	9	Expanded to 0.73"
.45 Colt	260	Dry Creek	Keith	0.300	1,290	11	Nose flattened significantly

Pressure

The first claim I began to question was that less pressure equals less recoil and less muzzle blast. Maybe if measured scientifically in a lab environment a difference could be determined, but that really doesn't matter. In shooting these nearly identical guns with nearly identical loads, I find recoil and blast to be, well, identical. For the life of me, I cannot tell a bit of difference between them. I chalk this claim up to theory and wishful thinking more than anything.

It's also claimed that lower pressure yields less wear on the gun. If the loads are within safe operating parameters for the gun in question, I seriously doubt that any thoughts about .45s outlasting .44s would bear any fruit. There's just not enough difference here to matter, and if you ever manage to wear out one of these guns, you will have surely gotten your money's worth out of it.

Size Matters

Size does matter, but not in the way that most seem to think. One thing I find to be very interesting is that while bullet diameter and weight are always factors in the comparison, meplat diameter is never mentioned. In fact, the diameter of the meplat is really the only meaningful dimension. It is the meplat that creates the wound channel, not the bullet's overall diameter.

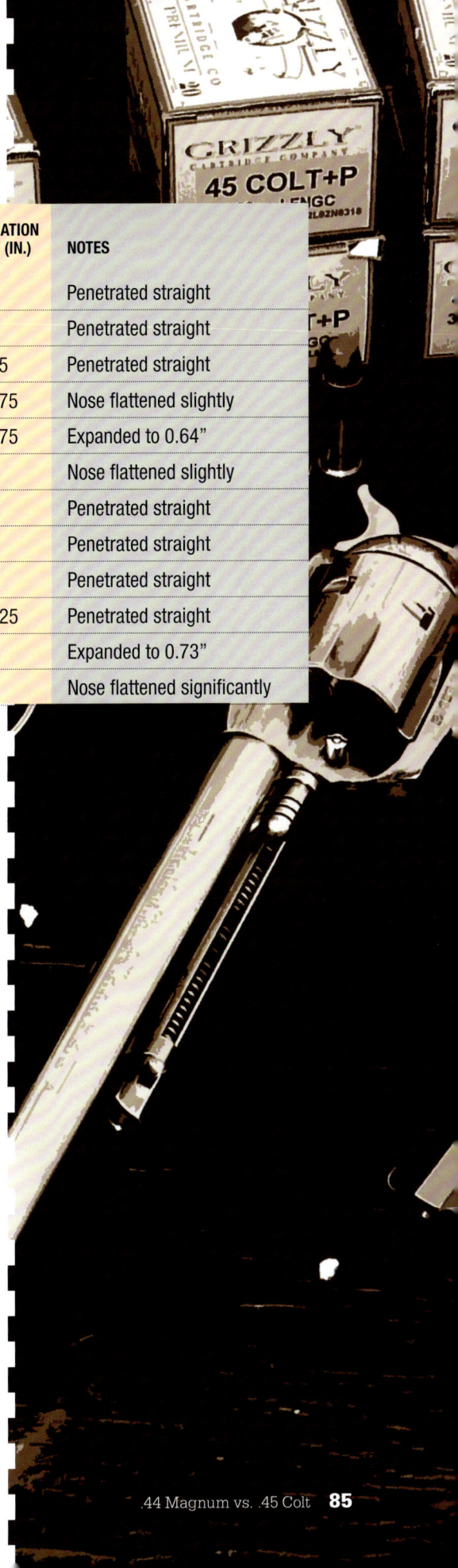

It is easy to discern from the chart that .45s are not always bigger than .44s. Sometimes, they are smaller! Note that the 310-grain .44 has a much larger .370-inch meplat than the 335-grain .45 at .345 inches. Their sectional densities are roughly the same, but despite the larger meplat and therefore greater drag, they penetrated close to the same depth. The 300-grain .45 load penetrated much better but has a very small meplat of .300 inches.

Note the 320-grain .44 load. It has a larger meplat of .340 inches compared to the 325-grain .45's .300 inches, yet they penetrated similarly. Which one is really the bigger hammer? Not so cut and dried, is it? So it is important to always address the operative dimension, the meplat. If the meplat is .300 inches it doesn't matter if the bullet behind it is .410 inches, .430 inches or .452 inches, with regard to the wound channel. With the understanding that for a given meplat diameter, a heavier bullet, or more precisely bullets that are heavier in relation to their diameter (sectional density), should penetrate deeper. It is even plausible that a larger bullet will encounter more friction and penetrate less, but we're really counting angels dancing on the head of a pin here.

Heavy Bullets

The argument here has always been that the .45 Colt handles heavier bullets "better." I don't know what definition is used for the term "handle," but it would seem to conflict with reality. The heavyweights in this test are within 5 grains of each other, while the 355-grain .44 bullet has a sectional density closer to that of a 400-grain .45 bullet. Yet, with maximum loads, they were within 70 fps of each other and only an inch separated them in the penetration test. The 330-grain .44 was within a measly 1 fps of the 335-grain .45 load.

There is a tug of war back and forth across the board, but the two are very close. I see no evidence here to support the theory that the .45 Colt does anything any better with heavy bullets. If there is an edge at all, insignificant as it is, it belongs to the .44 Magnum.

Penetration

It's obvious that the best penetrators were .44 loads. Not by much, although it's worth pointing out that an inch of Sim-Test has more significance than an inch of wet pack. It still only amounts to 4 percent. All of the heavy cast bullets that were tested penetrated very well and quite straight. It is a close race with no clear winner.

The heaviest bullets that did not deform penetrated the deepest. Bullets with smaller meplats seem to penetrate better than those with larger meplats. The heaviest bullets with the largest meplats matched the penetration of lighter bullets with smaller meplats, although some of the middle heavyweight bullets combine a very respectable meplat with very deep penetration, such as the 335-grain .45 and 320-grain .44. Even comparing the 310-grain .44 to the XTPs, it's easy to see that this load would create a very large wound channel and easily double the penetration of the jacketed bullets.

History

While the .45 fans love to claim history as a feather in their favorite cartridge's cap, both have it in spades, for the ancestors of the .44 Magnum predate the grand, old .45 Colt. Its pappy, the .44 Special, is no spring chicken. While the .45 harkens back to dusty cow towns and gunfighters, the .44's history is no less storied. Had it not been for Elmer Keith writing about his exploits, which led to the .44 Magnum's development, we wouldn't have those strong-frame .45s to load to 32,000psi.

Conclusion

There is no clear winner here, and that was not the end result we were seeking anyway. Our goal was only to shed some 21st Century light on a discussion that is often steeped in myth, legend and outdated information.

For all intents and purposes, the two cartridges perform nearly identical. Recoil is comparable with comparable loads. Both are capable of outstanding accuracy. Both are capable of taking the largest game that wanders the earth. Both cartridges fit into sixguns of the same size and weight. The point here is not to talk anyone into trading their favorite .45 for a new .44 Magnum, but rather that those with .44 Magnums ought not to feel the need to trade "up" to a .45 Colt. – *Craig Copeland*

The .44 Magnum versus .45 Colt: Part II

By Max Prasac

When this book was a mere concept and conversation, I wanted to revisit the .44 Magnum versus .45 Colt debate. I felt the testing I performed in Big-Bore Revolvers was fairly conclusive, but it seems that no amount of proof ever puts any debate completely to bed.

That said and acknowledged, let's do this thing again. To make this test even more waterproof, I reduce variables even further. My goal will be to see which cartridge is able to deliver the deeper, bigger wound channel. The bigger part should be a no-brainer with all else being equal (i.e., me-plat percentages being the same for the respective competing cartridges). For this reason I have pitted loads made by the same manufacturer against one another. This time around, though, we have even more loads and are

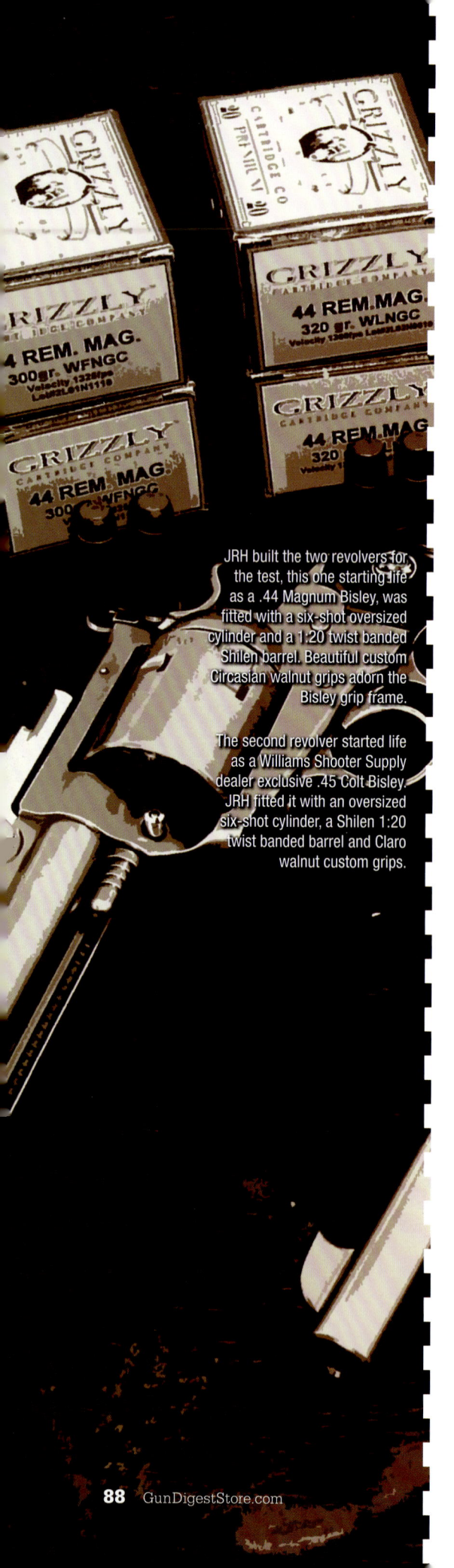

JRH built the two revolvers for the test, this one starting life as a .44 Magnum Bisley, was fitted with a six-shot oversized cylinder and a 1:20 twist banded Shilen barrel. Beautiful custom Circasian walnut grips adorn the Bisley grip frame.

The second revolver started life as a Williams Shooter Supply dealer exclusive .45 Colt Bisley. JRH fitted it with an oversized six-shot cylinder, a Shilen 1:20 twist banded barrel and Claro walnut custom grips.

utilizing an independent lab for all of the testing. A ransom rest was deployed to run all loads into the media, which was a mix of wet newsprint and magazines — tough material than in my first test.

Like the first test I ran between these two big-bore cartridges, I gathered a variety of loads from a number of ammunition manufacturers, as well as some well-crafted handloads. JRH Advanced Gunsmithing put together the two Bisleys fitted with oversized six-shot cylinders and 5.5-inch Shilen barrels, both with the same 1:20 twist rate. I don't want to be accused of stacking the deck in favor of one or the other by giving either an unfair advantage, perceived or otherwise; hence, the two new custom revolvers.

I even performed some impromptu penetration testing on a dead water buffalo while on a hunt in Texas. While this test was anecdotal, it was a bit surprising. I shot the shoulder of a dead cow with two loads a mere 2 inches apart through a shoulder bone. The two loads were on the extreme end of the spectrum, the .44 Magnum represented by Buffalo Bore's very serious 340-grain +P+ load and Garrett Cartridge's equally imposing 365-grain .45 Colt +P load. The .45 exited and was not found, the .44 stopped just under the offside hide. Keep in mind a dead animal is harder to penetrate than a live one. Again, this is all interesting, but anecdotal.

88 GunDigestStore.com

Penetration Test - .44 Magnum

BULLET/LOAD	VELOCITY (FPS)	PENETRATION (INCHES)	NOTES
330 Garrett	1,342	21.5	
	1,347	16.6	Meplat deformed
320 Double Tap	1,331	21.5	
	1,300	21.5	
340 Buffalo Bore	1,355	26	
	0**	26	
310 Garrett Low-vel	1,070	15	Veered out of box
	1,046	19	3 inches off course
355 Beartooth CL	1,171	23	2 inches off course
	0**	27	4 inches off course
240 Norma Triclad	1,393	14	Nose damage
	1,403	19	
300 WFN Grizzly	1,228	22.5	
	1,255	22.5	
310 Garrett Hi-vel	1,325	20	
	1,304	21	
330 Beartooth CL	1,256	29	
	1,252	29	
320 WFN Grizzly	1,087	19.5	
	1,023	20	
305 LFN Buffalo Bore	1,365	25	
	1,370	25	
240 SWC Double Tap	1,417	17	
	1,403	17	

*WFN = Wide Flat Nose, LFN = Long Flat Nose, SWC = Semi-Wadcutter, CL + Craig Copeland Handload

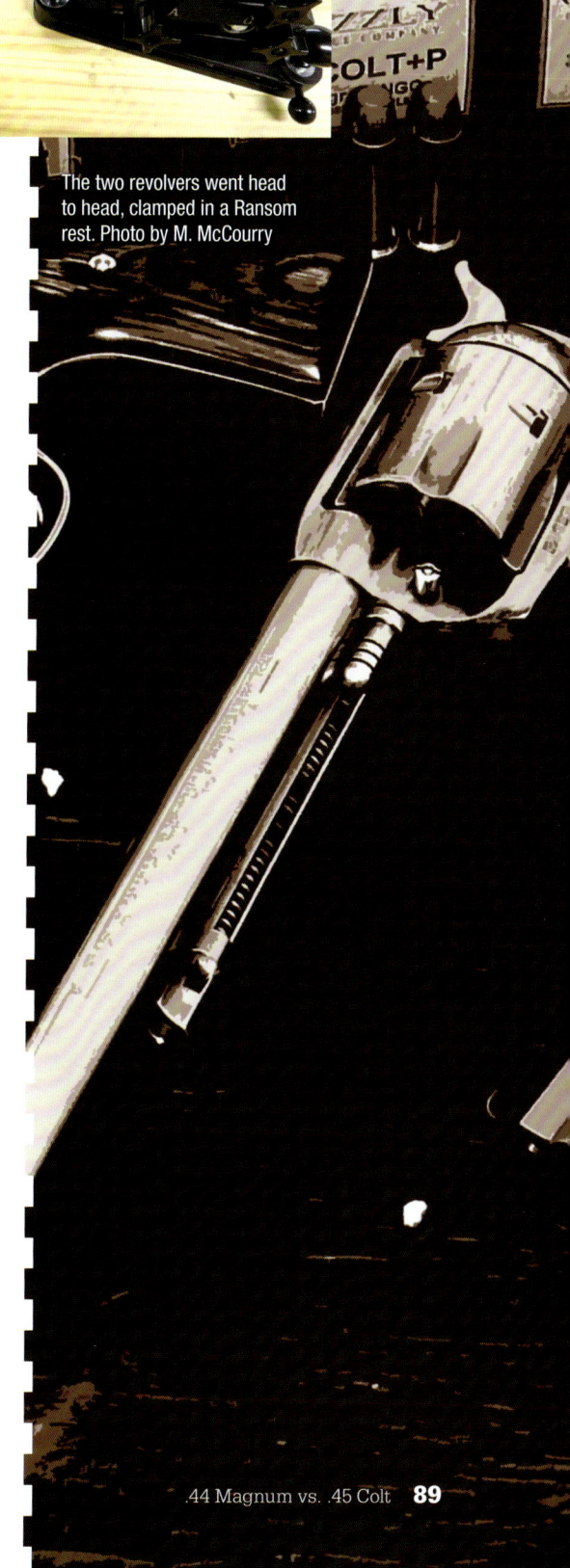

** No reading from chronograph, only penetration was measured.

The two revolvers went head to head, clamped in a Ransom rest. Photo by M. McCourry

.44 Magnum vs. .45 Colt

Penetration Test - .45 Colt

BULLET/LOAD	VELOCITY (FPS)	PENETRATION (INCHES)	NOTES
360 WLN CP — CL	1,315	18.5	Veered off course
	1,179	19	1 inch off course
300 LFN Grizzly	1,239	21	
	1,274	17	Meplat deformed
325 LFN Underwood	1,378	19	
	0**	18	Meplat deformed
325 WFN HSM	0**	13.5	Meplat deformed
	0**	15	
335 WLN Grizzly	1,298	20.5	
	1,298	21	
365 Garrett	1,117	18	4 inches off course
	1,138	20	4 inches off course
335 Double Tap	1,228	16	
	0**	17	
405 RHO Garrett	1,206	22	4 inches off course
	1,190	23	4 inches off course
360 Double Tap	1,136	18	
	1,137	17.5	
325 LFN Buffalo Bore	1,343	21	
	1,348	21	
265 WFN Grizzly	804	11	
	781	10.5	
265 Garrett	968	13.5	
	1,002	15	

*WFN = Wide Flat Nose, WLN = Wide Long Nose, LFN = Long Flat Nose, CP = Cast Performance, CL = Craig Copeland Handload, RHO = Redhawk Only

** No reading from chronograph, only penetration was measured.

And the Winner Is ...

If you looked at the chart of test results above, you will see that the old .45 Colt got soundly trounced — pretty much across the board, by the younger and smaller .44 Remington Magnum. Yep, the .45 Colt lost its shorts in the penetration test. A whole slew of serious load combinations went head to head, and in all honesty, most will serve you well in the game fields or for protection against angry critters.

Keep in mind that wet pack is a tough material. If your chosen bullet/load penetrates fairly well in wet newsprint, it will penetrate well in flesh. It's a material that will test the integrity of your bullet's nose. Once a cast bullet's nose is wiped off, penetration is compromised. You will notice in the photos of some of the bullets, the ones that went the deepest maintained their nose shapes better than bullets that failed to go deep.

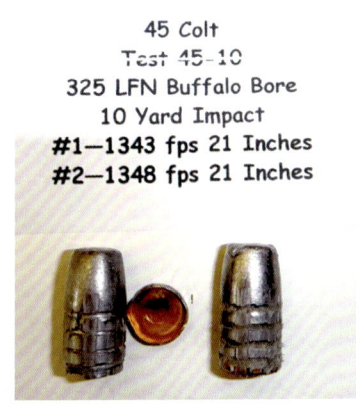

44 Magnum
Test 44-9
330 Beartooth Copeland
10 Yard Impact
#1—1256 fps 29 Inches
#2—1252 fps 29 Inches

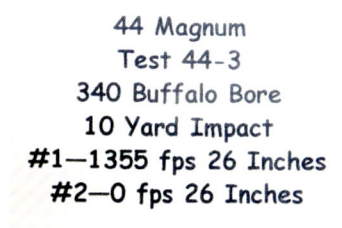

44 Magnum
Test 44-3
340 Buffalo Bore
10 Yard Impact
#1—1355 fps 26 Inches
#2—0 fps 26 Inches

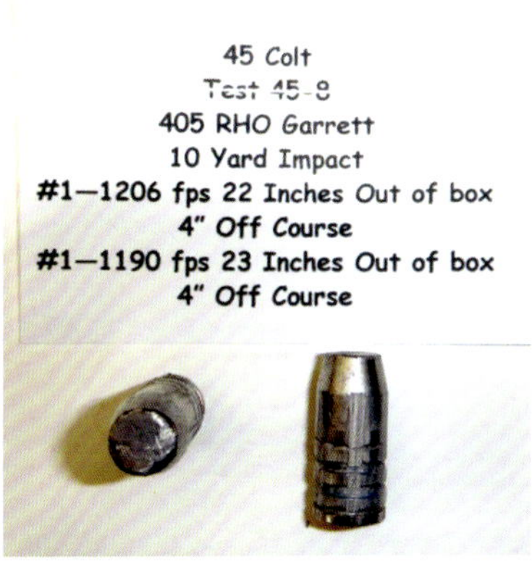

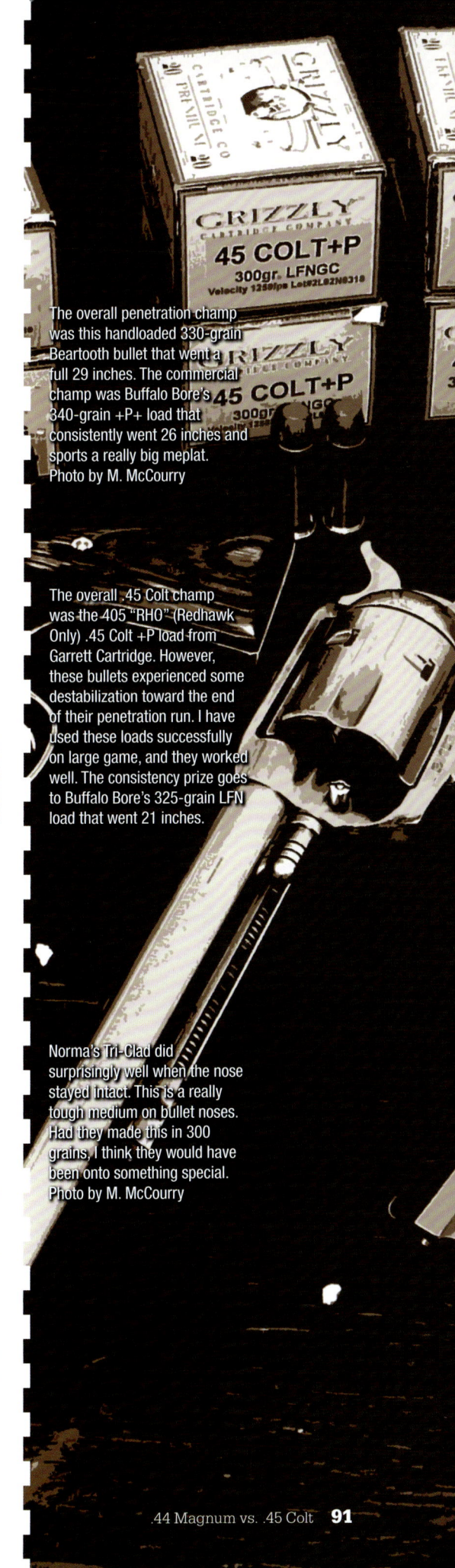

The overall penetration champ was this handloaded 330-grain Beartooth bullet that went a full 29 inches. The commercial champ was Buffalo Bore's 340-grain +P+ load that consistently went 26 inches and sports a really big meplat. Photo by M. McCourry

45 Colt
Test 45-9
405 RHO Garrett
10 Yard Impact
#1—1206 fps 22 Inches Out of box
4" Off Course
#1—1190 fps 23 Inches Out of box
4" Off Course

45 Colt
Test 45-10
325 LFN Buffalo Bore
10 Yard Impact
#1—1343 fps 21 Inches
#2—1348 fps 21 Inches

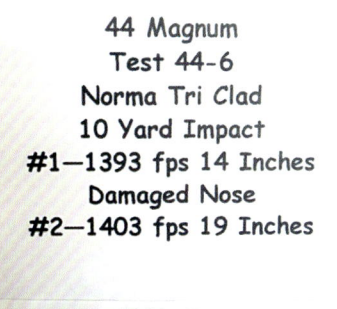

The overall .45 Colt champ was the 405 "RHO" (Redhawk Only) .45 Colt +P load from Garrett Cartridge. However, these bullets experienced some destabilization toward the end of their penetration run. I have used these loads successfully on large game, and they worked well. The consistency prize goes to Buffalo Bore's 325-grain LFN load that went 21 inches.

44 Magnum
Test 44-6
Norma Tri Clad
10 Yard Impact
#1—1393 fps 14 Inches
Damaged Nose
#2—1403 fps 19 Inches

Here's where I hedge my bets. I will say it again and again. If you are an observant individual, you will notice that on large game, there still is no replacement for displacement. Bigger is better, all other factors, such as meplat percentage, being equal. Bottom line is a bigger diameter bullet will typically make a larger hole and do more damage. However, put any of these in the right place, and a dead animal will ensue. Given the choice of the .44 Magnum or the .45 Colt (+P) on really big game, I will still choose the old .45 Colt, despite its rather lackluster showing in this test session.

But before I wrap up, I also want to take this opportunity to thank Michael McCourry and his independent lab for performing this labor-intensive test thoroughly and expeditiously. Without McCourry, you would be reading about something else in these pages. Now, can I get my revolvers back?

Norma's Tri-Clad did surprisingly well when the nose stayed intact. This is a really tough medium on bullet noses. Had they made this in 300 grains, I think they would have been onto something special. Photo by M. McCourry

sighting systems

How you hunt with a revolver will help determine the optimal sighting system for your application. Also, your vision will dictate what is appropriate for you to meet with success in the field. What is the best system available? That depends. There are a number of factors that come into play — what is best for you may not be best for someone else.

You should ask yourself a number of questions first, to make a good and educated determination. Answering these should help you narrow down your choices. Are you hunting over bait from a stand? If so, how long of a shot do you expect and what is the maximum distance you could end up ultimately shooting? Will you be shooting off of a rest (for maximum stability)? Are you hunting with dogs? How good is your vision? Another thing to consider is recoil and making sure the sighting system you choose can withstand the considerable abuse generated by a high-powered handgun.

I have laid out three major sighting systems to consider and their optimal uses.

CHAPTER 6

Photo by G. Smith

Sighting Systems **93**

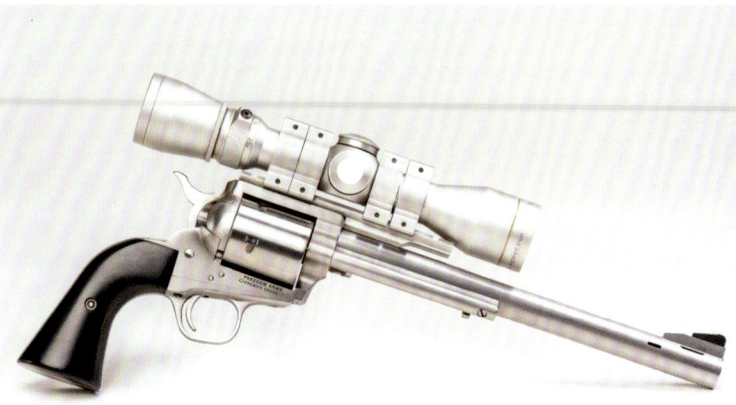

A Leupold 2.5-8x variable handgun scope mounted on a Freedom Arms Model 83 in .454 Casull. Photo by G. Smith

Sighting System 1: Scopes

There are a number of quality long eye relief scopes produced specifically for handguns today, such as those offered by Burris and Leupold, enabling their effective use on a firearm held at arm's length. Using a scope on a handgun requires some getting used to. All of the shakes and wobbles when shooting offhand are exaggerated when peering through a scope, especially when using a variable power set on high magnification. With a handgun, you don't have the benefit of whole-body support of the gun, which increases the movement of the firearm.

Because of the long eye relief, the light gathering ability of the exit pupil is compromised; therefore, some of the advantages gained by using a scope on a rifle don't quite translate over to a handgun scenario. There are simply physical limitations that are not the fault of design or manufacture,

Gary Smith took this Texas wild hog with a Smith & Wesson Model 57 Classic in .41 Magnum, topped with a Leupold 2X scope. Photo by G. Smith

94 GunDigestStore.com

Super Redhawk with Leupold FX-II H 4x28 Handgun Scope.

Leupold FX-II Handgun scope.

but the location of the scope relative to the shooter's eye. Good light does help a pistol scope's function. As with any system, before laying out your hard-earned cash, talk to the manufacturer about compatibility with your hunting or shooting rig. It may not be rated for your application.

Scoped handguns are best used with a solid rest, making them nearly optimal for hunting from a stand or blind over bait. They also offer the added benefit of magnification, allowing you to better assess and judge the animal. And, obviously, you can shoot at much longer ranges. Target shooting will be more accurate with a scope on a handgun, as the sighting system is more precise from an aiming standpoint.

All of that being said, I personally don't care for scopes on revolvers. They are difficult to use in a hurry. When you have the luxury of glassing an area and carefully picking your shot, scopes are fine. On the other hand, they can be detrimental in a defensive shooting situation for the aforementioned reasons. I know a number of very successful handgun hunters who use scopes on their hunting revolvers. But to me this is a very limited option that truly has a time and a place for use.

Sighting Systems **95**

OPTIC OPTIONS

Many people, myself included, have trouble with open sights even under the best of conditions. So what are your options? If you're a hunter, you'll want to equip your revolver with some sort of optic. You can have your revolver drilled and tapped (assuming it didn't come with mounting provisions already in place) for a scope mount from a number of manufacturers such as Leupold and Weigand.

However, if you don't want to have holes drilled into the top of your gun's frame, you have several viable options. I tried three types, and they all have their merits. The simplest, smallest and least intrusive is from JP Enterprises and consists of a small mount that fits in the recess that houses the rear sight. It will accept one of their JPoint holographic-type sights (I went with a 4 MOA unit). If you want to mount something larger, like a scope or a tube-type red dot, Weaver produces a slick mount that is a no-drill, no-tap variety, but you will be limited as to what you can actually mount as the rail is rather short. I sourced the Weaver base from Brownells, and while it's perfect for a scope, it is a bit problematic for a tube-type red dot.

Enter Weigand Combat Handguns, Inc. I got my hands on a prototype model of the new scope base (also a no-drill, no-tap type) that was made specifically for this application. This base was designed to withstand the stresses associated with the .454 Casull and to offer no compromise with regard to stability. The rear portion is mounted to the rear-sight recess, and the front part of the base encapsulates the front sight base (minus the front sight blade) giving two solid mounting points. With this sight base, the sky is the limit as far as optic options are concerned, as the rail is adequate in length. We used all three throughout this test, and all delivered. It just boils down to preference.

Sighting System 2: Red-Dot Sights

Red-dot sights offer no magnification but superimpose a red, lighted dot over your intended target. This is a personal favorite of mine for most hunting and target shooting applications. The dot on the better scopes can be adjusted for brightness to compensate for changing light conditions in the field or out on the range. It is probably the best solution for low-light hunting situations, making target engagement easy to attain in a hurry. Some red-dot type sights also feature an adjustable dot size, enabling you to adjust diameter up or down to better serve the conditions. In low light, where black crosshairs may be hard to see, the red dot can be adjusted to shine brightly.

One of the author's personal favorites is the Ultradot 30. The 30 denotes the tube size of 30mm. These sights are remarkably durable.
Photo by J. Miner

Sighting Systems **97**

The relatively new Ultradot 6 features four dot sizes and two reticle patterns.

Left: One of the best holographic red dot-type sights available today is the Trijicon RMR.

The author took this wild hog in North Carolina with an Ultradot 30 equipped BFR in .500 JRH.

There are essentially two types of red-dot sights: a tube type that resembles a riflescope and is adjusted and mounted in the same manner, and the holographic sight that projects a red dot on a small screen. The holographic-type is quite compact and may not necessarily add any bulk to your hunting rig. However, it may not be the best choice in inclement weather as it can be difficult to keep the screen clean for an unobstructed view of your target. Holographic types also tend not to be as rugged, as much more of the mechanism is exposed and not enclosed in a tube — something else to consider.

However, there are some very good units available, such as the Trijicon RMR. In general, red-dot sights are light

98 GunDigestStore.com

Ultradot offers two holographic sights, the Pan-A-V (above) that features multiple reticles, and the L/T (right).

in weight and don't change the balance of your gun in any significant way. Be sure to speak to the manufacturer prior to spending your money. Make certain the red dot you choose is up to the task of withstanding the recoil of your handgun (a recurring theme here!).

In any case, a good warranty goes a long way in customer confidence. Ultradot produces a whole line of economical and rugged red dot-type sights that come with a lifetime warranty. I am a big fan of Ultradot's products for a number of reasons, but mainly for the reliability of their products.

I have had an Ultradot 30 (this is a 30mm tube diameter, hence the designation) on a number of my heavy recoiling revolvers and can report that it has exceeded my expectations by a dozen miles. Thousands of full-tilt .475 Linebaugh rounds (420s at 1,350 fps) and a full complement of heavy load development for my .500 JRH BFR have tested the very integrity of that Ultradot. The poor unit even resided on my ultra-abusive lightweight Ruger Super Redhawk in .500 Linebaugh. The only failure I have experienced was a set of rings that broke from the vicious recoil generated by the .475. But the Ultradot 30 never missed a beat. To add insult to injury, I even mounted that sight on my 8-pound .416 Remington Magnum Mauser (yup, I do own a rifle) for load testing.

I have not been kind to my Ultradot. But like a loyal dog, it keeps coming back, tail always wagging. The only drawback with any red-dot sight is that battery failure can leave you high and dry at the worst moment. Remember to always carry a spare battery and the tools necessary to change it in the field. From supported and unsupported shooting positions, the red dot shines.

Sighting Systems **99**

This is the Bowen Target Sight, the finest rear sight available for your revolver, in the author's opinion.

The Bowen Rough Country sight is another great option. Once sighted in, it can be locked down to protect the settings.

Sighting System 3: Open Iron Sights

Iron sights are adored by revolver purists. While there are a couple revolvers on the market that come with fixed sights — such as the Ruger Vaquero — virtually every hunting or target revolver has a set of adjustable irons up top. They work well as long as you have adequate light. They are quick to acquire, but because you aren't peering through a tube, you have a full view of what is happening around you.

Why is this important? Just ask those who hunt bear or wild hogs with dogs why it is crucial to see all that is going on around you in the chaos of a hunt with hounds. You must be able to respond quickly, assess the situation, pick your shot and make absolutely certain that no dogs are in the way. Open sights in this situation have no equal. One of the greatest advantages open sights enjoy is their ultra-reliability and resistance to recoil.

There is no glass to break or batteries needing replacement. The only real limitation is your vision and ability to line up the front and rear sights on the target. With open sights, it seems the older you get, the better you were.

In my humble opinion, the best aftermarket adjustable rear sight is manufactured by Hamilton Bowen of Bowen Classic Arms. This is by far the best adjustable rear sight available for a revolver. It is precise, easy to adjust and well made.

Whatever you choose, you need to practice enough to completely familiarize yourself with the sighting system. Some sights take some getting used to, but once you do, their use should become second nature.

The Assassinator light can be used with any sighting system, including open irons.

HUNTING AT NIGHT

Hunting in the dark is perfectly legal in many — though not all — states. Wild hogs in particular are treated by some state game agencies as varmints, thus there are no set limits. As a bonus, it just so happens they make the perfect test medium for various guns, calibers, bullets and loads.

My home away from home is an outfit called Hog Heaven Outfitters of Johnston County, N.C. More often than not, particularly in the hot summer months, I hunt at night. Now, if there is a light source where the hogs are feeding, any sighting system will work. But, if there is no light source, there is a great solution. You simply bring your own light to the party with one of Hog Heaven's Assassinator hunting lights. The Assassinator is a small flashlight with a colored lens, the most popular being red or green, that attaches to your optic or gun barrel thanks to an easy mounting system. The light comes equipped with a number of different activation switches, including a traditional on/off button on the end and a pressure or remote switch with cable. It also comes with two long-lasting rechargeable batteries and a charger. Once mounted, you are ready to bring your own light source to the fight.

I've used the Assassinator on a number of nighttime hog hunts. It's an affordable alternative to expensive thermal or night-vision optical equipment. The Assassinator is appropriately named and works as advertised. As the photos indicate, it delivers the goods. In the field, before shooting, I turn the Ultradot on, flip the switch on the Assassinator, acquire my target and let lead fly. Works like a charm. Photo by C. Magera

Sighting Systems **101**

revolver holsters for the field

Whether you are hunting with a revolver as a primary gun or as a backup, you need to have a good holster. The physical size of the revolver is what makes it so attractive to carry in the field, as long as you can comfortably strap it on. Once you do, you will free up your hands for other uses, such as camp chores, clearing brush or climbing up a ladder stand. A revolver is particularly useful when skinning out an animal in bear country when your rifle is propped up against a tree, inevitably out of reach — keeping your personal defense gun close to your body. In some places, a rifle shot is a dinner bell for hungry brown bear. We all know bear attacks are rare, but why chance becoming a statistic?

I'm going to limit this discussion to open carry in the field and not touch on concealed carry. There are two basic types of holsters for outdoor carry that I recommend, yet there are subcategories and variations on each theme. They are typically made of either leather or nylon. The two types of holsters are belt holsters, which obviously strap to your waist, and shoulder holsters, which are slung over your shoulder.

CHAPTER 7

Photo by W. Daems

Holster selection will be determined by your needs. We are blessed in that there are many holster options available to handgun hunters today. There are many mainstream and boutique holster manufacturers across the nation. Obviously, the type and size of sidearm, and whether or not it is equipped with an optic, will determine where you can feasibly carry it. Do you really want a 10-inch barrel revolver with a scope strapped to your waist? The type of hunting you are participating in — stand hunting, spot and stalk, with dogs, etc. — should factor into your decision, as it will present differing equipment requirements.

Obviously, when you are chasing bear down with dogs, you want to travel light, and your revolver needs to be accessible. Are you carrying any gear around your waist? Are you using a daypack or a full-framed pack? Are you wearing bulky winter clothes? Are you working in the woods in bear country and carrying tools? And don't leave out personal preference, meaning what type of holster works best for you. Which one is easiest and most comfortable to carry and offers the easiest access? This is very important, as you will want unimpeded access to your sidearm, particularly in an emergency situation. Hunting bear with dogs taught me that you need to be able to draw and fire your revolver at the drop of a hat, as the dynamic on the ground between bear, dog and man changes constantly and rapidly. There is no time for fumbling to clear leather, as lives are at stake.

There are many different holster types that boil down to your needs and preferences. A number of mainstream manufacturers produce quality holsters, such as Bianchi, Galco, El Paso Saddlery and Safariland, to name a few. Smaller, high-end boutique makers such as Barranti Leather, Graveyard Jack's Custom Sixgun Leather, Big Rob's Gun Leather, 7x Leather, Mitch Rosen, Milt Sparks and Simply Rugged will cost a bit more, but you get what you pay for. There are also mass-produced, relatively inexpensive holsters such as nylon units from Uncle Mike's that may serve your needs.

Revolver Holster for the Field

This is the Northwest Mountain Companion by Barranti Leather. It's great for the range or field with minimalist styling and a covered triggerguard. This is one of Barranti's most popular models. Photo by M. Barranti

Belt Holsters

Belt holsters come attached to a belt dedicated to supporting just the holster, or they attach to your chosen belt worn around your waist to hold up your pants. You can carry your revolver on your strong side — that is the side your shooting hand is on, or in crossdraw fashion, depending on preference. There are many differing quality levels of this type of holster, but they all basically do the same thing.

An important feature, and perhaps the most important, is the retaining strap. This also pertains to shoulder holsters. The retaining mechanism needs to be strong enough to keep your revolver in your holster when performing physical feats such as climbing, running, jumping or even falling, but also needs to be quickly undone with one hand if you must bring your piece into action. Quality holsters can retain your revolver

A Paladin for the 5-inch Ruger Bisley, this time with a full overlay of "vintage bark" elephant hide by Graveyard Jack's Custom Sixgun Leather. Photo by C. Copeland

Left: The author wearing his Barranti "Threepersons" holster and a .45 Colt Bisley on a Virginia black bear hunt.

without a strap, but I like the added safety measure.

One of the less expensive brands I've had good luck with is Uncle Mike's, which are affordable and durable. I particularly like the thumb break of the retaining strap, as it is very intuitive to use. But, like all nylon holsters, they don't form to the shape of your firearm, a feature only afforded by leather. Some folks dislike the feeling of a 3 pound gun pulling their trousers down, and for them the shoulder holster is a better option.

This is the Barranti No. 5 model with Ruger Logo. The George Lawrence Company took input from the late Elmer Keith in the design of their version of the 'Threepersons' style holster, also known as the Keith/120 model. The early Lawrence pattern dating from the 1920s was made prior to the addition of adjustable sights on revolvers. It featured much more graceful lines than later models and was the inspiration for the No. 5. Photo by M. Barranti

The Paladin, by Graveyard Jack, featuring a tension screw, full coverage for the triggerguard and a hammer shield, for a 4 5/8-inch Ruger Bisley. Photo by C. Copeland

Right: Graveyard Jack's version of the Threepersons for a 4 5/8" medium frame Blackhawk. Photo by C. Copeland

Revolver Holster for the Field **105**

The No. 5 on Universal Chest Rig and Hank Sloan by Barranti. The Universal Chest rig harness and adapter allow you to convert nearly any strong-side holster into a chest rig. Photo by M. Barranti

Diamond D chest rig for a 5-inch Ruger single action. Photo by C. Copeland

Shoulder Holsters

The shoulder holster is the preferred method of carrying any revolver that is larger and heavier than a back-up firearm. Your gun may be wearing a scope or red dot-type sight, making the piece bulkier. Or, you may be wearing other gear around your waist that impedes the carry of a wheel-gun on your belt. A shoulder holster is worn opposite of your strong side, enabling you to grasp your gun by reaching across your chest. This is a really good way to carry a large, heavy handgun because the weight gets distributed around your torso in an even fashion.

Some shoulder holsters position the gun more toward your chest. They can also be adjusted under your arm on your weak side, with an attach-

Right: The author's favorite chest rig is this one produced by 7x Leather, housing his Super Redhawk in .480 Ruger with an Ultradot 30 mounted up top. Shown here on a bear hunt in Maine.

106 GunDigestStore.com

This is the Signature Series Northwest Hunter by Barranti. The top-of-the-line chest rig features bear and deer track carvings on the holster and shoulder strap, cartridge slide, lining and chest strap. Photo by M. Barranti

This belt and cartridge slide was produced by 7x Leather and is useful for a belt holster or to anchor a shoulder rig.

Left: This rig, by Pistol Packaging Inc. of Maple Plain, Minn., features a Bandito holster with a removable flap for carrying a scoped or open-sighted revolver.

ment point for added stabilization from your belt to the bottom of the holster. Others are positioned over both shoulders and attach to both sides of your belt to anchor the firearm and prevent it from swinging loosely. These holsters are harder to get in and out of without twisting the straps. They may require an additional pair of hands to set up.

A high-quality holster is a good investment that can provide many years of reliable service while hunting all manner of game. It offers protection from the elements for your firearm and, when broken in properly, can be as comfortable as a good pair of boots.

There are many options available, but don't discount regular production holsters, as there are many good ones on the market. Before choosing a holster for carrying your hunting revolver into the field, make a list of requirements to narrow down your choices. That way, you will make a more informed decision.

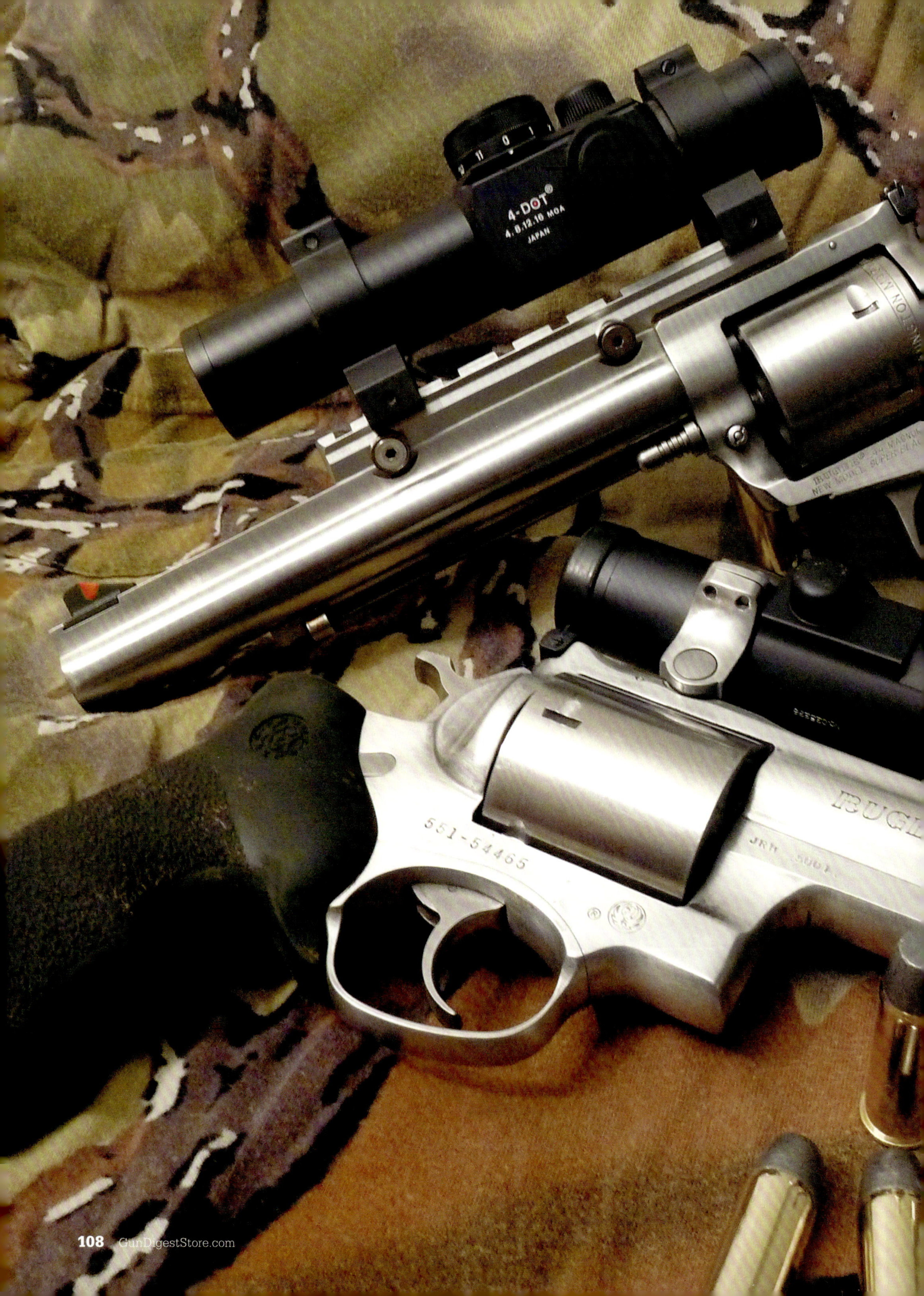
4-DOT
4, 8, 12, 16 MOA
JAPAN
551-54465

CHAPTER 8

big-game hunting revolvers

T This chapter will examine the currently available revolvers in both single- and double-action that are suitable for hunting big game, grouped by manufacturer, beginning with the largest producer of firearms in the world, Sturm, Ruger & Company.

Sturm, Ruger & Company

Probably the most produced modern single-action revolver in circulation is Ruger's Blackhawk and its .44 magnum derivative, the Super Blackhawk. Strongly built and affordable, this is the single-action revolver for the masses. These revolvers have a number of innovative design features that set them apart from other revolver makes in modern form, particularly the transfer-bar safety system — introduced with the "New Model" designation in 1974. The transfer bar allows the revolver to be safely carried with a live round under the hammer.

New Model Blackhawk. Ruger photo

Ruger Blackhawk

Ruger's large-framed single-action revolver is available in a plethora of configurations to suit just about anyone's tastes. It's available in blued and stainless steel, with barrel lengths of 4 5/8, 5.5, 6.5 and 7.5 inches, in both a standard "plow handle," or Bisley grip frame. Convertibles can also be had in .357 Magnum/9mm, and .45 Colt/.45 ACP. There are too many combinations available to list individually, including dealer exclusives. Check out www.ruger.com for all offerings.

The Blackhawk is available in the following calibers:

- .357 Magnum
- .41 Magnum
- .44 Special (Mid-frame "Flat Top" only)
- .44 Magnum (Bisley only)
- .45 Colt
- .30 Carbine

Ruger Super Blackhawk — The Blackhawk Grows Up

The legend begins in the winter of 1955-56 with a Ruger employee handing William B. Ruger a number of once-fired, unmarked cases, claiming to have found them in the dumpster of a local scrap yard. Bill Ruger's curiosity was aroused enough to delve into a little detective work. Ruger's investigation led him to the office of Remington's Dewey Godfrey where, with a little prodding, he learned of the super-secret new project they were conducting in conjunction with Smith & Wesson. That project was none other than the .44 Remington Magnum, a powerful handgun cartridge the likes of which had never before been seen. Bill Ruger was obviously a persuasive fellow, as he left Godfrey's office with enough specifications and technical details in hand to start his own company's ball rolling in the new realm of super revolvers.

The first .44 Magnum prototypes built by Ruger engineers were on the small .357 frame. Purportedly, they held together well until proof loads in the 90,000 psi realm bulged a cylinder. It is not clear whether or not the top strap let go; I've heard both versions of the story from various sources. However, Great Western Arms Company also produced a revolver that was Single Action Army-esque and found top-end .44 Magnum loads to be problematic. Ruger responded by building a larger frame.

New Model Super Blackhawk. Photo by L. Martin

Super Blackhawk

Four changes separated the Super Blackhawk from its predecessor, the Flat-Top .44 Magnum Blackhawk. Evidently, there were enough complaints about the recoil in the first Flat-Top Blackhawk .44s that Ruger decided to do something about it. The improvements made by engineers came in the form of the Super Blackhawk. The grip frame, the main culprit, was made larger in the old Colt Dragoon style, and it was made of steel instead of the previous aluminum alloy. More changes included a wide trigger and hammer, and the top of the frame was modified to more or less encapsulate the rear sight with ribs on both sides for further protection. Gone was the standard and somewhat odd 6.5-inch barrel in favor of a 7.5-inch tube. The fluted cylinder was replaced by an unfluted one. Lastly, the Super Blackhawk was fitted with a wide-spur target hammer and corresponding wide serrated trigger. Oddly enough, the Flat-Top .44 Magnum and the Super Blackhawk were simultaneously produced until 1963 when the .44 Flat Top was dropped from production.

The Super Blackhawk is available in blued and stainless steel, with a plow-handle grip — the Dragoon style square-back trigger guard, with the shorter-barreled versions receiving the smaller XR3-RED plow handle from the Blackhawk— and lastly, they are also available with a Bisley grip frame. Barrel lengths of 3.75, 4 5/8, 5.5, 7.5 and 10.5 inches are available. The Super Blackhawk is available in .44 Magnum.

Bisley in .44 Magnum.

While it took them awhile, Ruger heard the outcry for bigger calibers and made it happen with the introduction of the all-new Super Blackhawk Bisleys in .454 Casull and .480 Ruger. This is the revolver we've all been clamoring for, and now we've got it — and it's a dandy. Equipped with a 6.5-inch barrel, a long ejector rod housing (that was first seen on the .357 Maximum revolvers of the early 1980s), a five-shot counter-bored cylinder made from special, super-tough 465 Carpenter steel, a locking base pin and a Bisley grip frame. It's available as a Lipsey's dealer exclusive, so get yours while supplies last.

Super Blackhawk in .480 Ruger.

Super Blackhawk Hunter

The Super Blackhawk Hunter series of revolvers was introduced in 2002 as a dedicated hunting piece. Chambered in .41 and .44 Magnum, a limited run were also chambered in .45 Colt. Built with integral scope mounting points (scallops) along the dedicated rib on top of the barrel, the only barrel length offered is 7.5 inches. The revolver can be had in two different grip configurations — standard Ruger Super Blackhawk (plow handle), or the Bisley grip frame. Which is better? It boils down to prefer-

Ruger Bisley Hunter in .44 Magnum.

ence. I personally prefer the Bisley, particularly in heavy-recoiling chambering. I find that the Bisley handles recoil better than the standard, or plow-handle grip, and moves around less in the hand.

Available in the following calibers:

- .41 Magnum (plow-handle grip only)
- .44 Magnum (plow-handle and Bisley grips)

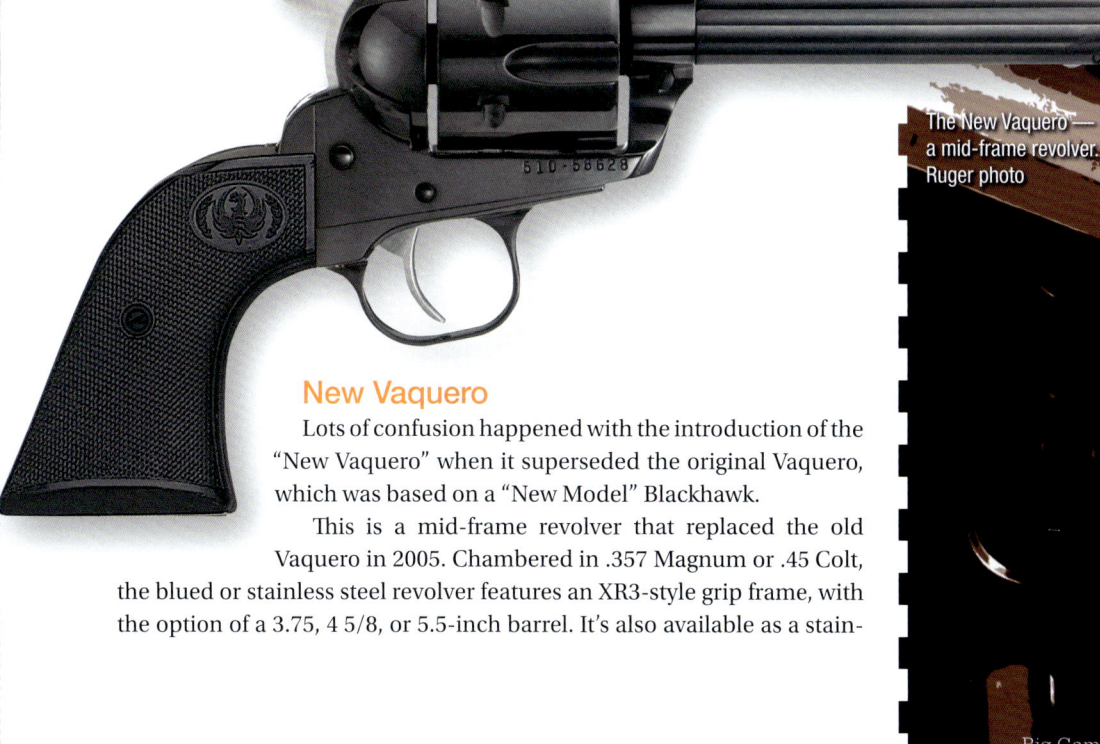

The New Vaquero—a mid-frame revolver. Ruger photo

New Vaquero

Lots of confusion happened with the introduction of the "New Vaquero" when it superseded the original Vaquero, which was based on a "New Model" Blackhawk.

This is a mid-frame revolver that replaced the old Vaquero in 2005. Chambered in .357 Magnum or .45 Colt, the blued or stainless steel revolver features an XR3-style grip frame, with the option of a 3.75, 4 5/8, or 5.5-inch barrel. It's also available as a stain-

The Vaquero — not to be confused with the New Vaquero — is a full-size revolver.

less or blued steel dealer exclusive with a Birdshead grip in .45 Colt or .45 ACP. Convertible models in .45 Colt/.45 ACP are also in the catalog.

New Model Bisley Vaquero

This is the same mid-frame revolver as the New Vaquero, save for the Bisley grip frame, trigger and hammer. It's available in .357 Magnum or .45 Colt, a 5.5-inch barrel, simulated ivory grip panels, fixed sights, a six-shot cylinder and is made of stainless steel.

While I like Vaqueros, new and old, I find that the fixed sights are a limitation. You really have to tinker with your loads to find what will work with sights that cannot be adjusted. Many folks adjust the elevation by modifying the front sight's height. Make mine with adjustable sights.

The Bisley Vaquero. Ruger photo

RUGER GRIP FRAMES —
THE PLOW HANDLE AND THE BISLEY

Ruger revolver arguments nearly always center on the grip frames that are collectively grouped into two types, the so-called plow handle and the Bisley. Big-bore revolver enthusiasts seem to be equally divided as to their preference, except when moving up to the really heavy recoil producers, where the Bisley seems to edge a slight lead in preference.

But, let's talk plow handle first. A generic term encompassing three different, albeit similar grip frames: the XR3, XR3-RED (RED for redesign) and the Dragoon style. Many pages can be dedicated to the Ruger single-action grip-frame discussion, but I don't want to burden you with the minutiae. For an absolutely detailed rundown of the grip frames used by Ruger over the years, I would recommend the excellent piece by Bill Hamm, with photography by Bill Hamm and Boge Quinn, on Gunblast.com. It is the most definitive work I have seen to date.

Anyhow, for this discussion, the XR3 was first introduced in 1953 on the Single Six and the .357 and .44 Flat Top Blackhawks. The Dragoon-style grip frame with the squared back trigger guard made its debut on the Super Blackhawk in 1959. This grip frame is longer than the XR3 toward the bottom of the grip. The XR3-RED made its first appearance in 1962 on the Single Six, Super Single Six, Hawkeye, Old Army and, most importantly for this discussion, the Blackhawk. All three of these plow-handle grip frames share a similar contour, the main differences being the length of the grip. I am admittedly way oversimplifying here, but there have been so many variations that we simply don't have the luxury or space to explore further. I have purposely left the Birdshead grip out of this discussion as I personally feel it doesn't belong anywhere on or near a revolver that generates substantial recoil.

The Bisley grip frame is patterned loosely on Colt's Bisley model, with a more vertically profiled grip, which made its debut in 1986. Master gunsmith, Hamilton Bowen, states in his excellent book, *The Custom Revolver*, that: "Without the Bisley grip frame, with its longer, more vertical grip, the ultra big-bore revolver boom would never have materialized. The .475 and .500 Magnum guns would be unshootable fitted with any other grip frame."

I agree completely with this sentiment. One of the most common complaints leveled at the Bisley is the close proximity of the shooter's fingers to the trigger guard, leading to uncomfortable contact.

Which one is better? This question is subjective at best. The plow handle tends to pivot upward in the hand, while the Bisley acts somewhat like a double-action revolver, pushing back into the web of the hand. I find it much easier to control a Bisley grip on a heavily recoiling revolver than one fitted with a plow-handle. It's just a preference, and each individual will require something different. I would recommend trying both before drawing a conclusion. I have found that a custom set of grips, made for your hands, goes a long way toward making any revolver more controllable and enabling you to shoot more accurately.

Ruger's excellent Bisley grip frame (above) compared to the Dragoon-style plow-handle grip frame (below).

Big Game Hunting Revolvers

Ruger's Double Actions

Like all of Ruger's products, the double-action revolvers are over-engineered with uncompromising strength. You will see that none of Ruger's double-actions are spindly in construction, making them more bulky, but also giving you confidence and peace of mind.

Yes, Ruger double-action revolvers have a reputation for bulk. This is an oft-cited criticism that I see as a nonissue. I am not alone in my beliefs, as you will see later in the custom revolver segment of this book. Those who build or repair custom guns see Ruger durability as a clear asset. To paraphrase master gun builder Hamilton Bowen, you will not shoot a Ruger Redhawk loose. The same cannot be said for Smith & Wesson's various offerings. Don't read me wrong here when I say that I, too, appreciate Smith & Wesson revolvers, because I own a number of them and will continue to shoot them. But when I am serious about going afield, a Ruger revolver normally gets the nod. With that bulk comes reliability, the most important asset you can have when your life depends on such a tool for survival.

Ruger didn't get into the double-action racket until the 1970s, but when they did, a whole slew of iconic hunting revolvers were the result.

Ruger's GP 100 .357 Magnum revolver.

GP100

Designed to be used by police and for personal defense, the GP100 was released in 1985 as a .357 Magnum with a 3-, 4-, 5.5- or 6-inch barrel and an adjustable rear sight (though a few models meant for defensive use have fixed rear sights), available in blued or stainless steel. Unlike the competition, the GP100 features a full, rather than a half or sideplate style frame, and a dual-cylinder locking system. The GP100 is of very stout construction. The grip is cast integral to the cylinder frame.

GP100 is available in the following calibers:

- .22 LR
- .357 Magnum

The Ruger Redhawk in .44 Magnum. Photo by L. Martin

The Redhawk

The 1980s ushered in Ronald Reagan, New Wave music, bad fashion and the all-new Ruger Redhawk. The Redhawk represented a new era of .44 Magnums — big, bold, bulletproof (so to speak), and able to digest ammunition no Model 29 could ever hope to take on and still survive. A trend emerging with handgun hunters demanding the use of ever-heavier bullets for big-game hunting necessitated a platform that could take the extra punishment from handloaders pushing the ballistic envelope. It was clear that the Redhawk had arrived and was up to the task.

The Redhawk began its storied existence as the ultimate double-action revolver. Later iterations were made available in .357 Magnum (interchangeable with .38 Special) and in .41 Magnum. Since the Redhawk proved more than up to the task of withstanding the abuse of the larger .44 Magnum, the smaller caliber versions were even stronger due to thicker cylinder walls.

The Redhawk was available in both blued and stainless steel, the grip in walnut. Blued-steel versions in .44 Magnum were made available with a 5.5- or 7.5-inch barrel or a 7.5-inch barrel into which were machined scope ring mounting points, an option that became available in 1986.

The Redhawk features heft in all of the right places. That's the result of an exceptionally strong revolver built around a particular cartridge, the .44 Remington Magnum, instead of adapting a cartridge to an existing platform as was the case with Smith & Wesson's Model 29.

The .41 Magnum Redhawk

The Ruger Redhawk was the "first double-action properly scaled to the .44 Magnum cartridge," according to master gunsmith Hamilton Bowen. Introduced in 1979, the Redhawk epitomized Ruger's propensity for over-engineering. "In general," Bowen went on to say, "Redhawks are perfectly suited to large, high-performance sporting cartridges."

What did he mean by this? Well, to start with, the cylinder is considerably larger than that of the Blackhawk and much larger than any other double-action revolver in existence, save for Smith & Wesson's super-sized, crew-served X-frame. The barrel shank is the largest of all production revolvers. The frame sports a thick top strap and a unique crane locking system.

According to Bowen, "Redhawks rarely ever go out of time or shoot loose." Cylinder notches are placed between chambers and not directly over the thinnest part of the cylinder. These offset bolt notches leave a lot more metal around each chamber. Worth noting is that Ruger didn't really have to offset the notches. Center positioning them would have provided enough "meat" for the .44 Magnum. By over-building it in 1979, however, they already had the basis for the .454, which came later in 1999 in the Super Redhawk. Center-cut stops on the .454 would have necessitated a five-shot cylinder design. In short, the buffer — or margin — that Ruger builds into their firearms allows them to upsize or power-up on the fly, without having to re-engineer.

The most frequent complaint I have heard about the Redhawk is in the grip frame. The Redhawk uses one spring to operate the hammer and trigger. This design makes tuning the action a more difficult and somewhat problematic undertaking. That's because by lightening the trigger pull, the hammer is also lightened, which can result in light hammer strikes. Light hammer strikes can compromise primer ignition, which isn't a good thing, particularly when your Redhawk is performing bear-protection duty in the field. It would be a hell of a time to find out you have ignition problems when an 800-pound Grizzly bear is chewing on you. This issue was addressed with the advent of the Ruger Super Redhawk by virtue of its GP-100 grip frame utilizing separate springs for the trigger and the hammer.

The Redhawk is available in the following calibers:

.41 Magnum

.44 Magnum

.45 Colt

.45 Colt/.45 ACP convertible

The Super Redhawk

First introduced in 1987 amd chambered in .44 magnum, in 1999 a .454 Casull version was added, and in 2001, Ruger's very own .480 Ruger entered the marketplace. The snub-nosed Alaskan model was first introduced in 2005 chambered in both the raucous .454 Casull and the .480 Ruger. A .44 Magnum version of the Super Redhawk Alaskan joined the others in 2007.

The Super Redhawk is built like a tank. While it's almost dimensionally identical to its parent the Redhawk, the addition of a frame extension at the front of the frame from which the barrel protrudes gives the illusion of mass — much more mass. While it feels solid and substantial, I don't find its weight to be a negative, particularly when shooting loads from the upper end of the spectrum. In this case, mass is your friend.

When introduced, the Super Redhawk was intended to supersede the legendary Redhawk, addressing a number of its perceived shortcomings. Ruger felt the frame could be extended to accommodate another mounting point for a scope or other optic.

Another point of contention addressed by the new Super Redhawk is the grip frame. The Super Redhawk received the superior grip frame of the GP100, as engineers had heard the gripes about the action of the Redhawk for years but had a fix in the GP100's frame.

Though they look quite different from one another, the Redhawk and

Super Redhawk are more similar than meets the eye. Aside from the frame extension and the GP100 grip frame, the Redhawk and the Super Redhawk are basically the same. The integral scope ring mounting points take the stresses off the barrel shank, placing them squarely on the frame, increasing longevity and improving balance. That said, the greatest advantage enjoyed by the Super Redhawk over its sibling is the aforementioned action.

Originally offered in .44 Magnum, the Super Redhawk became the launching point of Ruger's foray into truly big-bore cartridges, namely the .454 Casull. Not content with addressing the .454's high operating pressures by simply going to a five-shot cylinder, Ruger sourced a special high-strength steel called 465 Carpenter. This steel was torture tested by Ruger to make absolutely certain it was up the task of repeated 65,000 psi abuse that the .454 Casull would dish out. The new .454 Super Redhawk even looked different from the .44 Magnum versions that came first in that the cylinders were unfluted and were originally offered in a unique, graphite gray finish called "target gray." Received with mixed emotions by the gun-buying public, the finish proved tough. Interestingly, it was actually not conceived, but accidental. The finish just happened during the parts tumbling process, and the powers that be at Ruger decided to run with it. It is no longer available, unfortunately. I am one of those who liked the target-gray finish as it is unlike any other offered by any factory or the aftermarket.

Super Redhawk in .454 Casull.

The Super Redhawk also offered a unique opportunity to introduce the .480 Ruger, the first cartridge to ever bear the company's name. The .480 Ruger is essentially a shortened .475 Linebaugh, from 1.40 inches to 1.28 inches. It's a cartridge well known and respected by big-game handgun hunters, featuring a .476-inch diameter bullet in a range of weights, with a SAAMI maximum pressure of nearly 48,000 psi.

Ruger also opted to house this chunky cartridge in a six-shot cylinder in the aforementioned 465 Carpenter steel. The release of this new cartridge came at an inopportune time, sandwiched between Smith & Wesson's most powerful .500 Magnum and highest velocity .460 Magnum, neither of which the new Ruger cartridge could match.

The big news in 2013 was the re-release of the .480 Ruger Super Redhawk following a three-year hiatus. The .480 is available on a 7.5-inch Super Redhawk or the bulldog-esque Alaskan model with a 2.5-inch barrel. Ruger is again marketing this powerhouse with renewed vigor. The big Ruger is back and hopefully here to stay, but this time it is sporting a stainless steel finish instead of the first iteration's target-gray color, with the exception of the Alaskan model that has always been stainless.

I asked Ruger about the change, and they cited that the wear characteristics of the gray finish were not up to their standards. Apparently, once it became worn, the finish could not be touched up or reapplied. Since it met with mixed reviews from the start, the decision was made to discontinue target gray. As I stated before, I was one of those enthusiasts who actually liked the unusual gray finish in that it was unlike anything else out there, further setting the .480 and .454 Super Redhawk apart from their contemporaries. Oh well. That said, the stainless finish looks very sharp, giving off a menacing, all-business appearance.

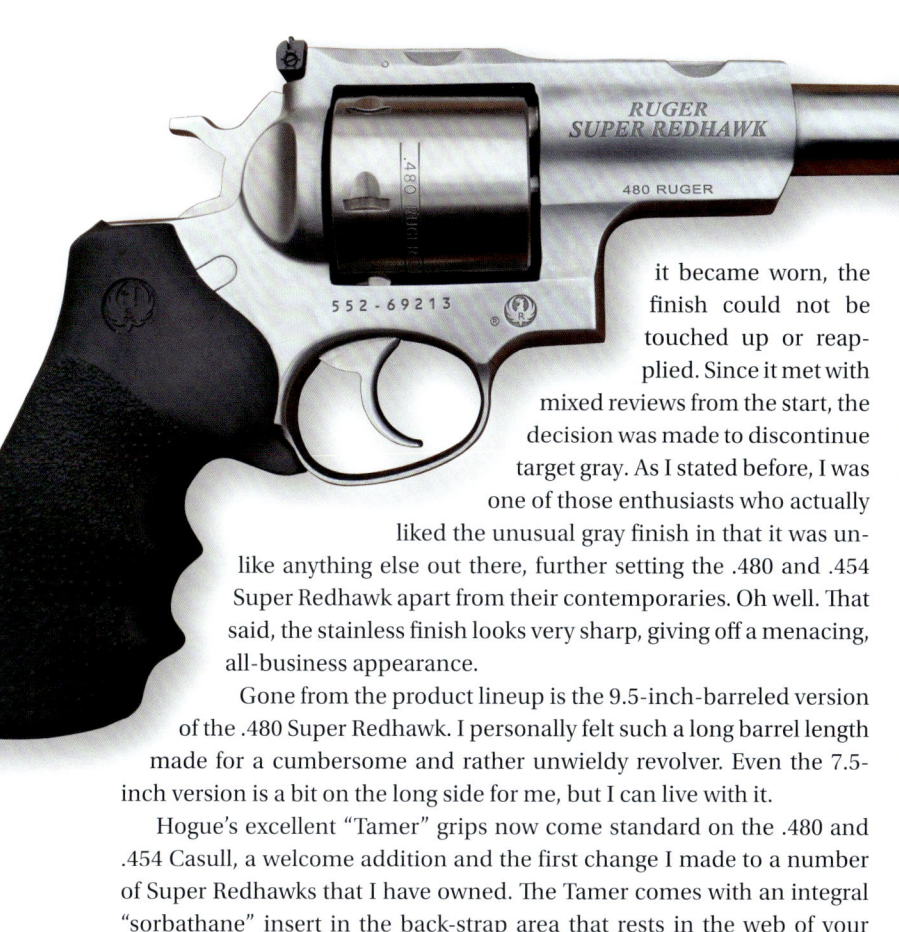

Gone from the product lineup is the 9.5-inch-barreled version of the .480 Super Redhawk. I personally felt such a long barrel length made for a cumbersome and rather unwieldy revolver. Even the 7.5-inch version is a bit on the long side for me, but I can live with it.

Hogue's excellent "Tamer" grips now come standard on the .480 and .454 Casull, a welcome addition and the first change I made to a number of Super Redhawks that I have owned. The Tamer comes with an integral "sorbathane" insert in the back-strap area that rests in the web of your hand, precisely where double-action revolvers deliver their punishment. This is a vast improvement over the old rubber grips with wood inserts, plus they feature finger groves that improve your grip consistency.

The Super Redhawk is available in the following calibers:

.44 Magnum

.454 Casull

.480 Ruger

Super Redhawk in .480 Ruger.

Super Redhawk Alaskan in .480 Ruger.

Big Game Hunting Revolvers **121**

TESTING RUGER'S ALL-NEW SUPER BLACKHAWK

I was asked by Ruger to perform some testing on new single-action Super Blackhawk models in .454 Casull and .480 Ruger under a veil of secrecy of a strict embargo. I put nearly 1,000 rounds through the .454 and almost 5,000 rounds through the .480 model. Appropriately dubbed an endurance test, I wasn't sure whose endurance we were testing — the guns or mine. I had no support crew or relief shooters. Just me, the revolvers and piles of ammunition. I am happy to report that I survived and my hands are still somewhat intact.

I can't figure out what's wrong with me. I have an inability to say no when asked to test firearms that I find irresistible, irrespective of the parameters of the test. When I was first approached about these projects by Ruger engineers last year, I was told that I was on a short list to test the .454 Casull and .480 Ruger Super Blackhawk single-action revolvers. They said something about being recoil-proof and a glutton for punishment in explaining why I had been chosen for this honor. My wife neatly sums up these qualities with one word — numb. "No problem," I said, "and thanks, I think."

Ever since Sturm, Ruger & Company released the .480 Ruger in the love-it or hate-it Super Redhawk back in 2001, revolver aficionados have been brow beating Ruger to release this cartridge in their popular single-action revolver lineup. The combination of Super Blackhawk and .480 Ruger is debated incessantly, yet Ruger's reticence to actually make this happen has frustrated handgun hunters who have long wanted to see this marriage come to fruition.

Basically, a shortened .475 Linebaugh, the .480 Ruger is a serious big-game hunting round that, even when loaded to spec, isn't too abusive to the one pulling the trigger. Ruger has finally relented by offering not only their .480 Ruger in the Super Blackhawk line, but also the raucous .454 Casull. The Super Redhawk in .454 Casull has been available since the late '90s. Handgun hunters everywhere have reason to rejoice as two of their favorite calibers can be had in the revolver they love in an affordable package. Available through Lipsey's as a distributor exclusive, I cannot imagine supplies will last long.

Here's what you need to know. The new revolvers are based on the old revolvers. Ruger used the standard Super Blackhawk frame in 415 stainless steel. The barrel is 6.5 inches in both models (at least initially) and made from 15-5 stainless steel, with a 1:24 and 1:18 twist for the .454 Casull and .480 Ruger, respectively. The barrel is straight, no taper, and features a front sight base that is silver soldered on with a pinned sight blade and a standard Ruger adjustable sight in the rear. The cylinder is carved from 465 Carpenter steel, the super-strong, hard-to-machine material that first made an appearance in the company's Super Redhawk in .454 Casull and later in the .480 Ruger version. The cylinder is a five-shot configuration, with counter-boring to encapsulate the case heads. Dimensionally, the cylinder is like that of the .44 Magnum Super Blackhawk, save for a tiny bit more length to the rear to compensate for the recessed case heads. The new revolvers were fitted with an extra-long ejector rod housing that made its first appearance on the limited run of stretch-frame .357 Maximum revolvers of the early 1980s. A Bisley grip frame is the only one offered and the only one Ruger deemed acceptable for these applications. A locking base pin prevents it from walking out under recoil, a nice touch.

I tested both models thoroughly with factory fodder. Both pre-production models suffered from teething pains, which we have been assured have been sorted out, but are to be expected of test guns. Chronic screw loosening (the grip frame in particular), plagued the .454, but a drop or two of thread lock fixed that issue. The ejector rod housings on both loosened regularly, and both launched their front sights, ironically on the 480th round out of the .480 model. The .480 also had its barrel unscrew, but Ruger promptly fixed it and had it back in my sore hands to resume testing.

Recoil means something different to each shooter. While I am no stranger to the phenomenon, these relatively lightweight powerhouses pack a wallop on both ends. Not the worst you may encounter, but a considerable step up from the venerable .44 Magnum. The .454 Casull Super Blackhawk kicks noticeably harder than its .480 Ruger counterpart. This is no doubt due to the higher pressure levels to which .454 Casull ammunition is loaded, and while the .480 delivers a heavy push, the .454 has a snappy and much sharper recoil impulse.

Both revolvers delivered outstanding accuracy. The only limit was my eyesight with open irons, so I equipped both models with red-dot optics of radically different designs. I own a number of more expensive revolvers that cannot compete with the accuracy these two new Rugers displayed, as you can see in the accuracy tables.

I got the opportunity to test the new .454 Bisley on pork flesh at Hog Heaven Outfitters of Johnston County, N.C. I got lucky on the first morning when a 214-pound boar made the mistake of showing up. The shot was broadside at about 20 yards and required only one Garrett 365-grain .45 Colt +P Hammerhead to seal the deal. My testing was now complete.

In summary, Ruger and Lipsey's have finally given us what we want. What was once a custom-only and cost-prohibitive proposition is now just a phone call and less than $1,000 away. Evidently Ruger is listening. We all have reason to rejoice.

Big Game Hunting Revolvers **123**

ACCURACY TABLES

.454 Casull Super Blackhawk

LOAD WEIGHT/TYPE	ADVERTISED VELOCITY	GROUP SIZE (IN.) 25 YARDS	50 YARDS
Garrett 365-gr HC	1,350 fps	1.311	1.589
Buffalo Bore 325-gr. HC	1,525 fps	1.350	2.494
Hornady 300-gr. JHP	1,650 fps	1.380	2.463
Hornady 240-gr. JHP	1,900 fps	1.783	3.064
CorBon 360-gr. JFP	1,300 fps	.895	1.505
Speer 300-gr. JFP	1,625 fps	1.653	2.614
Federal Fusion 260-gr. JHP	1,350 fps	1.030	3.189
Double Tap 250-gr. SCHP	1,850 fps	1.021	2.124
Double Tap 335-gr. HC	1,600 fps	2.076	3.896
Double Tap .45 Colt +P 360-gr. HC	1,200 fps	.712	.957
Garrett .45 Colt +P 365-gr. HC	1,250 fps	1.224	2.232

.480 Ruger Super Blackhawk

LOAD WEIGHT/TYPE	ADVERTISED VELOCITY	GROUP SIZE (IN.) 25 YARDS	50 YARDS
Hornady 325-gr. JHP	1,350 fps	1.331	2.151
Hornady 400-gr. JHP	1,100 fps	1.298	1.367
Speer 325-gr. JFP	1,350 fps	1.511	2.632
Buffalo Bore 275-gr. SCHP	1,500 fps	1.086	2.416
Buffalo Bore 370-gr. HC	1,300 fps	.963	1.114
Buffalo Bore 410-gr. HC	1,200 fps	.579	1.422

• Indoors/Sandbags/Best Groups at 25 and 50 yards/ 5-Shot Group/ Abbreviations: JFP (Jacketed Flat Point); JHP (Jacketed Hollow-Point); HC (Hardcast); SCHP (Solid Copper Hollow-Point)

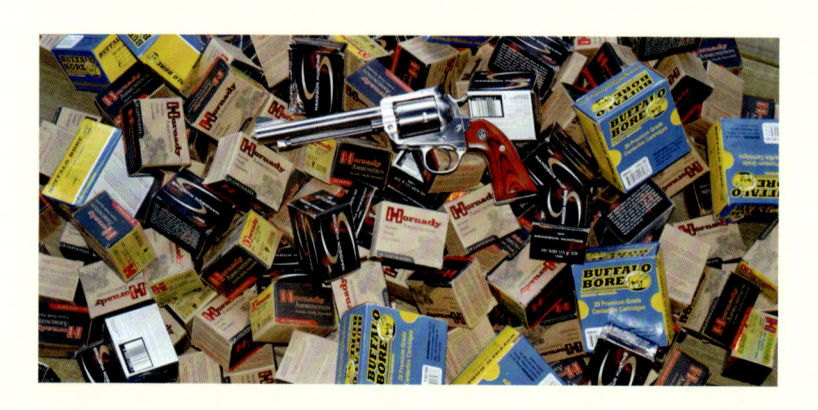

The heart of the new Super Blackhawk is the five-shot cylinder machined from special 465 Carpenter steel. A standard Ruger six-shot .45 Colt cylinder is on the left for comparison.

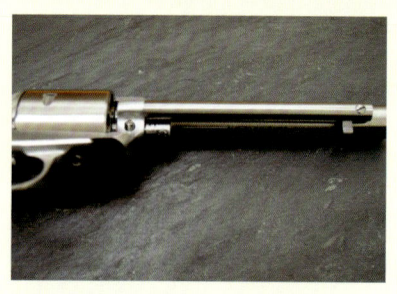

Both new models feature a locking base pin and a long ejector rod housing, which were first used on the Ruger .357 Maximum revolvers of the early 1980s.

Typical 400-round .480 SBH endurance test session.

This is what a pile of 5,000 rounds of ammunition (weighing over 400 pounds) looks like. What can't be seen is the pain inflicted by such a feat.

Smith & Wesson

Smith & Wesson only builds double-action revolvers, but they have the distinction of building some of the finest examples in the world. The three we are most interested in discussing are the L-, N- and X-frames. The N-frame was the largest offered by Smith & Wesson until 2003, when the X-frame was introduced. Smith & Wesson revolvers are known for their quality fit and finish, as well as distinctive actions. Distinctive how? The word superb comes to mind. They are characteristically smooth and only become smoother with use.

One of the newest L-frame Smith & Wessons is the Model 69, a 5-shot, medium framed .44 Magnum. Photo by L. Martin

L-Frame

The L-frames are Smith's mid-sized revolvers, comparable in size to Ruger's GP-100. There are a number of configurations available in six- and seven-shot .357s with a variety of barrel lengths well suited to hunting. The 386 XL Hunter features a scandium frame, seven-shot stainless steel cylinder, full-lug 6-inch barrel, Hi-Viz fiber optic front sight and a matte black finish. The big news in the L-frame world was the introduction of the Model 69 in 2014, a five-shot .44 Magnum L-frame weighing in at a mere 37 ounces. Available with a 4-inch barrel, this revolver could serve double duty as a primary hunting weapon and back-up.

The L-frames are available in the following calibers:

.357 Magnum

.44 Magnum

Smith & Wesson's ubiquitous Model 629 .44 Magnum. Photo by V. Ricardel

N-Frame

The N-frame was first introduced in 1908 as the Hand Ejector model in .44 Special and went through a number of iterations during its production history. But, the N-frame was made famous with the introduction of the .44 Remington Magnum in 1956, and these are the models we are most interested in discussing. The Model 29 received a second wind with the release of the film "Dirty Harry," starring the Model 29 in .44 Magnum, with Clint Eastwood playing a supporting role.

The big Smith features some of the nicest lines to ever make their way down a revolver production line. It feels good and well balanced in the hand, even with a longish 6-inch barrel. The Model 25s in .45 Colt are also of interest to the big-bore revolver enthusiast and aside from caliber are identical to the Model 29. The model designation changed to "629" when production changed to stainless steel.

The "Classic" series blued-steel revolvers harken to the pre-stainless steel days, with the Model 25 Classic, a six-shot .45 Colt featuring a 6.5-inch barrel, the Model 27 Classic .357 Magnum available with a 4- or 6.5-inch barrel, the Model 57 Classic, a six-shot .41 Magnum with 6-inch barrel, and, lastly, the Model 29 Classic in .44 Magnum with a 4- or 6.5-inch barrel.

The stainless 629 .44 Magnum comes in a number of configurations suitable for field use, to include barrel lengths from 2 5/8, 4 and 6-inches, as well as the Classic 629 available with 4- and 6.5-inch barrels with a full underlug.

Smith & Wesson's Performance Center is the company's "race" shop that churns out many interesting revolvers with unique features such as the 629 Stealth Hunter with a 7.5-inch barrel and a matte-black finish. The Model 629 .44 Magnum Hunter is also a Performance Center offering with a two-tone finish that comes from the factory with a red/green-dot-type sight.

The stainless-steel full-sized .357 Magnum Model 627 is available in a number of barrel lengths, and Performance Center versions are also offered if you wish to hunt with a full-sized .357 Magnum.

The lightweight 327 scandium-framed .357 Magnum is available in two barrel lengths — a snub-nosed 2-inch model, and one with a 4-inch barrel. The scandium-framed 329PD is a .44 Magnum available with a 4-inch barrel and a titanium-alloy cylinder, weighing in at a feathery 25 ounces empty. Lots of punch in a light package!

With so many iterations of the large N-frame being offered by Smith & Wesson, I would recommend contacting them directly as their offerings are subject to change, even as this book goes to print.

The scandium-framed 329PD weighs just 25 ounces and makes for sheer packing pleasure with .44 Magnum firepower.

Smith & Wesson has the distinction of offering the only forged-steel frames in the industry, and the N-frame is no exception. They are strong, relatively light in weight and will deliver years of reliable service if not abused. Many iterations of the Model 29 have been created in over five decades of production.

Smith & Wesson N-frames are available in the following calibers:

.357 Magnum

.41 Magnum

.44 Magnum

.45 Colt

X-Frame

The X-frame is the largest revolver Smith & Wesson has ever built. The shear mass of the X-frame was necessitated with the decision to build revolvers around the new oversized Smith & Wesson cartridges, the .460 and .500. Large and rather heavy, the X-frame isn't for everybody.

Picking up Smith & Wesson's .500 X-frame, one cannot help noticing the mass of the revolver and the cumbersome weight. Upon firing it, the "why" behind the bulk becomes clear. When you are burning that much powder, pushing a heavy bullet at high speed, it has to kick because it has no choice. It's physics, pure and simple.

With high nominal pressures on the menu, Smith & Wesson addressed the issue of strength in their new X-frame by supersizing the entire package and attaching what amounts to a K-frame grip size to the massive frame. As mentioned, the frame is forged. While stronger than a casting in the direction of the grain, they really don't offer a strength advantage over a quality investment casting. Testimony to the strength of the X-frame is the fact that it can operate all day long at the pressures created by the .460 and .500 cartridges.

2003 marked the year that Smith & Wesson snatched the most powerful handgun crown back from the .454 Casull. Back in 1983, when the Casull debuted in the Freedom

The X-frame in .500 Smith & Wesson Magnum, equipped with a 6.5-inch barrel. Photo by author

Just to put things into perspective, the top revolver is an X-frame, the bottom a Model 29 N-frame. The X-frame is big on size and even bigger on power. Photo by author

Arms Model 83 as a production cartridge, the crown was unceremoniously stripped away from the ubiquitous .44 Remington Magnum. Then in 2003, Smith & Wesson rolled out a whole new super-sized platform, the X-frame, chambered in a really big cartridge, the .500 S&W Magnum. Not only was the crown back on Smith & Wesson's head, it was cemented in place.

Based loosely on the .500 Maximum, or .500 Linebaugh Long — a wildcat created by Wyoming gun builder John Linebaugh — the .500 S&W Magnum took its case length from the Maximum, a full 1.6 inches, but with a slightly smaller diameter of .500 compared to its parent's .510 diameter. But here's the rub, the SAAMI pressure spec for Smith & Wesson's wonder cartridge is a full 62,000 psi! In 2005, the .500's smaller sibling, the .460 was unleashed on the public featuring a full case length of 1.8 inches, also with a ceiling operating pressure of 62,000 psi, just like the .500 S&W Magnum. The .460 completed Smith & Wesson's one-two punch on the big-bore revolver world.

If you have never seen or handled an X-frame Smith & Wesson in person, you may be surprised by the sheer size of the piece. The X-frame is the largest and strongest frame Smith & Wesson has offered to date, handily unseating the N-frame in sheer bulk.

The Smith & Wesson .460 XVR with an 8 3/8-inch barrel is the velocity champion.

I tested Smith & Wesson's .460 XVR a number of years ago, and the first impression is that this is a no-nonsense, long-range hunting tool, and that is precisely what it is. Weighing in at 72.5 ounces empty with an 8 3/8-inch barrel, this five-shot revolver comes in a satin stainless-steel finish with interchangeable compensators, one for jacketed and the other for cast bullets. With a 15-inch overall length, it's not a revolver you can stick in your jacket pocket or wear comfortably on your hip, but it was never meant to be. With its extra-long, gain-twist rifling barrel — meaning the rifling twist rate progresses down the length of the barrel, which purportedly aids in the stability of bullets — Smith & Wesson sought to produce the highest-velocity production revolver in the world. They succeeded in spades, with some factory loads achieving an incredible 2,300 fps!

So, what constitutes long range? If your eyes are as bad as mine, I

Three different calibers can be safely shot in a .460. From left to right, the .45 Colt, .454 Casull and .460 S&W Magnum.

would say anything over 100 yards with open sights, but within this discussion, I would say 200 yards. Game starts looking really small at that range, and open sights become a real challenge, despite the excellent HIVIZ front blade and adjustable rear sight of the XVR. But this is a gun that truly deserves a scope.

Recoil is negligible as the muzzle brake does an effective job at keeping the kick down to more than acceptable levels, as does the excellent wrap-around rubber grip it wears. The trigger is typical Smith & Wesson, meaning that it is very good and will only get better once the revolver is broken in. It exhibited no creep and broke cleanly.

A versatile chambering, the .460 X-frames boast the ability to safely shoot three types of ammunition, the .45 Colt, .454 Casull and the .460 S&W. You may not see optimal accuracy using the shorter-cased siblings of the .460, but they can be used in a pinch. Best accuracy will be seen with the full-length case of the .460.

The .500 is available with a 4-, 6.5- or 8 3/8-inch barrel, and two Performance Center models are available with 7.5- or 10.5-inch barrels. The .460 can be had with a 5- or 8 3/8-inch barrel, but to really take advantage of the .460's long-range capability, Performance Center models are available with 10.5-, 12- and 14-inch barrels — the 14-inch comes with a bipod, but it probably should have wheels as well.

The X-frame is a large, uncompromising gun that makes no apologies. It's available in:

.460 S&W Magnum

.500 S&W Magnum

quick test: LIGHT HEAVYWEIGHT

Smith & Wesson has been building .44 magnum revolvers since 1956, when they unleashed the venerable Model 29 N-frame on the shooting world. The first truly high-performance, big-bore, double-action revolver evolved over the years and has culminated into the space-metal, high-tech 329PD.

The company produces other scandium-framed lightweight revolvers, but I was interested in testing the biggest in the series, in one of our favorite calibers, the .44 Remington Magnum.

If you've never handled a 329PD, prepare to be shocked as unloaded it only weighs 25 ounces. Featuring a scandium-alloy frame, and a cylinder made of titanium alloy — a material that is stronger than most steels, corrosion-resistant and used extensively in the aerospace industry — Smith & Wesson has created a revolver that is both strong and very light in weight. The 329PD holds a traditional six rounds and sports a 4-inch barrel topped with a light-gathering red HI-VIZ front blade and an adjustable v-notch rear sight. The 329 comes with a nice finger-grooved wooden grip, and a recoil-absorbing rubber set. I tested all loads with the rubber grips. Though a bit on the heavy side, the trigger was typical Smith & Wesson in that it broke cleanly, but it clearly needed some breaking in as all revolvers do. The revolver is finished in matte black that is all business.

Surely this much punch in such a lightweight package must produce severe recoil, shouldn't it? Well, yes and no. While it kicks considerably more than my all-steel Model 29s, I never found it debilitating, but then again, I may not be the best judge with my big-bore revolver track record. Let's just say that it kicks less than it should.

I ordered a whole bunch of different loads from DoubleTap Ammunition and tested a number of them all the way up to my favorite 320-grain WFN, which incidentally recoils the most of all I've tried. I've used this load successfully in the past on a number of wild hogs. The .44 Special loads were an outright pleasure to shoot. I was unable to produce good groups at my usual 50 yards as the HIVIZ sights are an up-close combat sight and thereby a close-range proposition. At 25 yards, this revolver is at home. I envision the 329PD as a back-up piece. It is really quick to press into action due to its light weight and superior Smith & Wesson double-action ergonomics. It comes on target easily, and the sights are a snap to acquire. The most accurate load tested was the 225-grain XPB that printed a half-inch five-shot group at 25 yards. This gun is a pleasure to use for quick-fire drills.

I can say this about the Smith & Wesson 329PD: it is the most pleasurable big-bore revolver I have ever carried in the field. You don't even know it's there when strapped to your side. I have had a love affair with Smith & Wesson Model 29s in every flavor and have owned them for decades, and this one is no exception. Smith & Wesson has produced the ultimate back-up wheelgun in the 329PD. Big power, great handling, and light in weight.

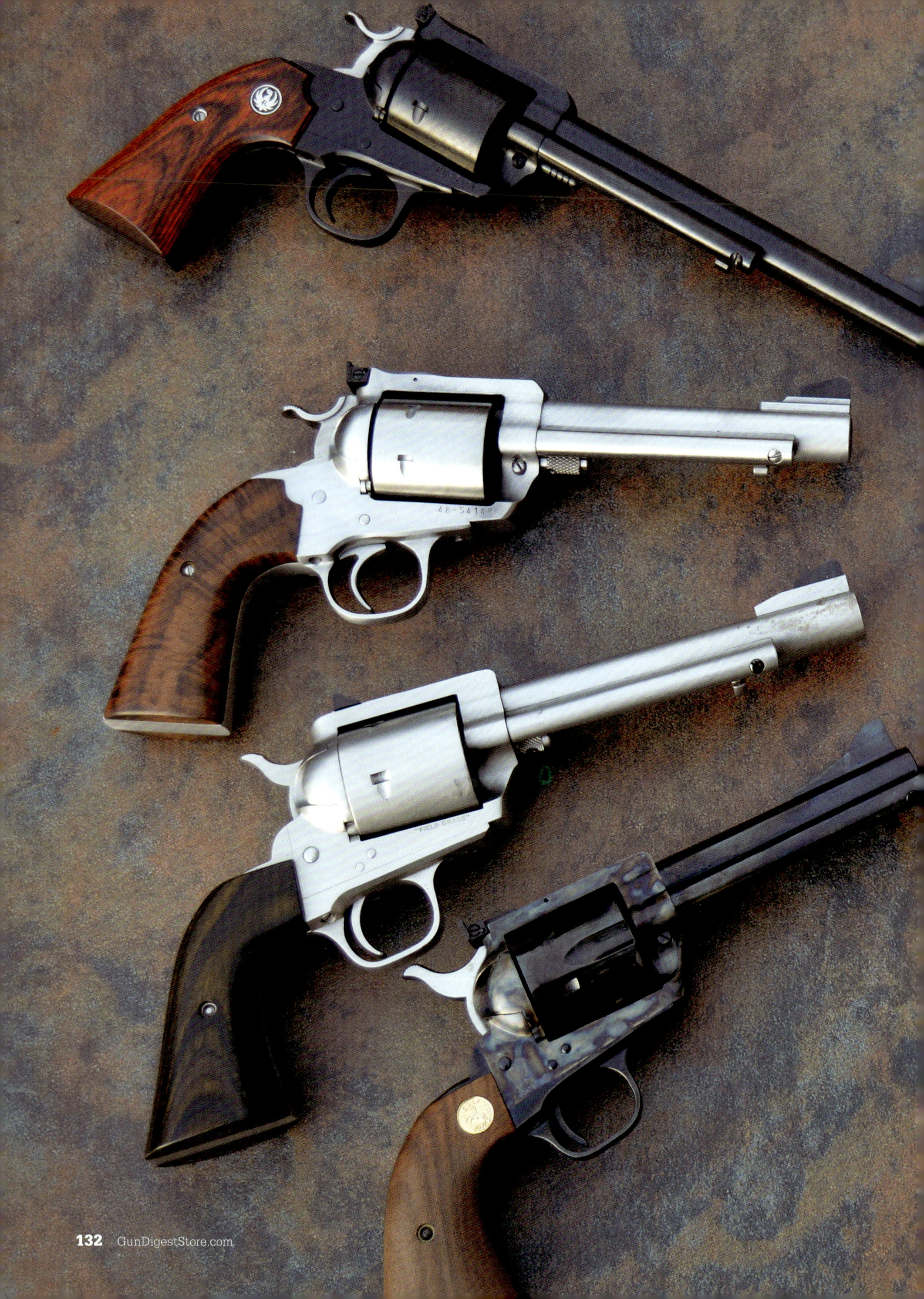

SINGLE VS. DOUBLE ACTION:
Which One is Right for You?

Revolvers come in many flavors, shapes and sizes, and almost limitless configurations. The two main platforms are the single and the double action. Single actions derive their name from the fact that they can only be fired by cocking the hammer and squeezing the trigger one shot at a time, whereas the double action can be fired in the same manner as the single, or by simply squeezing the trigger to fire, hence the term "double action."

All modern single-action revolvers are based, however loosely, on the Colt Single Action Army (SAA). So prolific was Colt's design that it is still in wide use today. There are a number of manufacturers of single-action revolvers today including Ruger, Freedom Arms, Magnum Research, Uberti and Colt.

Double-action revolvers are available from Smith & Wesson, Colt, Ruger and Taurus on the new and used market. Colt's excellent Anaconda is no longer in production, but used models can be found and are an excellent choice for hunting or back-up.

Both types of revolvers can be had chambered in calibers adequate for both big-game hunting and protective back-up duty, but each handle recoil differently. Double actions tend to transfer all of their recoil straight back into the web of your hand, while single actions have a propensity to exhibit barrel rise and are designed to roll upward (particularly in the case of ones equipped with "plow handle" type grips). Which one is best for you is ultimately a matter of preference. The one that is most comfortable in your hand and, more importantly, the one you can shoot most accurately, is the one you should choose.

Before that decision can be made, you will need to define the intended purpose of the revolver. Is the handgun going to be used as back-up, or as a primary hunting tool, possibly doubling as back-up? This is important because a primary weapon may be fitted with a longer barrel than one that will strictly be used as a back-up revolver, and it might be sporting an optic such as a scope or red-dot-type sight. A revolver that is intended only for back-up duty may ride on your belt for years without ever being drawn and used, so it probably won't have a very long barrel or an optic mounted up top, with more of a nod toward comfortable carry.

The external finish of the revolver is also something to consider. If the revolver will spend more time riding in a holster on your belt as back-up, stainless steel may be the most durable finish. Not only can bluing wear off in a holster from rubbing, it is more vulnerable to rust when exposed to the elements. In the case of back-up work, a double-action revolver offers a couple of distinct advantages over its single-action counterpart, including the ability to fire by simply pulling the trigger without having to yank the hammer back, and the option to open the cylinder to load and unload more easily compared to a single-action revolvers where one round at a time can be loaded and unloaded.

Oddly enough, like many people, I shoot double-action revolvers in single action almost exclusively. This sort of negates a perceived advantage. That said, I would rather have a double-action revolver if underneath an animal trying to make a meal of me as that would be the time to press the handgun's double action capability into service. As mentioned, the other advantage the double action holds over the single is the ability to load and unload a cylinder at a much faster rate. Of course, this virtue is only an advantage if a situation arises where a speedy reload is necessary. I have yet to experience this need in the field.

In North America, dangerous-game animals are not that common. That said, nearly any and every bear can potentially pose a danger, especially when wounded or feeling threatened. We all know that the chances of actually being attacked by a bear are slim, but that small percentage of opportunity carries substantial negative consequences.

Caliber choice in this discussion is a moot point, as either configuration can be chambered in a significantly powerful caliber. If you're hunting big game with a revolver or carrying one in bear country for protection, you should choose the biggest caliber you can accurately shoot without a flinch or fear of recoil. I like to think of the .44 Magnum as the minimum reliable caliber, and it is a good choice particularly if you do not reload, as there is an abundance of available factory ammunition for the popular caliber.

The grand old .45 Colt is perhaps the most overlooked, probably due to so much of the factory load

Big Game Hunting Revolvers   **133**

offerings being on the weak side due to all the older guns that are in circulation. However, loaded to its potential in a modern firearm from Ruger, Freedom Arms or Magnum Research, there is little the .45 Colt cannot tackle, and some specialty ammo manufacturers, such as Grizzly Cartridge, Buffalo Bore Ammunition, DoubleTap Ammunition, Underwood and Garrett Cartridges offer modern, higher pressure .45 Colt loads.

You have two platforms to consider when choosing your revolver. My suggestion would be to first define its use, and second, figure out which one you can shoot the best. This is the one that will inevitably be the most comfortable in your hand and inspire the most confidence. There is no substitute for actually doing a side-by-side comparison before making this critical decision. They both have their advantages and disadvantages, but both will reliably do the job. I must confess that I like both, but I have found that the single action points more intuitively.

Determining Your Needs

Picking a revolver to carry in the woods isn't necessarily an easy decision or one that should be taken lightly. Your sidearm should become an extension of yourself if you are carrying for protection — from two- and four-legged predators. If your revolver is to be used as a primary hunting tool, you have a bit more leeway in your decision between single- and double-action options. Chances are good that your double-action hunting piece will be shot single-action style anyhow, negating any advantages — perceived or real — between one type or the other.

So, put all of your needs up front when it comes time to make your decision. I've compiled a partial list to get you started in singling out what will be your perfect revolver:

• Primary use — What will the revolver be used for? Protection or hunting? Protection against what (this will help determine the caliber)? Double duty? A back-up piece will only need to be accurate at short distances where it will be used to save your bacon, so a short barrel will be preferable.

• Carry method — How will you carry your revolver? On your belt? In a shoulder holster? In a pack? Size, optics and overall weight will help you hone in on how you carry your chosen firearm, and your carry preference will also limit your options.

• Optics — If you are gifted with the vision of an adolescent, then open sights are attractive from a number of perspectives. However, we often need a little help to accurately place our bullets on target. A scope will limit your revolver to hunting duty, as the long eye relief found in handgun scopes does not lend itself to quick target acquisition in an emergency situation. You will likely mount a scope on a revolver with a longer barrel for longer shot expectancy. A red-dot-type sight offers a bit more flexibility than a scope as they are easier to acquire, yet they still add bulk to the revolver.

• Recoil tolerance — If you're sensitive to recoil, you may find double-action revolvers to be harder to shoot in the hotter calibers. The recoil tends to come straight back into the hand, whereas a single action tends to rise, deflecting recoil by reducing or redirecting the thrust upward. Many simply find the single-action revolver, even in large calibers, easier to shoot and not nearly as abusive. What is on the menu? Are you hunting really big game? If the answer is yes, a large caliber will be necessary and the platform you choose will determine what you, the shooter, will experience on the recoil front.

Dr. Larry Rogers, of West Virginia, took this white rhino with his .475 Linebaugh Ruger. The 420-grain Cast Performance hardcast bullet performed flawlessly. Photo by L. Rogers

Big Game Hunting Revolvers 135

Freedom Arms

Model 83

The Freedom Arms Model 83 is the Cadillac of the single-action revolver world. Freedom Arms was started by entrepreneur Wayne Baker with a revolver design brought to the table in 1978 by Dick Casull, a veteran designer and originator of the modern, high-pressure five-shot revolver. The first guns manufactured by Freedom Arms were actually mini revolvers of Casull's design. The biggest and most notable result of that union was the Freedom Arms Model 83 released in, you guessed it, 1983 and chambered for the .454 Casull. The introduction of the Model 83 also debuted the .454 as an honest-to-goodness production cartridge. Freedom Arms takes its name from the location of its plant in Freedom, Wyoming.

Though a traditionally styled single-action revolver, the FA 83 is all contemporary on the inside and produced of modern 17-4PH stainless steel, though in a five-shot configuration, a lesson learned by Casull after decades of experimentation and development. When handling a Freedom Arms revolver, the lack of cylinder play becomes readily apparent. The company prides itself on hand-assembling each and every unit to tight and exacting tolerances. It is a true hand-built production revolver, and the tolerances are tight enough to necessitate regular cleaning to avoid problems in moving parts (a condition that could prove detrimental when facing an angry critter higher up on the food chain than the user).

Unlike other commercial revolver producers, Freedom Arms has the distinction of performing machine work that is normally a custom shop-only proposition, a procedure known as line boring. Once the cylinder has been externally machined and fitted to the frame, the cylinder is heat-

The first Freedom Arms Model 83 revolvers were chambered in .454 Casull. Photo by V. Ricardel

treated. Once heat-treating is complete, the cylinder is then placed in the frame of the revolver, a face-boring fixture is fitted where the barrel will be attached, and each chamber is drilled through this fixture, which mimics the barrel. Thus, each hole is bored in precise alignment with the barrel, and it is one of the reasons Freedom Arms revolvers shoot as well as they do. All this extra attention will cost you more, but perfection isn't cheap.

The grip frame bears mention here. It is not at all like the plow handle of single-action revolvers of old (and some new), but instead it's much more like the Bisley interpretation by Ruger. It angles down much sharper than the traditional plow-handle that sweeps back before plunging downward. And, much like the Ruger Bisley, the FA 83 grip frame handles recoil much better, in my opinion, than the standard plow-handle, as it is not designed to roll up in the hand. This is very beneficial when shooting a revolver that generates considerable recoil.

Fast forward to 2016, and Freedom Arms not only continues to produce the Model 83, but it does so in a number of different calibers and in two different grades, Field and Premier. The FA 83 is available in the following calibers:

- .22 LR (Field grade only)
- .357 Magnum
- .41 Magnum
- .44 Magnum
- .454 Casull
- .475 Linebaugh
- .500 Wyoming Express

One can also opt for cylinders in compatible calibers such as .45 Colt (with .454 Casull), and .480 Ruger (with .475 Linebaugh). The Premier-grade revolvers feature a brighter brushed finish, fully adjustable rear sight, laminated hardwood grips and a limited lifetime warranty. Field-grade revolvers have a matte finish, a rear sight that can only be adjusted for elevation, a one-year warranty, and rosewood or rubber grips.

This Model 83 is chambered in Freedom Arms' proprietary and very lethal cartridge, the .500 Wyoming Express. This is a serious big-game cartridge. Photo by K. O'Neill

Model 97

Freedom Arms also produces a smaller-framed revolver, more in line with the size of the Colt Single Action Army, the Model 97, for those who wish for a trimmer package on their hip. The 97 is available in the following calibers:

.17 HMR

.22 LR

.224-32 FA (a wildcat of Freedom Arms' design)

.327 Federal

.357 Magnum

.41 Magnum

.44 Special

.45 Colt

Freedom Arms Model 97 .45 convertible engraved in commemoration of the 31st Safari Club International Convention. Photo by K. O'Neill

As the Model number suggests, the 97 was introduced in 1997. This revolver is a departure from the Model 83 mechanically in that it features a transfer-bar safety system similar to that of Ruger design, which allows for safe carry with a round under the hammer.

Also of note is the size difference between the 97 and the 83. When newly introduced, the 97 was only offered as a six-shot .357 Magnum, and the line was later expanded to include the .41 Magnum and the .45 Colt in five-shot configurations. Tim Sundles of Buffalo Bore Ammunition even loads special .45 Colt ammunition for the smaller 97, with a 300-grain bullet at moderate velocities and pressures, loaded to a shorter overall length to accommodate the 97's shorter cylinder. The Model 97 makes for a really fine packing revolver.

In summary, these revolvers have no equals with regard to fit and finish. Tolerances are very tight, and the grip frame is superb. Just like single-action Colts of old, the Freedom Arms 83 should not be carried with a cartridge under the hammer or an accidental discharge can result. Loading and unloading is performed with the hammer in the half-cock position, allowing the cylinder to spin — another nod to the Colt Single Action Army. In all, Freedom Arms produces true modern-day classics.

Magnum Research

BFR

Magnum Research entered the revolver building business in 1999, with the introduction of the BFR — the "Biggest Finest Revolver" — chambered in the ubiquitous .45-70 Government. They've since redesigned their revolvers and changed the moniker to stand for "Big Frame Revolver." As you are well aware, it takes a large cylinder and equally large frame to house a cartridge as big as the .45-70 and, as a result, the BFR has comic-book proportions. Today, Magnum Research produces both long- and short-frame revolvers in a range of calibers to suit just about anyone's needs.

Photo by V. Ricardel

Let me start out by saying that today's consumer would be very hard pressed to find a higher quality and more accurate firearm without spending twice what the BFR sells for. In appearance, they look like a Ruger Super Blackhawk on steroids, having been beefed up in key areas such as the bottom of the frame and the top strap. Consequently, they weigh a bit more than similarly sized revolvers but are second to none with regard to strength.

Made entirely of 17-4PH stainless steel, the BFR features a plow-handle grip frame like standard Ruger Blackhawks and Super Blackhawks. The counter-bored, unfluted, five-shot cylinder features a free-wheeling pawl, making loading and unloading a snap. The transfer-bar safety system is borrowed directly from Ruger, allowing for safe loaded carry in the field. The barrels are match grade and feature a fast 1:15 or 1:16 twist rate, depending on the caliber. All BFR frames come pre-drilled and tapped and include an aluminum Weaver-style scope base. You can specify rubber, ivory or black Micarta grips.

The following calibers are available in the short-framed revolver:

.44 Magnum

.454 Casull

.50 AE

.475 Linebaugh (Precision Center only)

.500 JRH (Precision Center only)

Long-framed revolvers are available in the following calibers:

.30-30 Winchester

.38-55 Winchester (Precision Center only)

.375 Winchester (Precision Center only)

.460 S&W Magnum

.45-70 Government

.450 Marlin

.45-90 Winchester (Precision Center only)

.500 S&W Magnum

.50 Beowulf (Precision Center only)

This is BFR's long-framed revolver in .45-70 Government.

Customized revolvers from the Precision Center (Magnum Research's custom shop) can be ordered in a number of less mainstream calibers. You can specify barrel length, the action gets some extra attention, and Precision Center guns also receive an 11-degree crown.

My only criticism of the BFR is a subjective one. The grip frame, as mentioned above, is standard Ruger plow handle. I am a self-professed Bisley man. That said, the Bisley grip frame is not for everyone, and if you ask any group of handgunners their preference, they will likely come down on one of the two sides evenly. However, Magnum Research has been listening and developed their own version of a Bisley-type grip frame, which is a great departure from the plow handle and similar in design to Jack Huntington's modified plow handle.

Overall, BFRs are outstanding revolvers delivering reliable performance at a reasonable cost. In my humble opinion, BFR should stand for "Bang For the Revenue."

Taurus

Manufactured in Brazil, Taurus offers a full line of big-bore revolvers for many uses. There are a number of models of differing frame sizes. At Taurus, variety is evidently the spice of life. While I consider the .357 Magnum to be a bare minimum for big game, Taurus offers a number of different models that I would consider for hunting. I have left off the smaller-framed revolvers that were designed to conceal and use as defensive firearms, instead starting with a medium-framed revolver, the Model 65, a six-shot .357 Magnum available in blued or stainless steel.

The medium-framed revolvers can be had in .38 Special, as well, but the nod goes to the .357 as one can safely shoot the milder .38 Special with the option of stepping up to the higher pressure .357 Magnum. The mid-frame is also offered as a seven-shot .357 called the Model 66, available in blued and stainless steel, with a 4- or 6-inch barrel length. The Model 66 comes in at 38 ounces and 40 ounces in 4- and 6-inch varieties, respectively.

The Tracker series is my favorite of the Taurus offerings. It's considerably smaller in stature than the Raging Bull and also has a five-shot configuration. It's available in .357 (a seven-shot), as well as .44 Magnum, and offers an easy packing alternative for field use. Available in matte stainless or blued steel with a 2.5- or 4-inch barrel, the Tracker is quite an attractive package. The 4-inch .44 Magnum version weighs in at a light 34 ounces empty. Trackers also come equipped with Taurus' excellent "Ribber" rubber grips.

The Tracker is available in the following calibers:

.357 Magnum (seven-shot)

.44 Remington Magnum

The Taurus Tracker is a rather compact revolver available as a seven-shot .357 or a five-shot .44 Magnum. Taurus photo

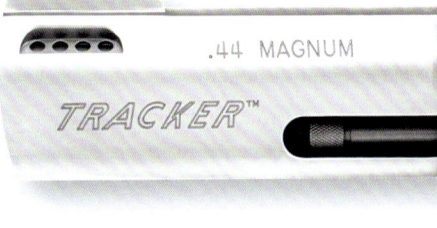

Big Game Hunting Revolvers **141**

The last step before the Raging Bull is the large-frame line of revolvers available in two calibers: an eight-shot .357 Magnum and a six-shot .44 Magnum. The .357 version can be had with either a 4- or 6.5-inch barrel, the .44 Magnum with a 4 , 6 ½- or 8 3/8-inch ported barrel. Built on a full-sized frame and available in stainless steel, the heaviest of the large frames weighs in at 57 ounces (.44 Magnum with 8 3/8-inch barrel).

Taurus' largest offering is the Raging Bull, available in .44 Magnum and the raucous .454 Casull. Taurus photo

The Taurus Raging Bull, introduced in 1998, is their largest-framed revolver, and is all business. It's of particular interest to this discussion as it has been chambered in the past in some of the most powerful revolver cartridges in production, including the .480 Ruger, .454 Casull and the mighty .500 S&W Magnum. The most powerful Raging Bull currently in production is the .454 version. The Raging Bull can be purchased new in a six-shot configuration in .41 and .44 Magnum, and in a five-shot platform in .454 Casull. New or used, the Taurus Raging Bull offers good value for the price of admission.

Available in a high-polish, matte-stainless, or blue finish, Taurus made sure there was something for every enthusiast, even with the most discerning taste. The Raging Bull is fitted with a bull barrel available in 5-, 6.5- and 8 3/8-inch lengths, with a full underlug and a vented rib, adjustable sights and effective rubber grips — effective in that they provide a good cushion to the shooter's hand. Barrels all feature porting to cut down on felt recoil, even with the stoutest of loads. The porting also serves to up the noise quotient, so one should always wear hearing protection. Unfortunately, they cannot be had without the porting. I simply dislike the additional noise porting creates, despite the positive role it plays. The package is rounded out with a large five-shot cylinder. The Raging Bull certainly looks the part and lives up to its name.

Note: While no longer chambered in .480 Ruger, a resurgence in the popularity of this caliber may bring it back into the lineup. That said, the Raging Bull was offered in .480 Ruger, and they do become available on the used gun market from time to time. The .480 Raging Bull was available only in a five-shot configuration, with a 5-, 6.5- and 8 3/8-inch barrel length in high-polish stainless, matte-stainless or blue finish.

The Raging Bull is currently available in the following calibers:

.44 Remington Magnum

.454 Casull

Taurus also produces an answer to Smith & Wesson's scandium-framed lightweight revolvers in their Ultralite series. These are large-framed .44 Magnums featuring a construction of titanium alloy. Available with either a 2.25- or 4-inch barrel in either a "Titanium Blue" or "Titanium Stainless Steel" finish, these lightweights weigh 27.3 and 28.3 ounces for the 2.25- and 4-incher, respectively. The six-shot revolver can be carried day and night without even the slightest burden, and it would make for a great backup gun for the outdoorsman. The Ultralite is available in .44 Remington Magnum.

Another Taurus revolver that has exceeded all expectations, as far as popularity is concerned, is the Judge. This long-framed revolver is chambered in .410 bore and .45 Colt. A variety of different configurations are available, culminating in the "Public Defender Polymer" Judge, an ultra high-tech revolver with a steel frame and polymer exterior over-molded onto the steel frame. The popularity of the Judge series has spurred the design and production of "Judge only" .410 shotgun loads to accommodate the short-barreled revolver with a focus on home defense, something the .410 has never been loaded for commercially. Performance with either type of ammunition in the Judge has proven to be a bit lackluster.

I liken the Judge to an Enduro motorcycle — on- and off-road capable. It can do both, but neither well. It's an innovative idea, but it falls a bit short of my expectations. Having said that, even Smith & Wesson has jumped on the .410 shotgun/.45 Colt revolver bandwagon, with their own Governor, proving the popularity of these platforms with shooters. Not to be outdone, Magnum Research has also introduced a .410/.45 Colt single-action revolver to their extensive lineup.

Taurus offers a wide range of quality revolvers for a wide range of usage.

Taurus' ultra-popular Judge is a .410/.45 Colt available in a wide range of configurations. Taurus photo

Big Game Hunting Revolvers **143**

Colt

Photo by C. Copeland

The company that really started it all still produces a version of the famous Single Action Army (SAA) today. Sometimes called the "Peacemaker," virtually all modern single-action revolvers are loosely based on Colt's classic design. A truly iconic piece of Americana, the Colt Single Action Army is probably the most recognizable gun in American film history. Three generations of Colt SAAs have been produced since its inception in 1873.

The first was produced from 1873 through the start of World War II. During this time, the classic army-style revolver was available and later joined by the Sheriff and Storekeeper models that featured shorter barrels and no ejector housings. In the late 1880s, a flat-top SAA target model was added to the lineup. The Bisley model, a competition-style revolver, was introduced in the early 1890s that featured a distinct vertical grip frame and low-spur hammer, fixed or adjustable rear sight, and a removable front sight blade. Production ceased during the war and didn't begin again until 1956.

The granddaddy of all single-action revolvers is Colt's Single Action Army. This one was produced in 1897 in .45 Colt and is exceptionally accurate. Obvious care was taken in the production of this revolver.
Photo by D. Bradshaw

The army-style model continued to be produced, and the only variation was the "New Frontier" model that was a target-style revolver with modern adjustable iron sights. Production ended in 1974, only to resume in 1976. Significant changes in design marked the third-generation guns, including a different barrel shank thread pitch and a solid cylinder bushing. By 1982, regular production faltered even though the factory custom shop continued producing revolvers on a special order basis. By 1993, the Colt Single Action Army was back in Colt's catalog and is available today.

The granddaddy of all modern single action revolvers is alive and well. The Single Action Army is available in the following calibers:

.357 Magnum

.45 Colt

This Colt New Frontier was produced recently and is chambered in .45 Colt and equipped with a 5.5-inch barrel.

The New Frontier is available in the following calibers:
.44 Special
.45 Colt

Other Colts

Colt had only one offering in the big-bore double-action arena, and that is the excellent Anaconda. Produced from 1990 to 1999, the Anaconda represented Colt's foray into double-action .44 Magnum revolver production to compete with Smith & Wesson's Model 29 and Ruger's Redhawk. Looking much like a scaled up and stainless Python (which in and of itself is not a bad thing), the Anaconda features a full underlug, six-shot cylinder, ribbed barrel, adjustable sights and all stainless steel construction. Unlike the competition from Smith & Wesson and Ruger, the Anaconda was never produced in blue, though Colt did offer it in a Realtree camo version for a time.

Colt .44 Magnum Anaconda.
Photo by R. Quiroz

Big Game Hunting Revolvers **145**

The Custom Option – Have It Your Way

There was a time when owning a true big-bore revolver — excluding the .44 magnum and the .45 Colt — was a custom proposition only. Many custom handguns were built on Ruger platforms in cartridges that, 20 years ago, were wildcats but now have become production calibers. Those days are gone, but you can take any factory revolver and improve upon it significantly or simply personalize it. It may not be about making it necessarily better or more reliable, but making it more to your liking. Examples of personalizing are custom grips that fit your hand perfectly, sights that are easier on your eyes to use more effectively, or a trigger pull that is lighter and smoother than the one with which the revolver left the factory. Nothing improves shooting confidence like a smooth trigger that is easy for you to control.

No discussion of custom revolvers would be complete without looking at Elmer Keith's famous No. 5 Colt revolver, probably the first custom to grace the pages of the popular gun media of the late 1920s. Keith's No. 5 was a collaborative effort between a number of talented individuals and the brainchild of Harold Croft of Philadelphia, Penn. But before the No. 5 was born, four other revolvers from Croft were unveiled in the September

1928 issue of the American Rifleman. The four numbered variations based on Colt Single Action Army revolvers featured modifications to the receivers, sights, hammers and grip frames and were turned into true high-performance, lightweight self-defense guns. Keith had the good fortune to shoot extensively a number of Croft's Colt SAA creations and came away impressed not only with Croft's innovation, but also the workmanship of gunsmiths Neal Houchins and R.F. Sedgley. Clearly these guns ignited a fire in Keith that got him thinking and speculating in print about the perfect revolver for the dedicated outdoorsman.

The result of all of Keith's vocal (and written) speculation was what is known as the Keith No. 5 Colt that made its debut in the April 1929 issue

This brace of Ruger Bisley Hunter models is owned by Greg Wilburn. From left to right: .44 Magnum (P. Grashorn Dall sheep grips), .41 Magnum, Harton created .414 SuperMag (on Ruger .357 Maximum frame), and lastly a .45 Colt (also with Grashorn Dall sheep grips). All have been massaged by Alan Harton's capable and talented hands. Photo by G. Wilburn

JRH custom Bisley in .500 JRH with 5.5-inch PacNor barrel and Turnbull CCH.

Big Game Hunting Revolvers **149**

THE 'SMITHS

I don't have the space here to profile all of the talented custom gun builders in this segment, but I have compiled a list for you to peruse. Some you will immediately recognize, some you may not, but I hope you take the time to research and consider one or more of them for your next custom revolver project.

- John Linebaugh's Custom Sixguns (John Linebaugh)
- JRH Advanced Gunsmithing (Jack Huntington)
- Bowen Classic Arms (Hamilton Bowen)
- Single Action Service (Alan Harton)
- Andy Horvath (Andy Horvath)
- Clements Custom Guns (Dave Clements)
- Gary Reeder Custom Guns (Gary Reeder)
- Gallagher Firearms (John Gallagher)
- Ben Forkin

Bowen Nimrod in .475 Linebaugh with bighorn grips by Rob Rowen. Photo by G. Needleman.

of American Rifleman, in an article entitled, "The Last Word." The No. 5 Colt, in .44 Special, embodied many of Croft's innovations, with a number of Keith's, resulting in what has been described by Hamilton Bowen in his book *The Custom Revolver*, as "what was probably the first practical, dedicated revolver for the serious outdoorsman." The Keith No. 5 was undoubtedly the most influential and most photographed custom revolver ever built, and the virtual progenitor of all custom single-action revolvers to come.

One of the first true customs I remember reading about was the Seville that Ross Seyfried commissioned John Linebaugh to build in 1986, in .45 Colt. The Seville started life as a .44 magnum and was fitted with a custom, oversized six-shot cylinder and a Douglas barrel. It was able to handle loads somewhere in the 60,000-psi range that were unthinkable in any other platform of the day. Seyfried truly pushed the limits when loading his .45 Colt Seville, but it held up well. That Linebaugh Seville was made famous in the pages of *Guns & Ammo*, culminating in the successful killing of a Cape buffalo by Seyfried in Africa.

Dustin Linebaugh built .475 Linebaugh Bisley with bighorn sheep grips by Rowen Custom Grips. Photo by G. Wagner.

tip from the field

ALL IN THE GRIP

One thing to consider with regards to heavy recoil is your revolver's grips. In order to make your big-bore revolver as manageable as possible, it's important to have a good set of grips that actually fit your hand well. This will make all the difference in the world as far as shootability is concerned. Some aftermarket grips seem as if they were made for your hands, in which case you are lucky as they tend to cost less than a custom set — typically a lot less. If you cannot find aftermarket units that fit your needs, I am of the opinion that custom grips are a worthwhile investment. Good grips can mean the difference between being able to enjoy your big bore and shooting it well, or dreading to touch it off. The choice is yours.

Custom walnut grips by JRH Advanced Gunsmithing.

John Linebaugh built .500 Linebaugh Bisley with banded 5.5-inch barrel. Photo by M. Distin

There are a number of great gun builders and gunsmiths that can turn the ordinary into the exotic, limited only by your imagination, the capabilities of your chosen gunsmith and the depth of your pockets. Yes, custom work is costly, but a revolver's function should not be taken lightly. It is a serious piece of equipment that requires a skilled hand to modify. So, it costs money and time to customize properly.

Without a doubt, the most popular platforms on which custom big-bore revolvers are based are the Ruger Blackhawk and Super Blackhawk single-actions. The "new models" are built strongly and provide a tough foundation. While rough in factory trim, they can be massaged to perfection. The transfer-bar safety is a reliable system, making for safe loaded carry in the field and trustworthy ignition.

Martin custom .500 Maximum with 6.5-inch barrel and hard-chrome finish. Photo by Lee Martin

Big Game Hunting Revolvers **151**

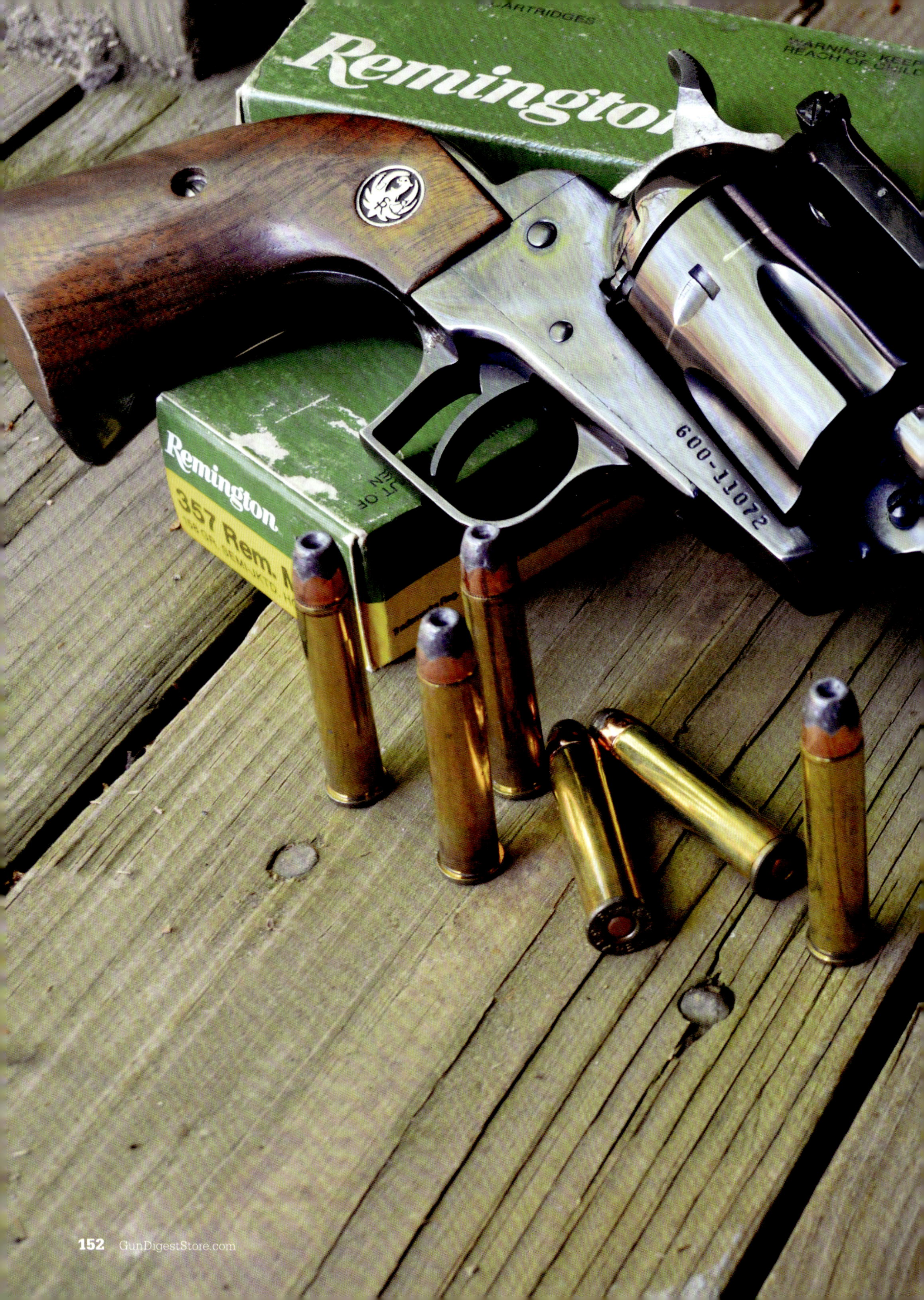
CARTRIDGES
Remington
Remington

CHAPTER 9

the .35s

The various .35 calibers make for great small to medium game getters. Many hunters, myself included, have used the .357 Magnum on big game, and while placement trumps all else, the smallish .35s don't leave much margin for error. However, in the case of whitetailed deer and smaller wild hogs, the .35s can be quite effective. If you are going to choose a caliber from this category, it is wise to pick one that can sling heavy-for-caliber bullets at acceptable velocities. For this reason I have left the .38 Special off the list.

Clay Ralston shot this coyote at 125 yards with a Freedom Arms M353 .357 Magnum using 180 Nosler Partitions. It's topped with a M8 4x Leupold.

Durward Thomason, of North Carolina, shot this mouflon with his Freedom Arms Model 353 in .357 Magnum, loaded with 140-grain Barnes XPBs. The revolver is topped with a 4x Leupold scope and the shot was made at just over 50 yards.

The .35s 153

Left, the .357 Magnum, right, the .44 Magnum.

.357 Magnum

Introduced in 1935, the .357 Magnum was the first cartridge to wear the name "Magnum." While not a big bore, this is one of the first truly high-performance handgun cartridges ever produced, boasting velocities never before seen from a revolver cartridge.

Dimensionally, the .357 Magnum is a lengthened .38 Special loaded to much higher pressure levels. The case was lengthened to prevent unintentional use in the structurally weaker guns chambered only for the .38 Special (you can, of course, use .38 Special rounds in any revolver chambered for the .357 Magnum), a wise tactic to save some folks from themselves.

While this round has proven an effective defensive caliber throughout its colorful history, we find it to be on the light side for big-game hunting. However, proper placement with a good bullet, matched to the game being hunted, will put meat on the table. But due to diameter limitations, the .357 Magnum is on the marginal side. That said, there is still no replacement for placement. Loaded with heavy hardcast bullets, penetration can be quite impressive.

The .357 Magnum is a good starting point for the beginner or novice, as the mild recoil makes mastering a revolver in this caliber a snap. There are many fine makes and models of this caliber available new and used.

quick facts

BULLET DIAMETER
.358 inches
CASE LENGTH
1.29 inches
OVERALL LENGTH
1.59 inches
MAXIMUM PRESSURE
35,000 psi

hunt report

NEW MEXICO BLACK BEAR

This black bear hunt took place in August 2014, in New Mexico's Lincoln National Forest with Little Joe's Big Game Hunting. The hunt would be conducted from the south end of a northbound pack of hounds. This is no terrain for the faint of heart. The hunt was scheduled for seven days. A whole week is a good idea, because you never know what you'll encounter even with a talented pack of hounds. Basically, Pasquarello hunted his backside off for days. Up one hill, down another, the dogs catching a trail three times only for it to go cold.

The fifth day started early with lots of muscle aches, coffee and a fistful of ibuprofen. They were riding in the truck with the sun barely creeping over the horizon, signaling the start of another brutal day, when the dogs struck a trail. The guide cut the hounds loose, and his intuition served him well as 15 minutes later the dogs had a color-phase black bear up a tree.

The last climb to the tree was difficult, but Pasquarello was motivated. They tied the dogs off, and he positioned himself for the shot. He was using his trusty Ruger GP100 in .357 Magnum, stoked with 158-grain JSPs. The bear was 30 feet up a tree on a limb, but Rich positioned himself on a hill that put him 10 yards and eye level from the agitated bear. The first shot broke cleanly at the broadside target, right behind the shoulder. His second shot clipped a tree limb, but his next four shots were true and all wound up in the lung area. The bear was sick, but Pasquarello did the prudent thing and kept pumping rounds into the beleaguered bear until his revolver audibly went click.

He began to reload when the bear toppled over and out of the tree, and that was all she wrote. The bruin went an estimated 450 pounds and made the fact that Pasquarello blew his knee out on that last approach well worth the agony.

Who:	Richard Pasquarello
What:	Black Bear
Where:	Lincoln National Forest, NM
Range:	10 yards
Revolver:	Ruger GP100
Caliber:	.357 Magnum
Bullet:	158-grain JSP Sellier Belloit

Rich Pasquarello killed this big black bear in New Mexico with a Ruger GP100 in .357 Magnum. Photo by R. Pasquarello

.357 Maximum left,
.44 Magnum right.

.357 Maximum

Truth be told, the .357 Maximum was the brainchild of Bill Ruger Junior before Elgin Gates released a long-cased .357 that was ultimately called the .357 SuperMag, the first in a series of metallic silhouette cartridges. This all, despite conventional wisdom crediting the late Elgin Gates with the creation of the cartridge.

The .357 Maximum has a maximum case length of 1.6 inches. Unlike the .357 Magnum, which was lengthened to prevent loading in guns chambered in .38 Special, the Maximum increases the payload of the cartridge to enable it to throw heavy projectiles at reasonable velocities for metallic silhouette shooting and hunting. The .357 Magnum simply did not provide enough punch to knock over the steel targets with any consistency in this style of competition at extended ranges and has proven marginal on really large game animals.

In 1982, Ruger produced a special Blackhawk single-action revolver with a lengthened frame to accommodate the requisite longer cylinder. These revolvers were produced for just one year (see segment on Ruger's .357 Maximum revolver) and experienced some purported trouble with particle and gas erosion to the forcing cone and the underside of the topstrap, an issue that was only evident when loaded with light bullets at high velocity. The gun media of the time was complicit in spreading this misinformation. It was never intended to be loaded in this manner, but instead to shoot heavy bullets in the 180- to 200-grain range at the same velocities as lighter bullets from the .357 Magnum.

quick facts

BULLET DIAMETER
.359 inches
CASE LENGTH
1.605 inches
OVERALL LENGTH
1.990 inches
MAXIMUM PRESSURE
52,000 psi

Ruger's .357 Maximum.

Sig Himmelmann, of Seville fame, brought a .357 Maximum that was marked as a .357 SuperMag to market in 1981, even before the brass and ammunition was available from Federal. Ruger, with the assistance of David Bradshaw, on the other hand, took their time and did extensive testing of the gun and loads before shipping them in late 1982. Ruger was prudent and thorough in their design, testing and production. Dan Wesson, a force in metallic silhouette at that time, also offered a revolver in the .357 Maximum chambering (albeit they were designated as .357 SuperMag), a double-action revolver that proved accurate and popular.

For me, the .357 Maximum by Ruger represents a high point in Sturm, Ruger & Company's revolver development. The gun was produced with extra care, as its purpose was to compete in metallic silhouette competition and to dominate in the hunting fields. Many International Handgun Metallic Silhouette Association (IHMSA) competitors immediately pressed their .357 Maximums to service in hunting. This was a race-bred machine from the factory. A finite number of these revolvers still exist, and they are beginning to command a premium as the collecting world is finally realizing the unique nature of the guns.

The .357 Maximum still enjoys popularity and is very viable today.

The .35s **157**

hunt report

VERMONT WHITETAIL

As told by David Bradshaw:

For an upcoming deer hunt, Ruger had sent me the SRM-4 Blackhawk .357 Maximum prototype on loan. I loaded Hornady's .357 158 JHP, the predecessor of the XTP, for the Maximum's first foray into the wild. Inspired by a case full of Hercules 2400, the 158 JHP averaged 1,956 fps.

When it finally came time to hunt, a snow suitable for tracking greeted us as we commenced to swing the flank of a five-mile long mountain. Cutting no track through the hardwoods, my hunting partner and I split to work our way up the mountain with the intention of rendezvousing in a high saddle in an hour or two. In the event either of us cut good sign, that hunter would take the track, at which point he would be on his own.

Who:	David Bradshaw
What:	Whitetail
Where:	Mountains of Vermont
Range:	40 yards
Revolver:	Ruger .357 Maximum Blackhawk
Caliber:	.357 Maximum
Bullet:	158-grain JP Hornady

I reached the saddle without cutting a track, let alone one worthy of a buck. Easing over a knoll of mixed hard woods, I paused to eyeball a somewhat open bowl. A buck sliced into the peripheral of my right field, gliding effortlessly through the woods.

Upon seeing the buck, I drew the Maximum upward, the thumb of my drawing hand cocking the hammer. With the revolver sights crossing the buck's torso, sweeping past its nose, tunnel vision set in and closed the deal, as the deer folded to a neck shot.

Ruger's .357 Maximum was born to shoot steel and to hunt.

This is the very first production Ruger Blackhawk .357 Maximum revolver, with spare barrel and cylinder. Photo by D. Bradshaw

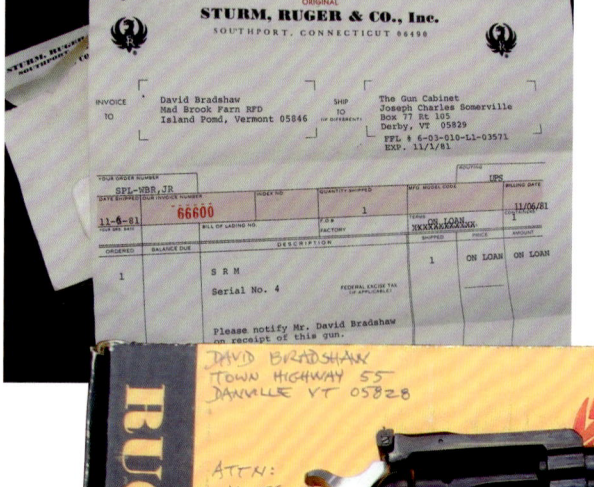

1 Kim Ralston shot this Merino Ram at 35 yards using a Ruger GP100 .357 mag with 6-inch barrel, topped with a 2x Nikon Monarch scope. He was shooting a 180-grain Nosler Partition over a max dose of H110.

2 One of Kim Ralston's hunting revolvers is this Ruger GP100 .357 Magnum with 6-inch barrel, topped with a 2x Nikon Monarch and Weigand Mount.

NATIONAL RIFLE ASSOCIATION
T. SLOW FIRE PISTOL TARGET
MATCH #
RELAY #
TARGET #
STAGE #
S&W 57 Classic
50 yards
Winchester 240 PTHP
5-shots
2"
1204 fps.
LEUPOLD
41 MAGNUM
20 Centerfire Cartridges
Cartouches à percussion centrale
THE NATIONAL TARGET CO
3958-D DARTMOUTH CT. • FREDERICK, MD 21703
MANUFACATURERS AND DISTRIBUTORS OF OFFICIAL N.R.A. TARGETS
N.R.A. LICENSE NO. 1
OFFICIAL 50 FT. SL
NATIONAL
B-2

G. SMITH

CHAPTER 10

the .40s

In my opinion, the big-bores actually start with the .41 Magnum. The following calibers are effective big-game getters that won't subject you to a heap of abuse like some of the calibers in subsequent chapters. The .40 calibers are an excellent choice for the novice and experienced alike.

Right: This whitetail buck was shot at 12 yards using a Field Grade Freedom Arms M654 .41 mag with 7.5-inch barrel, no front sight. It was loaded with Barnes 180 XPB over 23.0 grains of H110. Photo by K. Ralston

Left: This water buffalo cow was killed by Jason Menefee with the custom .41 Magnum Ruger revolver he built, loaded with Buffalo Bore's 265-grain hardcast loads.

.38-40 Winchester left, .44 Magnum right. Photo by R. Millette

.34-40 Winchester

Despite the ".38" in its designation, the .38-40 Winchester actually features a .401-inch diameter bullet. Even though this one is a bit on the eclectic side, it possesses some attributes that make it very attractive.

Originally known as the .38 WCF (Winchester Centerfire), this blackpowder warhorse has enjoyed a bit of a resurgence in popularity despite its "middle of the road" attributes. Even though it wasn't known as a particularly good performer from both an accuracy and power standpoint back in the day, with modern powders, bullets and quality (read: strong) revolvers, it can be a very good performer that doesn't beat the shooter up. This is a good cartridge for the recoil sensitive.

quick facts

BULLET DIAMETER
.401 inches
CASE LENGTH
1.29 inches
OVERALL LENGTH
1.590 inches
MAXIMUM PRESSURE
36,000 psi

Durward Thomason shot this boar at 62 yards with a Freedom Arms 97 in .41 Magnum, stoked with 210-grain Speer Gold Dot hollow points. Photo by D. Thomason

hunt report

THANKSGIVING BUCK

As told by Rob Millette:

I have taken many deer with my .38-40 Bisley, but the first is special for a couple of reasons. My second son and I have never had a very close relationship, so we decided he would come up and visit while everyone else was gone for the Thanksgiving holiday. We were able to spend several days hunting together.

Over the summer, I had found a supplier of good cast bullets that had a decent crimp groove that would hold well under recoil. I decided the 200-grain LFN profile was to my liking and worked up a load of 14.0 grains of HS-6 powder. This load gave me around 1,300 fps with extremely good accuracy. I was reading Elmer Keith's Sixgun Cartridges and Loads and discovered he had developed a very similar recipe using the .40-60-210 rifle bullet.

One afternoon, I decided we would go to a property just down the road from my house and sit there until dark. One of the property owner's grandsons met us,

Who:	Rob Millette
What:	Whitetail
Where:	Mississippi
Range:	20 yards
Revolver:	Ruger Super Blackhawk Custom
Caliber:	.38-40 Winchester
Bullet:	180-grain Flat-Nosed Hardcast

and we sat together for a while, letting the two boys visit. About an hour or so before dark, our visitor decided he had had enough of the cold and started walking back to his grandparent's house. Just as he reached the north side of a large group of trees, I heard a deer get up and move in our direction. I tried to get my son's attention, but he was daydreaming. So I took the shot, pass-shooting the deer as it ran down the edge of the field. I heard it pile up about 75 yards down the tree line.

Photo by R. Millette

.41 Magnum on left,
.44 Magnum right.

.41 Magnum

The "Goldilocks" of the original Magnum triumvirate, the .41 Magnum was meant to fill the gap between the .357 and .44 Magnum. If the .357 was too small and the .44 too big, the .41 Magnum was just right. Announced in 1964 by Remington at the same time Smith & Wesson unveiled the Model 57 chambered for the round, the cartridge was originally intended for law enforcement use. Some law enforcement agencies did press the .41 Magnum into service, but like many good ideas, lowering standards pushed this large cartridge out of contention. Some of the physically weaker officers evidently had trouble shooting the big revolvers and, thus, were ineffective with them. An officer of the law must absolutely be confident and competent with his or her sidearm, or it's all for naught. We saw a similar pattern of events unfold some years later with the 10mm when it was adopted by the FBI. That round, too, was emasculated until it disappeared and was replaced by a weaker sibling, the .40 Smith & Wesson.

It's more than a shame it never caught on like the .44 and the .357 did, as it is a very effective round. It does enjoy a loyal following outside the badged world and, in my experience, doesn't give up a whole lot to its bigger brother, the .44 Magnum, but it does perform with less recoil, even when loaded hot.

Very little is available in factory ammunition for the .41 Magnum today. This lack of on-the-shelf availability makes the round a wonderful handloading proposition, if one is serious about extracting the maximum performance from the cartridge. Exceptions to that rule include commercial ammo by Buffalo Bore, Grizzly Cartridge, Underwood and DoubleTap, all offering very serious, heavy .41 Magnum loads for hunting very large game. Buffalo Bore has one load consisting of a 265-grain WLN at 1,350 fps. I was witness to this load being used on a half-ton Watusi and can testify to its terminal effectiveness. This is a load to seriously consider if you are not inclined to handload.

quick facts

BULLET DIAMETER
.41 inches

CASE LENGTH
1.29 inches

OVERALL LENGTH
1.590 inches

MAXIMUM PRESSURE
36,000 psi

hunt report

TEXAS WATUSI

This hunt took place in Hondo, Texas, with Action Outdoor Adventures. Bovines were on the wish list, but this time an Ankole Watusi — a wild bovine from Africa — was on the menu. The shooter was Jason Menefee, a master gunsmith with JRH Advanced Gunsmithing of Sparks, Nev. Menefee was breaking in a custom revolver he had just put the finishing touches on. He sighted it in merely a few days before making the trek east to Texas, but he was ready.

We had played a game of cat and mouse with this Watusi bull for a good hour before a decent shot opportunity presented itself. Menefee was forced to take an offhand shot, but he was prepared for that as well. The bull was moving from our left to right at a paced-off 50 yards. When the bull cleared the trees broadside, Menefee gently pressed the trigger on the cocked Ruger. The 265-grain pill sped toward the high shoulder of the Watusi and dropped the animal like it had been struck by lightning. A more decisive result I cannot remember.

Had we left the bull to expire on its own, the next sequence of events may not have transpired. The Watusi was down in a segment of tall grass, but it was clearly visible and not moving. I unholstered my .500 Maximum as I slowly made my way toward the downed animal. My hunting partners, revolvers at the ready, approached some ways behind me in a line.

Who:	Jason Menefee
What:	Watusi
Where:	Hondo, TX
Range:	50 yards
Revolver:	Ruger Super Blackhawk Custom
Caliber:	.41 Magnum
Bullet:	265-grain Flat-Nosed Hardcast

When I got within a dozen or so feet from the bull, two things happened simultaneously. Our guide loudly proclaimed with some urgency to watch out because the bull was getting up. At the same time, the Watusi sprung to its feet, looking for a fight, clearly unhappy with us. As it stood, it whipped around looking for its first target, and I let 525 grains of lead fly, followed by yet another, in the Watusi's shoulder area, visibly rocking the half-ton of beef and driving it back to the dry Texas dirt. About then, a fusillade of booming big-bore revolvers off to my right rear opened up like an artillery battery firing for effect, raining lead down on the bull. When the smoke cleared, I looked over to my right at my two smiling hunting partners, both ejecting spent cases from their revolvers. Clearly, all is well that ends well.

Jason Menefee poleaxed this 1,000-pound Watusi with a custom .41 Magnum that he built. The shot was 50 yards, offhand.

.414 SuperMag

Designed by Elgin Gates in the mid-1970s, the .414 SuperMag is merely a .41 Magnum lengthened to 1.61 inches. Dan Wesson was the sole manufacturer of production revolvers in this specialized caliber. As with the other SuperMag calibers, the .414 was originally intended for competition in metallic silhouette. Like its smaller sibling, the .41 Magnum, when loaded with good bullets the .414 makes for a good medium- to big-game hunting cartridge. The rarity of this cartridge means you will have to reload, though a revolver so chambered will readily digest .41 Magnum fodder.

quick facts

BULLET DIAMETER
.41 inches
CASE LENGTH
1.610 inches
OVERALL LENGTH
1.975 inches
MAXIMUM PRESSURE
43,511 psi

Dr. Mark Key killed this bison with a Freedom Arms Model 83 in .41 Magnum loaded with both CEB 220 solids and 210-grain Swift A-frames. Photo by M. Key

tip from the field

WEAVER STANCE AND PRACTICING OFFHAND

I have found that there are no better ways to shoot your big-bore revolver offhand than the Weaver stance or, in my case, a modified Weaver. Basically, you need to find out what works best for you, and the only way to accomplish that is to get out there and burn powder.

Let's examine my offhand shooting technique. As I stated earlier, what works for me may not work for you, and you must find the best technique for yourself. Hopefully this will give you a foundation upon which to build or at least something to try.

Start by standing nearly sideways, with your left foot forward. This is a fighting posture, a modified Weaver stance, in which your knees are slightly bent. Grip the revolver in your right hand with your left hand under the butt, providing support. My supporting left elbow moves in and against my ribcage, creating a solid rest. This is what creates the stability, your elbow resting against your ribcage. This is a much more stable position than the isosceles stance where the revolver is almost free-floating in your hands. Apply the same trigger and breathing control to your shot.

When practicing for the hunt, I tend to shoot offhand, simply because it's the most difficult position to master. We've already discussed offhand stance, but let's talk practice for the hunt. I try to spend most of my time on the 100-yard line shooting pig silhouettes. The pig silhouette measures roughly 16 inches wide by 12 inches tall. It's a pretty small target at 100 yards. Sounds odd, but when you can consistently hit a 16-by-12-inch target at 100 yards, you are prepared for the worst-case scenario. Preparing for the toughest shots is a recurring theme in my hunting regimen. Some folks have different loads for different game, while I prefer to have one load that can do it all and perform well under the worst possible conditions. That is how I view practicing for a handgun hunt. Prepare for the worst, and the "normal" shots come easily when you are properly prepared. I realize this sounds extreme and that it can be difficult when you begin practicing in that manner at extended range. However, I assure you that when you can consistently hit16 by 12-inch targets at 100 yards, closer shots become quite a bit easier. Still, you never really know what you will encounter on the hunt. I can almost guarantee that if you don't prepare, you will face the worst-case scenario. Remember, Murphy's Law applies to hunting, which is why I practice offhand, as it seems inevitable that I will get an offhand shot.

BEFORE USING GUN-READ WARNINGS IN INSTRUCTION MANUAL AVAILABLE FREE FROM
RUGER
SUPER BLACKHAWK

CHAPTER 11

the .44s

This chapter should probably be called the .43s, but I won't quibble about the false moniker that was placed on the various .44s' birth certificates. Can you imagine the street cred' ".429 Magnum" would have had? I'm okay with maintaining the ruse.

This chapter will cover the .44 Special, .44 Remington Magnum and the .445 SuperMag in ascending order. This is a very popular category among the revolver faithful. The .44 Special is a very pleasant round to shoot for nearly every level of shooter. The .44 Magnum is a threshold cartridge and clearly over the limit for many from the standpoint of recoil. The .445, though no longer chambered in a production revolver, is still a great performer that is sometimes offered by custom gun builders.

Ken O'Neill shot this mountain lion in Idaho with his Smith & Wesson Model 629 in .44 Magnum, loaded with Sierra 240 JHPs over a stiff charge of 296. Photo by K. O'Neill

.44 Special left,
.44 Magnum right.

.44 Special

This cartridge was the darling of none other than Elmer Keith, and his high-performance loading efforts led to the design and introduction of the bigger and more potent .44 Remington Magnum. Still a viable performer when loaded correctly, this cartridge is a great big-bore alternative for the recoil-sensitive, as its low pressure delivers a relatively mild recoil impulse. Designed primarily as a defensive round, the .44 Special features a .429 diameter like its offspring, the .44 Magnum, but the case length is a nominal 1.16 inches. The .44 Special can be safely fired in any and every .44 Magnum-chambered revolver. This cartridge does indeed make for a great defensive round, as it can be easily handled and delivers a fairly large bullet. Loaded properly with heavy-for-caliber hardcast bullets, I wouldn't hesitate to use the .44 Special on reasonably big game.

quick facts

BULLET DIAMETER
.429 inches
CASE LENGTH
1.16 inches
OVERALL LENGTH
1.615 inches
MAXIMUM PRESSURE
15,500 psi

John Taffin shot this Ibex/Catalina goat cross with the Freedom Arms Model 83 in .44 Magnum. Photo by J. Taffin

170 GunDigestStore.com

tip from the field

SAFETY

Let's talk safety a moment, particularly when out on the hunt. Let's assume that you know a deer is approaching your position, so you are preparing to take a shot. You have carefully and quietly pulled the hammer back, but you are keeping your finger away from the trigger. Let's say that the deer changes course, forcing you to change your position before the imminent shot. Do you decock your revolver and risk the deer hearing you cock it again? It's not necessary if you simply place the thumb of your supporting hand between the hammer and the frame of the revolver, creating a positive stop (see photo). This way, you can safely move into a new position and be ready to let lead fly. This is simple, yet effective.

Putting the thumb of your supporting hand between the cocked hammer and the frame provides a positive stop for the hammer, making it safe to move positions without decocking.

The .44s **171**

.44 Remington Magnum

The .44 Magnum is a serious handgun round and the second revolver cartridge to bear the name "Magnum" on its headstamp. The .44 Remington Magnum arrived on scene in 1956. Both Ruger and Smith & Wesson vied for the distinction of being the first to market the new high-powered cartridge with the introduction of the Super Blackhawk and the Model 29, respectively.

Smith & Wesson was first to market, and, ironically, it was a little-known manufacturer called Great Western Arms Company that also beat Ruger to store shelves with a .44 Magnum. The .44 hit gun shops nationwide, and the world hasn't been the same since. But the big shot in the arm for the .44 Magnum from a standpoint of popularity was the 1971 film, Dirt Harry, starring Clint Eastwood, the tough San Francisco detective who carried a Model 29 in a shoulder holster.

As mentioned, the actual diameter of the .44 Magnum is .429 inches. This really is the quintessential big-bore round and what I consider a threshold cartridge, meaning that it is the upper limit for all but the most hardened handgunner and still needs to be approached with caution by neophytes.

The .44 Magnum put handgun hunting on the map as a feasible endeavor. Having read the big- and dangerous-game exploits of Larry Kelly and others, I harbored no doubts as to the effectiveness of the .44 Magnum. The cartridge remained at the top position of power until 1983, when it fell victim to the game of one-upmanship with the release of Dick Casull's wonder cartridge, the .454 Casull. It's a move that the powers that

quick facts

BULLET DIAMETER
.41 inches

CASE LENGTH
1.285 inches

OVERALL LENGTH
1.610 inches

MAXIMUM PRESSURE
36,000 psi

be at Smith & Wesson never forgot, but don't worry, they participated in one-upmanship themselves a couple of decades later when they released their .500 S&W Magnum. We are a consumer society after all, driven by clever marketing, and it doesn't necessarily take much to convince us we need bigger, better, faster, more powerful, etc. But do we really need bigger?

Still considered the classic big-bore revolver cartridge, to this day the .44 Magnum enjoys a strong following among big-bore lovers. There is no big-bore round that can claim the variety of available ammunition on the market with loads from mild to wild. If you're not a reloader, this is the cartridge for you, because every possible load is available commercially for virtually any and every application imaginable. The .44 Magnum remains the gold standard by which all big revolver cartridges are measured.

So when do you actually need something bigger? The answer isn't so cut and dried, but I'll say it: never, actually. Before you proclaim me a blasphemer, let me qualify my statement by saying when it's properly loaded, the .44 Remington Magnum can, will and has unequivocally taken virtually every game animal that walks the face of this planet. However, in my experience, there are better choices for really large game, and they begin at .45 and go up from there. There, I said it. In summary, will the .44 Mag work on really big game? Yes. Are there better choices? Yes again.

The .44 Magnum is a great deer cartridge, and while it will comfortably take much larger game, I prefer moving up in diameter with animals significantly heavier than deer. Bigger is better, as long as the shooter is capable of competently shooting stronger calibers. With the move up comes a sizable increase in recoil. Can't argue with larger diameter and heavier bullets.

So when do you really need more than the .44 Magnum? That is up to you and your abilities. You need to be honest with yourself and determine how much abuse you are willing and able to withstand. I know this sounds like I am sensationalizing recoil, but in all seriousness, very few people can shoot the .44 Magnum well. These big revolvers require a lot of practice to master, and, quite frankly, they are not for everyone. So, if the .44 Magnum is your limit, there is no reason to fret. If you can handle it and you intend to hunt large game, by all means step up. You will be well served. While the ubiquitous .44 Magnum is fully capable of most tasks of which it will be asked, moving up in diameter is a good idea when elk, moose or larger are on the menu. But, only you can determine if you really need more. In the meantime, the .44 Magnum will remain the quintessential big-game revolver round.

Mark Key bagged this lioness with a 30-yard shot from his 6-inch Freedom Arms Model 83. It was loaded with 325-grain Swift A-frames, chronographed at 1,550 fps. Mark is seen here with PH Bobby Hansen of Bobby Hansen Safaris. Photo by M. Key.

hunt report

RED STAG

As Told by Gary Smith:

My hunt started off focused on deer, but that was short-lived when I found out about a particular red stag on the ranch. The thought of a traditional European stag mount on my wall was very appealing. In reality, the animal I was after was a rather large-bodied bull that had never crowned out. Alas, he was just a 4x4 with three-foot tall antlers and a body half the size of a Rocky Mountain elk. It took me all of about two seconds to switch gears and go after the stag.

After a brief and unsuccessful sit in the morning, we relocated a pop-up blind at the edge of a cedar break with a commanding view of my field of fire. In two directions I could see out to about 500 yards of scattered trees and grasses. Shortly after getting settled in, I spotted the bull at several hundred yards. He was with five hinds and a satellite bull, which was a spike. For the next six hours he taunted me. Never coming closer than 380 yards, the group fed, bedded down, milled around, bedded some more and moved in and out of view. Several times I strongly considered making a stalk, but I also knew the cover I would have to use was loaded with deer because of the weather.

After being sufficiently irritated, the herd bull ran the spike off for the last time mid-afternoon. Ultimately, the youngster was the first to the alfalfa, which was encouraging. From some 300 yards out, the big bull stood motionless and watched the spike feeding for nearly a half

Who:	Gary Smith
What:	Red Stag
Where:	Bandera, Texas
Range:	50 yards
Revolver:	Freedom Arms Model 83
Caliber:	.44 Magnum
Bullet:	270-grain Spear Jacketed Softpoint

an hour. He appeared noticeably irritated, but it wasn't enough to pull him up the hill. The small bull moved off into the thicket, and the big bull and hinds disappeared off to the west.

I was really second-guessing my earlier decision to stay put, but now I was pinned down by deer in nearly every direction. Finally, the bull walked out looking for his harem, and when he saw his ladies feeding on the alfalfa, that did the trick. He sauntered into range, and when he stopped quartering toward me I touched the trigger on the Freedom Arms .44 Magnum and planted a Speer 270-grain soft point into his shoulder. If I've learned one thing over the years, it is to admire your shooting when the animal is down and not before. At about 120 yards he stopped at a decent angle, and I put another one into his ribs. He went another 30 yards and crashed in spectacular fashion.

Once again the .44 Magnum performed on a large animal with excellent results. I was unable to recover either bullet, though not for lack of trying. The first shot lodged somewhere in his stomach, but we couldn't find it even though three of us looked for several minutes. The second shot was a complete pass-through in the ribs.

My setup for the red stag was a Freedom Arms with a 10-inch barrel and a Leupold 2.5x8mm scope in TSOB bases and rings. The gun shoots those Speer bullets like a dart, and their bonded technology allows them to hold together on big, tough animals such as stag or bear. My load is a full charge of Winchester 296 powder with a muzzle velocity of 1,377 fps. — G. Smith.

Smith took this red stag with a scoped Freedom Arms Model 83 in .44 Magnum. Photo by J. Pace

.445 SuperMag left,
.44 Magnum right.

.445 SuperMag

As is the case with all of the SuperMag cartridges, the parent case of the .44 Magnum is stretched to 1.6 inches, which signifies a considerable increase in case capacity and velocity potential over the parent cartridge. A creation of Elgin Gates, the reasoning behind the development of the .445 SuperMag was better knock-down power in metallic silhouette shooting, where it did indeed excel. Only Dan Wesson offered revolvers chambered in this special cartridge, a gun based on the maker's stretched frame. It does make for a good hunting round and should not be overlooked. Aside from Dan Wesson revolvers found on the used gun market, this is a custom proposition.

quick facts

BULLET DIAMETER
.429 inches
CASE LENGTH
1.610 inches
OVERALL LENGTH
1.935 inches
MAXIMUM PRESSURE
40,611 psi

This North Carolina sow was brought down by the author with a Ruger Super Blackhawk loaded with Hornady's 300-grain XTP load. One shot at 50 yards was required.

The .44s **175**

1. Clay Ralston bagged this big buck at 70 yards with his Ruger Super Blackhawk Hunter topped with a 2x Leupold scope and loaded with 300-grain Beartooth WFNs over a stiff charge of H110. Photo by K. Ralston

2. This 150-pound boar fell to Gary Smith's Freedom Arms Model 83 in .44 Magnum. Photo by G. Smith

3. Maine black bear shot by K. Ralston at 35 yards using a Ruger Bisley Hunter in .44 Mag with an M8 2x Leupold mounted. The load was a 300-grain WFNGC from Montana Bullet Works over 19.0 grains of H110. Photo by K. Ralston

4 Amanda Key killed this black bear with her Ultradot-equipped Smith & Wesson Performance Center Model 629 .44 Magnum, loaded with Beartooth 265-grain hardcast bullets at 1,200 fps. Photo by M. Key

5 Lynn Thompson killed this Australian water buffalo with a Ruger Redhawk slinging Hornady 300-grain XTPs. Photo by L. Thompson

6 The author shot this large North Carolinian sow at night using a Ruger Bisley Hunter loaded with DoubleTap's 320-grain WFN load.

7 John Taffin took this Catalina goat with the TLA 7.5-inch West Texas Flat-Top Target .44. Photo by J. Taffin

8 Clay Ralston shot this merino ram at 90 yards using a Ruger Bisley Hunter in .44 Magnum with an M8 2x Leupold scope. His load was a 300-grain WFNGC by Montana Bullet Works over 19.0 grains of H110. Photo by K. Ralston

9 Gun writer extraordinaire, John Taffin, with an aoudad he took with a .44 Magnum. Photo by J. Taffi

10 A nice four horn ram taken by Craig Copeland, who used his .44 Mag Bisley Hunter and a 355-grain Beartooth WLN at 1,200fps. The range was 65 yards, and the ram only ran 20 yards before tipping over. Photo by C. Copeland

11 Larry "Mr. Whitetail" Weishuhn took this monster buck with his Ruger Super Blackhawk Hunter in .44 Magnum. Photo by L. Weishuhn

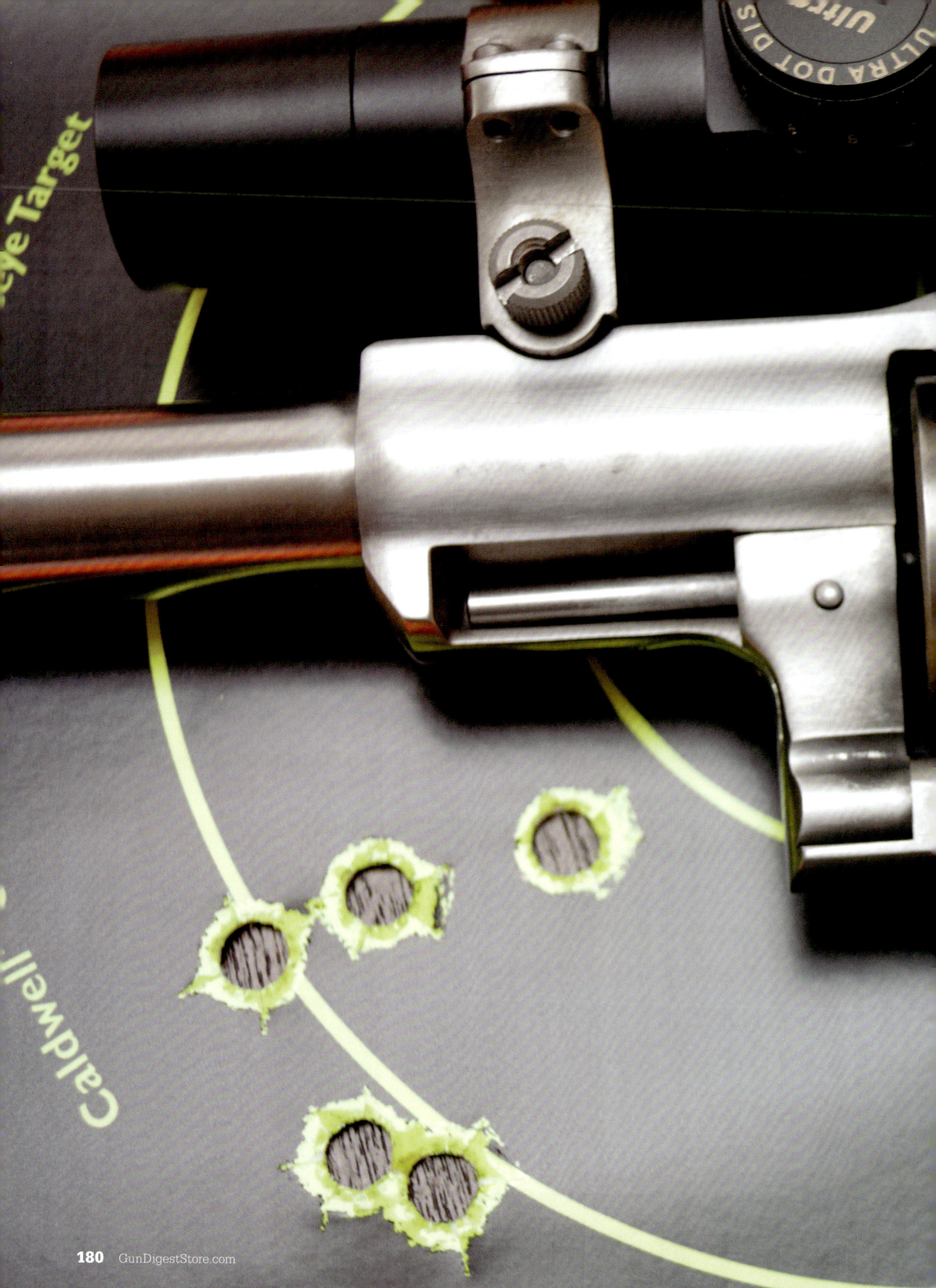
ULTRA DOT DIS
Ultra
Eye Target
Caldwell

CHAPTER 12

Gary Smith downed this 40-inch trophy Cape buffalo with his Freedom Arms 83 in .454 Casull, loaded with 325-grain Barnes Busters. Photo by G. Smith

the .45s

The .45s are a very versatile group of cartridges, ranging from the .45 Colt on the bottom end up to the high-velocity champ, the .460 S&W Magnum, at the top end. My personal favorite is the smallest and lowest pressure producer, the .45 Colt. Lower pressure leads to lower recoil and lower noise levels. I don't place a premium on velocity potential, but there is no denying that increasing velocity increases the range of effectiveness, if you want to reach out a bit farther than typical handgun hunting distances.

.45 Colt left,
.44 Magnum right.

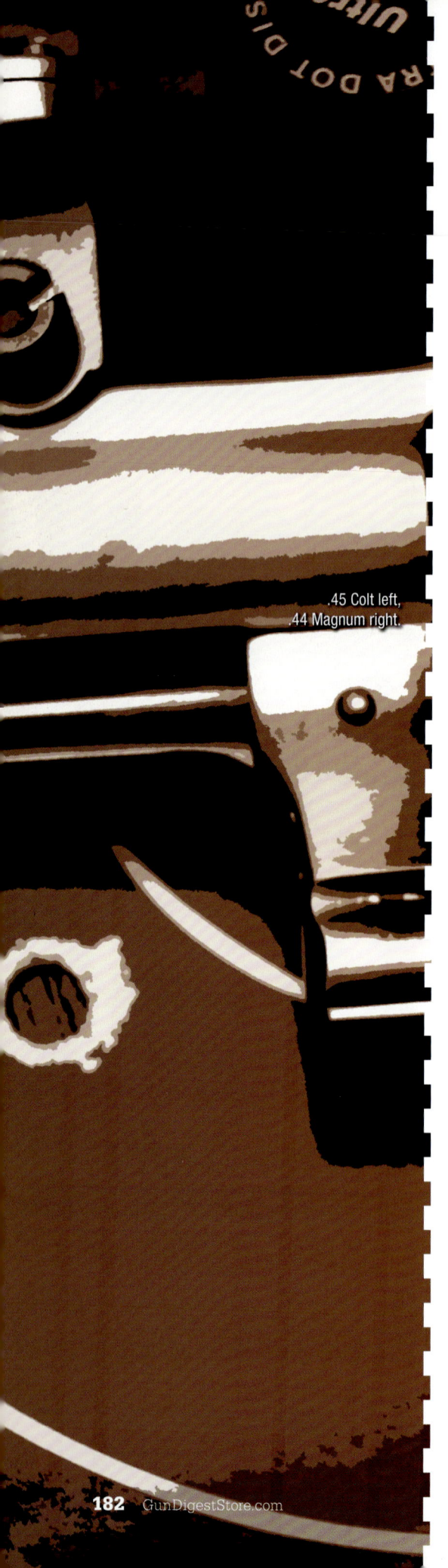

.45 Colt

This segment really is the story of two cartridges. Born in 1873, this old black-powder cartridge never seems to get its just due. Think of the .45 Colt as the Rodney Dangerfield of big-bore handgun rounds (a reference older readers will get!). Rarely is it loaded to potential from the factory because of the vast number of older revolvers in circulation that are incapable of handling the higher pressure, modern smokeless loads that would most likely reduce them to shrapnel. Basically, full-power loads in those old guns are lawsuits waiting to happen. So, due to liability issues, the .45 Colt is rarely ever viewed in the same vein as the .44 Magnum.

No slouch even in black-powder form, the .45 Colt in modern times really takes on a different persona. Load it to its full potential, and it will give the much-vaunted .454 Casull a run for its money and leave the .44 Magnum sucking wind in its rearview mirror. But before you roll out the hate mail, keep in mind that I own at least a half-dozen .44 Mags of all shapes and sizes. It's just that I am a bigger fan of the modern .45 Colt. If there ever was a do-it-all cartridge, the .45 Colt would be at the top of the heap.

Gun scribe Ross Seyfried is also a big fan of the .45 Colt and chose one to use against Cape buffalo in the mid-1980s. Seyfried evidently had a great deal of confidence in the capabilities of the round — when loaded to potential — and his own ability on the trigger. In an article in Handloader magazine, while discussing the merits of the .44 Magnum, Seyfried said, "In the midst of this I began working in Africa. It was a handgunner's paradise. Plenty of deer- and elk-like critters could be stalked within honest handgun range. Many could be taken with the .44 Magnum, but I always felt like I was asking a boy to do a man's job." Almost losing a trophy kudu shot with his trusty .44 Magnum further exposed that round as an under-

quick facts

BULLET DIAMETER
.452 inches

CASE LENGTH
1.285 inches

OVERALL LENGTH
1.60 inches

MAXIMUM PRESSURE
14,000 psi

Kim Ralston took this Maine black bear at 45 yards using Freedom Arms Model 97 .45 Colt with 5.5-inch barrel. It's topped with a 4 MOA JPoint sight and shoots a Hornady 250 XTP over 20.5 grains of 2400. Photo by K. Ralston

achiever of sorts on really huge game, and Seyfried's confidence in the .44 Magnum fell.

About this time, a gentleman by the name of John Linebaugh began pestering Seyfried with letters and phone calls touting the .45 Colt as a significant step up and over the legendary .44. The two finally met, and Linebaugh offered Seyfried the chance to shoot his .45 Colt over the chronograph. Ross declined, stepping back an adequete distance and taking cover, as he truly expected the revolver to come apart like a grenade in Linebaugh's hands. But, the chrono' told the true story — six times in a row, the 310-grain bullets traveling at 1,500 fps. Remarkable! The biggest shock came when Seyfried, expecting to pound the surely mangled cartridge cases out of their chambers, was able to lift them out with minimal effort. Linebaugh was definitely on to something, and Seyfried immediately commissioned him to build one of these super .45 Colts. As for my love affair with the cartridge, what's good enough for Ross Seyfried, is certainly good enough for me.

One need not load the .45 Colt to Casull levels to enjoy a leg up in effectiveness. Loaded to much lower pressure levels, the .45 Colt will not leave you needing more.

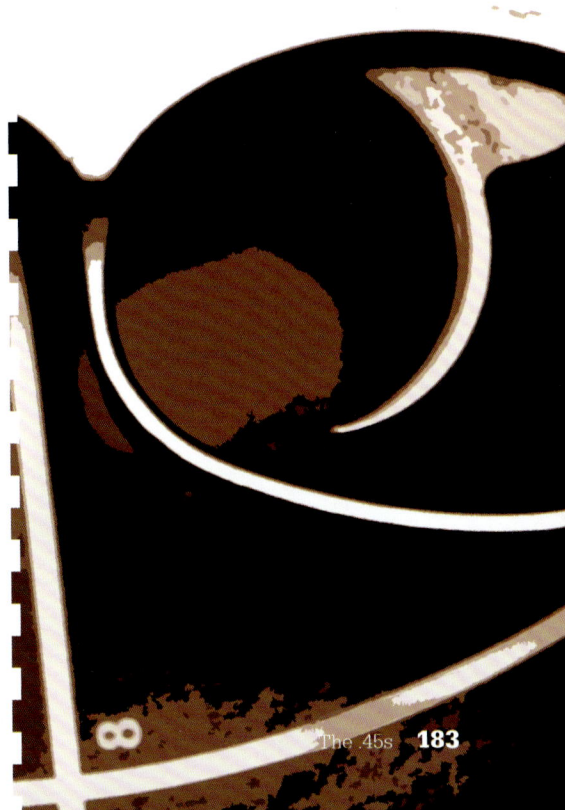

The .45s **183**

hunt report

TEXAS WATER BUFFALO

Action Outdoor Adventures of Hondo, Texas was the location. A big water buffalo bull was the goal. A .454 Super Blackhawk loaded with hot .45 Colt +P loads provided the means, and I was manning the trigger.

It was an unseasonably warm October afternoon. We'd glassed and spotted a large buff that would provide just the test we were looking for. We put a stalk on the lone bull and managed to get within 25 yards downwind of the big bruiser.

Using the fork of a small tree in the thick brush as a rest to stabilize the Super Blackhawk, I didn't want to take any chances when so close to such a strapping example of bovine flesh. My first shot had to count. The bull moved clear of the scrub brush that was obstructing the path my bullet would have to travel to make terminal contact. The hammer on the big Ruger was already thumbed back and ready to strike a primer. I centered the red circle of the Ultradot on the upper part of the shoulder of the broadside bull and squeezed off the first of five rounds. The Ruger barked and bucked as the heavy bullet twisted its way out of the barrel. The shot looked and felt good, but as animals weighing nearly a ton typically do, the bull ran off crashing through the thick foliage.

We took off in a sprint, attempting to flank the wounded bull. We made it to a clearing, setting up for the next shot that would surely come. The bull cleared the thick stand of trees and scrub. It saw us and, despite making us visually, still came anyway. Bovines, be they milk cows on the farm or Cape buffalo in the Selous, are unpredictable and, quite frankly, a bit scary. But the bull came, looking right

Who:	**Max Prasac**
What:	**Water Buffalo**
Where:	**Hondo, TX**
Range:	**25 yards**
Revolver:	**Ruger .454 Casull Super Blackhawk**
Caliber:	**.45 Colt**
Bullet:	**405-grain Flat-Nosed Hardcast**

at me. Since it seemingly didn't mind my presence, I took the opportunity to drive another Garrett 405-grainer into the beast's shoulder, triggering a sprint. I managed to put another behind the bull's shoulder as it was going away, but it crashed onward.

At this point we summoned for help to locate the wounded animal. Within 30 minutes of the last shot, we saw a dark lump lying motionless in the tall grass. On approach, Jack Huntington and I both put a couple more rounds in the beast just for good measure. It's unsettling when a "dead" buffalo finds its legs (See Jason Menefee's exciting hunt report in the Chapter 10 .41 Magnum segment!).

The big 405-grain bullets from Garrett did their job with aplomb. Two bullets were found in the skin of the offside shoulder, having actually pierced the skin. The third bullet exited. The big bull would strain the scales to the tune of 2,000 pounds. That's a lot of beef in anyone's book.

This large water buffalo bull required three Garrett 405-grain .45 Colt loads from a new Ruger Super Blackhawk in .454 Casull before it conceded defeat.

.454 Casull left,
.44 Magnum right.

.454 Casull

In the early 1950s, while Elmer Keith was hot-rodding the .44 Special, Dick Casull turned his attention to the .45 Colt and building special five-shot cylinders on Colt Single Action Army revolvers. In those days, with limited gunpowder options, one had to get creative in order to achieve high velocities. Casull was able to get a full 2,000 fps out of a 230 grain (one designed for use in the .45 ACP round) by loading two grains of Unique, 25 grains of H2400 and three grains of Bullseye. At the time, highly compacted triplex loads were the only path to achieving the pressures necessary to reach the velocities he sought.

quick facts

BULLET DIAMETER
.452 inches

CASE LENGTH
1.398 inches

OVERALL LENGTH
1.765 inches

MAXIMUM PRESSURE
65,000 psi

Manufacturers of .454 Casull ammunition have remained true to the original design parameters, offering some very high-velocity loads. However, with modern powders, the .454 is loaded to lower levels than the SAAMI maximum spec, as they are able to achieve the desired velocities without touching the maximum pressure ceiling. The pressures are still high, relatively speaking, but lower than the max allotted levels. The Casull also shines with heavy-for-caliber bullets, though care must be taken when loading them at high velocities, for such recipes have a propensity for testing the integrity of the crimp.

In 1983, the Freedom Arms Model 83 was introduced in Dick Casull's souped-up .45-caliber cartridge. Never before had such a high-pressure revolver round been produced nor a gun that could live under the abuse generated by it. Other manufacturers, such as Ruger and Taurus, followed suit years later with their own super-strong revolvers chambered in .454 Casull, as this round required a revolver of much stronger construction than any made for the .44 Magnum. This was not only because of the

Lynn Thompson, a masterful handgun hunter, killed this Cape buffalo with his Freedom Arms Model 83 in .454 Casull. Photo by L. Thompson

higher pressures, but also because Dick Casull specified a longer case to prevent the accidental use of .454 Casull ammunition in .45 Colt revolvers of inadequate strength. Additionally, Casull specified a small rifle primer pocket to strengthen the head of the case by virtue of leaving more material in this area.

I think of the .454 Casull as the .378 Weatherby of the revolver world, as neither is really pleasant to shoot when loaded to spec. The .454 Casull generates horrendous recoil and has caused its fair share of injuries. Most .454 Casull ammunition manufacturers load the cartridge short of its full velocity and pressure (SAAMI specification) potential. However, paper ballistics sell, and even loaded down a bit, the .454 can still boast potent numbers. There is no other commercially available handgun cartridge that has a maximum SAAMI pressure specification as high as the .454 Casull, though the .460 and .500 S&W Magnums come close.

At the end of the day, the .454 Casull is a very flexible cartridge, which was Dick Casull's vision from inception. What he wanted and what was ultimately delivered was a cartridge and revolver combination that can be loaded from mild to extremely wild, as the shooter's desires and needs dictate. I think Dick Casull succeeded impressively.

Federal's unbelievably accurate 300-grain Swift A-Frame load has delivered sub 1-inch five-shot groups at 50 yards on a regular basis.

quick test 454 REASONS TO REJOICE

Some guns just flat-out shoot. This Ruger Super Redhawk (SRH) in the rambunctious .454 Casull has exhibited exceptional accuracy from day one. Newly configured in 2014 with a barrel profile featuring no taper and a new front sight, the .454 SRH is otherwise unchanged.

Upon delivery I fitted the big revolver with an Ultradot 30 red-dot sight with Ruger's own 30mm rings. I shot my first targets at 25 yards to get on paper and after some adjusting pushed it out to 50 yards. Loaded with Federal's fantastic 300-grain Swift A-Frame loads at an advertised 1,520 fps, I've managed to shoot a number of sub 1-inch five-shot groups off of the bench, the best measuring a meager 0.75 inches!

I typically limit my hunting revolver testing to 50 yards as it gives a good indicator how it will perform up close and at distance. This revolver deserved further testing, so I stretched its legs out to 100 yards. Well, it didn't disappoint, delivering a number of 1.75-inch five-shot groups. The Ruger SRH/Federal Swift A-frame load combination is a match made in heaven.

Federal's 300-grain load routinely delivers 1.75-inch groups at 100 yards!

.460 Smith & Wesson Magnum left, .44 Magnum right.

.460 Smith & Wesson Magnum

Smith & Wesson's long-range wonder cartridge was introduced in 2005, housed in the company's X-frame platform. Boasting a case length of a full 1.8 inches, the .460 is basically a stretched .454 Casull. This new cartridge was designed in the same vein as the .454 — high pressure, high velocity, long range. The .460 S&W Magnum has the distinction of being the highest-velocity production revolver cartridge in existence, with some factory loads able to exceed 2,300 fps.

With an overall cartridge length of 2.30 inches, the .460 XVR will also safely chamber and fire .454 Casull and .45 Colt ammo. However, I have not been able to extract acceptable accuracy shooting various loads of .45 Colt or .454 Casull through my test XVR.

Not a terribly efficient round, the .460 excels with both light and heavy bullets, but it will not outshine the .454 Casull by much when mid-weight bullets are loaded. Similar pressures can be achieved, and, by increasing the payload, the results aren't dramatic. That said, in most factory loads, the .460 pushes a lightweight bullet at high speeds, just as intended. In this iteration, it does well on thin-skinned game, but light, frangible bullets at high velocity are a recipe for disaster on truly large animals. Fortunately, the .460 is very effective loaded with heavy bullets as well.

The price you pay for choosing the .460 S&W Magnum is the size of the revolver necessary to hold the oversized cartridge. Then again, every decision you make comes with a price.

quick facts

BULLET DIAMETER
.452 inches

CASE LENGTH
1.790 inches

OVERALL LENGTH
2.343 inches

MAXIMUM PRESSURE
61,931 psi

hunt report

ALASKAN GRIZZLY BEAR

As told by Ernest Holloway:

I had been talking with outfitter Don Martin for several years about doing a hunt for moose or grizzly bear in Alaska. I would be in the Wrangell Mountains hunting on the Chitina River. We decided that our best chance was that someone would take a moose the day before I arrived, and then I could get on the carcass and hope a grizz got to it before the wolves — a lot of ifs!

I had decided I would use the 260-grain North Fork cup point out of my 7.5-inch Smith & Wesson .460 Magnum, topped with a H1 Aimpoint red dot. I was also taking a Ruger No. 1 chambered in .460 as backup.

On the drive from Anchorage to Chitina airport, Don informed me a moose was taken the day before and we should work to get on the carcass as soon as possible. We flew from Chitina to the lodge and wasted no time in dropping off the nonessentials and getting out so we could make an early morning trek to the gut pile. We set up camp about two miles downwind from where we thought the carcass was and turned in for the night. The morning came quickly, and we left camp at first light. However, the wind had now done a 180-degree turn, and we would have to circle around and move even faster.

Who:	Ernest "Ruggy" Holloway
What:	Grizzly Bear
Where:	Alaska
Range:	17 yards
Revolver:	Smith & Wesson X-frame
Caliber:	.460 Smith & Wesson Magnum
Bullet:	265-grain North Fork Cup Point Solid

The need to circle added to the challenge of finding the gut pile, as the river bottom looked like a maze of willows and watercourses. Even Don was second guessing himself. The wind shifted 180 degrees once again, and we held out hope that we had not been made by the bear. We were within several hundred yards and crows were in the trees above so we figured the bear was on the carcass. We slipped off the packs and started our stalk. About 100 yards out, we dropped a few feet into a dry gravel bed and made an assessment. The gravel bed had willows on both sides and wound its way up to within 75 yards of the spot. No sooner had we taken a step forward when I looked over to see Don shoulder his rifle as a large grizzly charged straight for us. It covered 40 yards in about two seconds, and I heard Don yell, "Any time you can shoot!" With that I let the first one go. At 17 yards it rolled the bear to a stop, and I continued shooting, actually pulling the trigger two more times with an empty gun. Don tapped me on the shoulder and said we should move back, reload and give it a few minutes. A quick discussion of the events followed, and I found it had happened so fast there was no big adrenaline rush or even time to get excited.

We slowly made our way back to find one very dead bear about four yards from where the first shot had connected. At that moment the magnitude of the hunt caught up with me, and so did the adrenaline. Upon further inspection, four of my five shots had hit the bear, while three of four out of Don's .300 Win. Mag. had made contact.

The necropsy revealed that my first shot was through the neck, into the shoulder and through the top of the lung, stopping about 30 inches from the point of entry to just under the hide on the back. The bullet nose was completely flattened where the cup had been. Another round went through the neck, another in the shoulder through the lungs and out the other side, and the last went through the ribcage. – E. Holloway

Guide Don Martin with Ernest Holloway and the grizzly bear that charged them.

.45-70 Government left,
.44 Magnum right.

.45-70 Government

I know I'm going against the fabric of this book by including a rifle round in the lineup. Having said that, this is another cartridge worth mentioning, as it is popular in the one production revolver produced in this old workhorse of a caliber. That revolver is Magnum Research's BFR — Big Frame Revolver. This super-sized offering is big on size and power with surprisingly moderate recoil.

In its nomenclature, ".45" denoted the caliber and "70" the number of grains of black powder. This old warrior is still hanging around, more viable and youthful than ever. Introduced in 1873 at the U.S. Army's Springfield Armory, the .45-70 in modern form is quite the performer, one able to mimic the .454 Casull in a handgun, but at much lower chamber pressures. We are talking about modern smokeless powder loads here, not the .45-70 in black-powder form. Granted, it takes a lot of revolver to house the big .45-70 round, but the bulk of the BFR serves to tame the cartridge quite a bit over a lighter revolver loaded to similar levels as the .454 Casull. The nominal bullet diameter is .458 inches and the case length 2.10 inches.

I took delivery of a BFR in .45-70 with a 7.5-inch barrel. The long-framed revolver has surprisingly good balance, despite its exaggerated proportions. The trigger was good and broke cleanly at about 3.5 pounds. All BFRs have a free-wheeling pawl, and the fit and finish is very good.

quick facts

BULLET DIAMETER
.458 inches
CASE LENGTH
2.10 inches
OVERALL LENGTH
2.55 inches
MAXIMUM PRESSURE
28,000 psi

BFR's excellent .45-70 proved an accurate revolver. New BFR-specific loads from Garrett Cartridge were tested, slinging a 540-grain bullet at 1,200 fps.

quicktest

BFR .45-70

BFR's .45-70 is the first revolver in the company's lineup, thus I felt compelled to get my hands on one and put it through its paces. The original was based on a frame by D-Max, before Magnum Research brought their own design to the table, featuring more metal in key places, making for a considerably stronger revolver than the original offerings.

I ordered a standard .45-70 equipped with a 7.5-inch barrel. I have shot these revolvers in the past, but I am always a little shocked by the sheer size of this five-shooter. However, its bulk helps tame recoil. That said, with a 7.5-inch barrel (a 10-inch barrel is the only other option), the balance is pretty good, and I had little difficulty shooting it offhand. However, it is big and heavy, necessitating a good shoulder holster when out in the field.

The trigger on this particular revolver was exceptional, breaking cleanly with no creep at 3 pounds. It was equipped with their newly designed rubber grips. The factory sights are quite good, but in an attempt to take advantage of the revolver's accuracy, I utilized the factory scope base to mount an Ultradot 30 red-dot, using four aluminum rings from Ultradot. That also served to add some weight to the revolver in anticipation of heavier loads down the line.

The BFR .45-70 proved extremely accurate, delivering groups of which many a rifle would be proud.

Recoil, while subjective, is not surprisingly stout, save for a few offerings that were quite brisk. The big .45-70 case holds a significant amount of powder, and the lightest bullets tested weighed in at 300 grains. Standard pressure loads weren't too hard to control, but Buffalo Bore's +P offerings required significant grip tension to subdue. Exceptional accuracy is also what I have come to expect from BFRs, especially considering the fact that all loads tested (with the exception of one) were designed for rifles — rifles with barrels significantly longer than 7.5 inches.

As this book goes to print I have yet to draw blood with this impressive, albeit huge revolver.

All testing was performed with an Ultradot 30 on the Magnum Research sight base.

ACCURACY TABLE

.45-70 BFR

MANUFACTURER	BULLET	GROUP SIZE (IN.) 25 YDS.	50 YDS.
Double Tap	300-grain TSX	.951	1.489
Buffalo Bore	405 JFP (Mag load)	.825	.841
Garrett	540 hardcast	1.334	2.392

The .45s **193**

1 Alan Griffith shot this enormous Alaskan moose with a 62-inch spread using a Ruger Blackhawk in .45 Colt, stoked with 335-grain WFNs. Photo by A. Griffith

2 Michael King shot this black bear in New Mexico with his Ultradot-equipped Ruger Super Redhawk in .454 Casull. Photo by M. Key

3 Alex Key took this lioness with factory-loaded Barnes 275-grain XPBs out of an 8 3/8-inch Smith & Wesson .460 XVR. A Burris scope tops the big revolver. Photo by M. Key

4 This wild hog was shot by the author in North Carolina with a Ruger Bisley in .45 Colt. The load was Grizzly Cartridge's 335-grain WLN. Only one shot was necessary.

5 Lynn Thompson, proprietor of Cold Steel, stopped this charging water buffalo with a Ruger Super Redhawk in .454 Casull while spear hunting in Australia. Lynn never steps out into the field without a revolver. Photo by L. Thompson

6 Bryce Towsley took this black bear with a Freedom Arms Model 83 in .454 Casull. The wheelgun wears a Leupold scope and shot handloads with 300-grain Hornady XTP bullets. Photo by B. Towsley

7 Kim Ralston bagged this whitetail buck at 80 yards using a Field Grade Freedom Arms Model 83 .454 Casull with 7.5-inch barrel. It's topped with a VX III 2.5x8 Leupold scope, TSOB mount and Weigand mag rings, loaded with 260 Nosler Partitions over a max dose of H110. Photo by K. Ralston

The .45s **195**

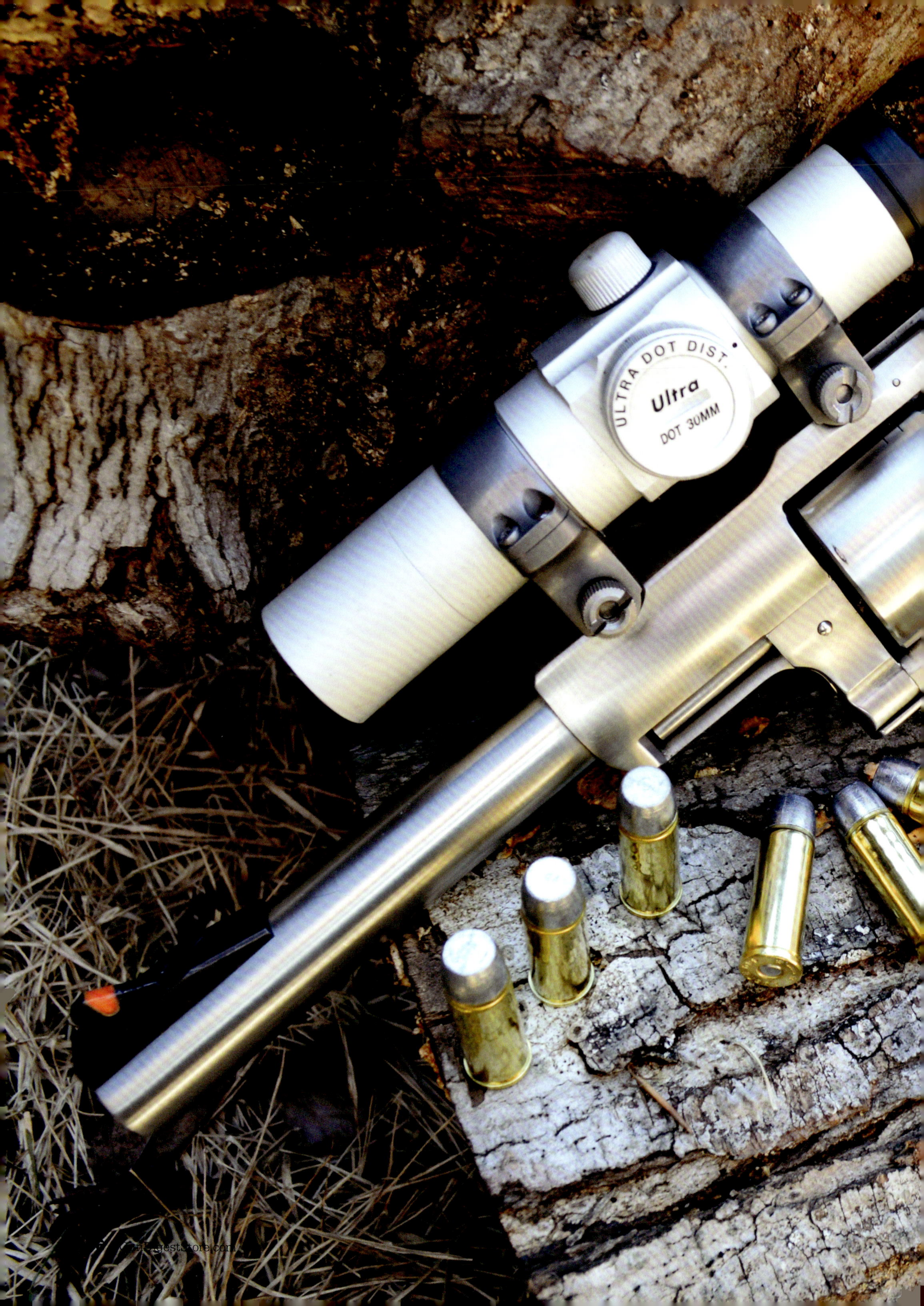
ULTRA DOT DIST.
Ultra
DOT 30MM

CHAPTER 13

Gary Smith shot this bruin at 130 yards in Alaska with a Freedom Arms Model 83 in .475 Linebaugh. Gary's bullet of choice here was a 325-grain Speer soft-point. Photo by G. Smith

the .475s

There are three notable cartridges in the .475-inch diameter category — the .480 Ruger, .475 Linebaugh and the .475 Maximum or Linebaugh Long. The progenitor of all three of these cartridges is the .475 Linebaugh, which spawned both the shorter .480 Ruger and the longer .475 Maximum. John Linebaugh is responsible for bringing his namesake .475 into this world by cutting the .45-70 Government down to 1.4 inches and necking the case to .476 inches. This caliber category is serious big-game medicine and represents a significant step up in terminal effectiveness from the various .45-calibers.

The .475s **197**

.480 Ruger left,
.44 Magnum right.

.480 Ruger

The .480 Ruger is, essentially, a shortened .475 Linebaugh. The first loads offered to the public did not show the true potential of the cartridge, featuring relatively light-for-caliber bullets at moderate velocities. It was also overshadowed by the aggressive marketing of the .500 S&W Magnum and later the .460 S&W Magnum. To that end, it never really stood a chance, as it could not boast being the biggest or the fastest. What Sturm, Ruger & Company did create, though, is a relatively mild recoiling and effective round that, in my opinion, is one of the better all-around choices for the big-game handgun hunter.

Released in conjunction with the Super Redhawk chambered in this caliber, the revolver was a good platform from which to debut the new round bearing the Ruger name on its head stamp. Recoil, while expectedly stout, still pales next to the .454 Casull loaded to spec, even though the .480 boasts a larger diameter. The .480 can be loaded close to the levels of the .475 Linebaugh but cannot achieve the higher velocities. Don't let that fool you into thinking the .480 Ruger isn't a serious cartridge. There is no game animal walking this planet that the .480 Ruger cannot comfortably take when loaded appropriately for the task at hand. Loaded to SAAMI specification pressure of just under 48,000 psi, only 2,000 psi separates the .480 Ruger from the .475 Linebaugh.

I like this round. Even when loaded with heavy bullets — 400 grains and beyond — the impulse is mild and creates more of a push than a sharp jab. Start pushing similarly weighted bullets up over 1,300 fps, though, and this is where the party starts. Plus, all factory revolver offerings in .480 Ruger are of sufficient bulk to tame even the hottest .480 loads. As a milder version of the .475 Linebaugh, what's not to like? This is a great choice if

quick facts

BULLET DIAMETER
.476 inches
CASE LENGTH
1.285 inches
OVERALL LENGTH
1.650 inches
MAXIMUM PRESSURE
47,862 psi

The Ruger Super Redhawk in .480 Ruger makes for effective big-game medicine.

you want big-bore knockdown power without debilitating recoil, all in a very controllable package.

I have a long relationship and history with the .480 Ruger that began in 2001 with the release of the new cartridge in the Ruger Super Redhawk. I was intrigued with the new chambering in the big, gray revolver and had to have it when I first laid eyes on it. With factory loads, that revolver proved very accurate. I took a number of Florida wild hogs with it and, thinking I needed more horsepower, eventually had it fitted with a five-shot cylinder in .475 Linebaugh. In that configuration I took a lot of big game. I tested a couple more .480 Super Redhawks over the years and was among the first to test the new Super Blackhawk in .480 Ruger, putting nearly 5,000 rounds downrange in testing. Long live the .480 Ruger!

tip from the field

SHOOTING REST

Finding a solid shooting rest in the field is extremely important when handgun hunting. I have found that it is best to set your hands on your chosen rest instead of the butt of the revolver. Resting on the butt may have an effect on the point of impact (POI) of the bullet, causing you to shoot over or under your intended target. The frame of the revolver can also be rested on a solid object for stability. You will have to see what works best for you. Some shooters report a shift in POI moving from offhand to a rest. If there is a shift, you will need to know it, and you will need to know where to compensate your hold. However, I have found that grip tension determines POI shift and not where and how I rest the revolver. If I use the same grip tension resting or offhand, POI remains the same. – Max Prasac

hunt report

THE SOUTH AMERICAN SAFARI

This hair-brained idea was hatched over more than a little sake at a local favorite Vietnamese restaurant. I explained to Olmstead (my editor at the time) my desire to take on the globe's most notorious bovine, the African Cape buffalo, with a handgun. No doubt this brilliant idea was fueled by what I would consider one of the most inspirational pieces to have ever graced the pages of a major gun magazine, Ross Seyfried's seminal piece, "The Ultimate Sport: Handgunning Cape Buffalo." Published in *Guns & Ammo* magazine back in April 1986, Seyfried conquered the fabled "black death" with a revolver chambered in .45 Colt without the benefit of a backup.

I'm pretty sure the sake was talking as well at this point, and Olmsted looked at me like I might need some professional help, a look he reserves for me on just such occasions. But, after a pause he said, "Go for it. Arrange it, write it and we'll run it. Don't get yourself killed."

With those marching orders, like a good Marine I set the wheels in motion. I had been planning this trip for more than a year. Well not exactly this trip, but a trip involving the bringing together of a large-bore revolver and a wild bovine of some sort at spitting distance. Zimbabwe was our original destination, and Cape buffalo the target. A plan was set, and several months before the intended departure, disaster struck. My PH suffered a stroke. Zimbabwe was off the table. Fortunately, my PH has made nearly a full recovery as this goes to print.

I was in a bit of a pickle. I had a shiny new Ruger revolver in hand, a great idea (some would argue the contrary) and nowhere to go on such short notice. I had been practicing all year with a variety of big-bore handguns to the tune of 2,100+ rounds with nearly 550 rounds out of the .480 Super Redhawk I intended to use. I was ready. If something went wrong, it wouldn't be for lack of practice. Plan B was pressed into effect.

Argentina has a rather large population of water buffalo — wild water buffalo. Not native to the region, Argentina's buffalo are nonetheless part of the flora and fauna of this southernmost South American country. Yes, Argentina was looking like the solution with each passing day.

As a hunting destination, Argentina had been on my radar for a very long time. My initial inquiries indicated the country was affordable — a relative term, but it isn't far out of reach, and the flights were significantly cheaper and mercifully shorter than Africa. I was really starting to like the Argentina option even more.

Fortunately, I have a friend who had handgun hunted there who was able to point me in the right direction. His outfitter, based in Buenos Aires, was Caza y Safaris (www.cazaysafaris.com). I contacted them with my ex-

Who:	Max Prasac
What:	Water Buffalo
Where:	Argentina
Range:	30 yards
Revolver:	Ruger Super Redhawk
Caliber:	.480 Ruger
Bullet:	CEB 340-grain Handgun Solid

pectations, and they responded promptly. A plan was set in motion for a five-day hunt in the province of Buenos Aires, about a three-hour drive outside of the city. Flights booked, paperwork done, gear packed ... and we were wheels up.

THE JOURNEY BEGINS

The next morning found me and my gear in a small van speeding toward the outer regions of the province of Buenos Aires. The three-hour journey landed us on a large parcel of land covered in swamps and marshes — the total and perfect breeding ground for mosquitoes. The lodge would have been inaccessible without four-wheel drive, as we got bogged down twice on our way to the hacienda. My driver and erstwhile guide was Dr. Martin Pouysségur, a lawyer by trade, and hunting guide by choice, and partner of this operation. Skilled at the wheel, fluent in English, Martin promised a fun-filled week ahead.

ON THE GROUND

The property is a wingshooter's paradise, teeming with waterfowl. En route we encountered what appeared to be a super-sized guinea pig, that by my estimation had to go over 100 pounds. It was a capybara, the world's largest rodent and a native of the region. It summarily dove into the water when it spotted us.

The lodge consisted of a main building for dining and food preparation, a bunkhouse and a couple of outlying support buildings. It's a beautiful old hacienda without power. The bunkhouse abuts a marsh, the flapping of wings a constant soundtrack. After lunch, we headed out for our first hunt of the trip.

THE HUNT BEGINS

The first day found us glassing vast tracts of marshland from a small rise in a stand of trees. We had water to our front and rear, giving us a good vantage point from which to observe. We'd walked a good mile from the lodge to begin our search for a shootable bull. The flat marshland was interrupted only by thick stands of trees. I was struck by the sheer volume of game in this part of Argentina, the land dotted with a number of different species of deer, some native and some introduced long ago. Sometime later we uprooted to another stand and glassed for a number of hours before spotting a couple of wild boar. The sun was dropping now, and our usable light was quickly fading. We played the wind and worked our way around the edge of the field to try and get within striking distance. At some point during the stalk, the boar

Over 1,500 pounds of wild Argentina water buffalo fell to the author's .480 Ruger Super Redhawk loaded with CEB solids.

.475 Linebaugh left,
.44 Magnum right.

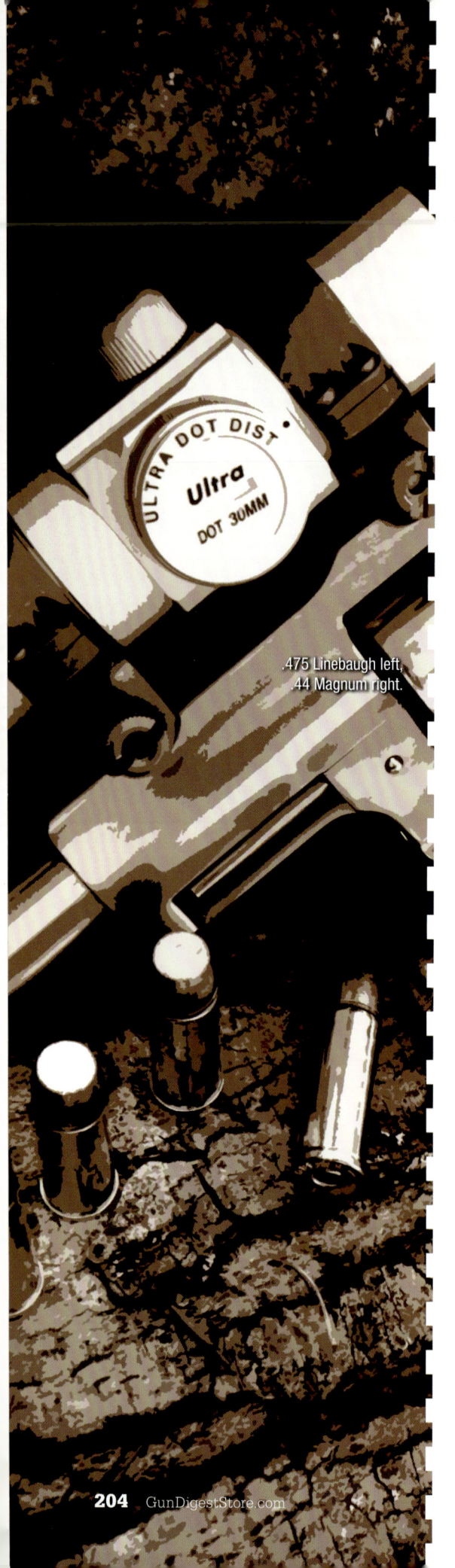

.475 Linebaugh

A personal favorite of mine, the .475 Linebaugh was unleashed on an unsuspecting handgun world in 1988 by John Linebaugh. The original parent case of the then-wildcat was the .45-70 Government cut down to 1.4 inches with a .476-caliber bullet. This cartridge is truly serious and has taken the largest and most dangerous game that Africa and the rest of the world has to offer, cementing its position in the realm of big-game hunting cartridges.

In its first iteration, it pushed a 400- to 420-grain bullet to speeds up to 1,400 fps. The recoil is stout by anyone's standards. This is not a cartridge for the uninitiated, as it kicks on both ends.

Ross Seyfried first wrote about the .475 Linebaugh in the pages of the May 1988 issue of *Guns & Ammo* magazine. The article was appropriately dubbed, ".475 Monster Magnum ... The 'Outer-Limit' Handgun." If that article hadn't gotten your blood pumping, he followed it up with an essay called ".475 Revolver Down Under" in the December 1989 issue of the same publication. In this article, Seyfried succinctly stated, "The .475 revolver cartridge was designed to be the ultimate big-game round for use in handguns. It represents a monumental step up from the .44s and a considerable increase in horsepower over any of the .45-caliber cartridges. This combination of long, heavy bullets and moderately high velocity makes even the highly touted .454 Casull seem small and ineffective."

Seyfried then proceeded to knock down all kinds of big game in Australia with a John Linebaugh-built Ruger Bisley .475, including feral goats, pigs, donkeys, wild cattle and even an Indian water buffalo. Seyfried's first

quick facts

BULLET DIAMETER
.476 inches

CASE LENGTH
1.384 inches

OVERALL LENGTH
1.75 inches

MAXIMUM PRESSURE
50,038 psi

shot on the water buffalo resulted in two broken front shoulders. The effectiveness of the cartridge on big game cannot be argued. The .475 Linebaugh represents a standard by which all big-game revolver hunting cartridges are measured.

Brass is readily available for handloading from two sources, Hornady and Starline. Loaded ammunition is available from a number of sources, including Hornady, Buffalo Bore and Grizzly Cartridge Company.

James Swidryk killed this warthog at 50 yards with a Freedom Arms Model 83 in .475 Linebaugh. The wheelgun was loaded with 400-grain Hornady XTP ammo. Photo by J. Swidryk

Gary Smith took this wild boar using a Freedom Arms Model 83 chambered in .475 Linebaugh. The revolver sports a 5.5-inch barrel. Photo by G. Smith

hunt report

SOUTH AFRICAN CAPE BUFFALO HUNT

As told by Darrell Harper:

I had the privilege of hunting Cape buffalo in South Africa with Kei River Safaris in 2013. Kei River is owned by Andrew and Sharyn Renton and Andrew also served as my Professional Hunter on this trip. He and I strategized during the one-and-a-half-hour drive to the property where the buffalo hunt would take place. Andrew wanted to approach the buffalo without being seen. "If he sees you he will either spin around and glare at you or run off," he explained. He didn't like the direct frontal shot because of the penetration requirements it posed.

I was hunting with a 6-inch Freedom Arms Model 83 revolver chambered for the .475 Linebaugh cartridge. The revolver was equipped with an Ultradot 30mm red-dot sight, and I was shooting handloads that chucked 400-grain WFN cast bullets out of the barrel at 1,325 fps. Andrew asked how my .475 would penetrate, and I told him the .475 Linebaugh has an excellent reputation for penetration and that it actually out-penetrates many rifles.

"That's great," he said. "How many animals have you shot with it?"

"Zero," I said, and I don't think that was the answer he was looking for, so he decided we should try for a broadside shot.

Andrew informed me that there were two old bulls that were hanging out together away from the main herd — these were our target animals. The other bulls that were still with the herd had not yet reached their potential. When we found the pair, we would first evaluate and then decide which one to go after.

Who:	**Darrell Harper**
What:	**Cape Buffalo**
Where:	**South Africa**
Range:	**30 yards**
Revolver:	**Freedom Arms Model 83**
Caliber:	**.475 Linebaugh**
Bullet:	**400-grain Hardcast WFN**

When we arrived at the property, the trackers climbed in the back of the Land Cruiser and we set out to find the buffalo. The trackers spotted one of the bulls lying in the shade alone. We searched around the area but couldn't find the other, but after surmising it was a good bull, we decided to give it a go.

Since the bull was lying down, Andrew sent the trackers around to approach it slowly, directly from the front. He hoped that the buffalo would stand and threaten for a while without crashing off. We thought this might distract the bull so that we could approach it from the side. Amazingly, this worked just as planned and the buffalo stood up and glared at the trackers. Andrew and I were able to move into position, and I got set up on the shooting sticks on the buff's left side only 30 yards away. Unfortunately, its shoulder was obscured by a bush, so I had to wait until being presented with a clear shot. This was probably a good thing, as it gave me an opportunity to get my nerves and breathing under control. As the buffalo continued to glare menacingly at the trackers, it finally inched forward enough to allow me a quartering-to shot.

"Do you see that crescent-shaped scar on his shoulder?" Andrew whispered in my ear. "Put the bullet at the very lower right-hand end of that scar."

The shot broke the buff's left shoulder, and it spun to its right and hobbled off in a stiff-legged gait. We moved quickly to our left and found that the bull had merely gone out of sight, turned 180 degrees and just stood there with its right side exposed. Again, the sticks came out and Andrew instructed me where to place my shot. Amazingly, the animal showed little to no reaction to the shot and made only a step or two forward. I fired two more shots into the chest/shoulder area, and incredibly, it just stood there soaking them up, taking only a step or two with each shot.

After what seemed like an eternity, the bull finally laid down on its left side. Andrew pointed out a spot in the bush where the buff's spine was exposed and he had me place a round there for insurance. After the buff stopped moving completely, Andrew cautiously approached the downed buffalo with his rifle. If the buff moved, he would fire a solid forward into the chest from the back of the ribcage. He gave the buff a couple of hard kicks to the pelvis and it showed no reaction. He was finished.

Cape buffalo have a reputation for toughness, and I witnessed this firsthand. Mine had traveled only 10 yards or so from where he had first been shot, but it had taken the animal quite some time to realize that it was dead! – Darrell Harper

DOUBLE-ACTION .475 LINEBAUGH

Many years ago, I convinced myself that my Ruger Super Redhawk in .480 Ruger needed more power. I've had more than a few automotive projects that have snowballed from "needing a little more power" to "this thing is out of control and no longer fun to drive." So you can see where I am going with this. It is not as if a .480 Ruger Super Redhawk is lacking in terminal performance or accuracy, I just couldn't leave well enough alone. I just needed a little more than the .480 Ruger had to offer, so I took this revolver that I bought new in 2001 and boxed it up and sent it off to JRH Advanced Gunsmithing, then located in Grass Valley, Calif., where it was fitted with a five-shot cylinder chambered in .475 Linebaugh. The stock barrel was retained and the action tuned, but the rest remained as it left the factory in New Hampshire. I added an Ultradot 30 red-dot sight with Ruger's own 30mm rings. This configuration demonstrated the toughness of the Ultradot 30.

That revolver proved very accurate with handloads consisting of a 420-grain flat-nosed hardcast bullet designed by a friend, Jim Miner, over a stiff charge of 296. Over the chronograph, these rounds averaged a consistent 1,350 fps, which would be considered a full-tilt .475 Linebaugh load. That recipe and gun accounted for quite a few deer and wild hogs over the years, never failing to put game down with authority. – Max Prasac

MY OWN CUSTOM .475 LINEBAUGH

I was lucky enough to come upon this custom .475 Linebaugh revolver in a trade. It is what I would consider the classic big-bore revolver by John Linebaugh. It's a stainless steel Ruger Bisley, with a banded 5.5-inch barrel and a five-shot cylinder. The action is butter smooth, and the accuracy is notable — something to be expected when a revolver is built correctly. This is exactly the revolver I coveted back when I was a college student poring over the materials John Linebaugh sent me when I wrote to him. I just had to wait a couple of decades before I got one! But they say good things are worth waiting for, and in the case of this revolver, those words ring true. – Max Prasac

.475 Maximum left,
.44 Magnum right.

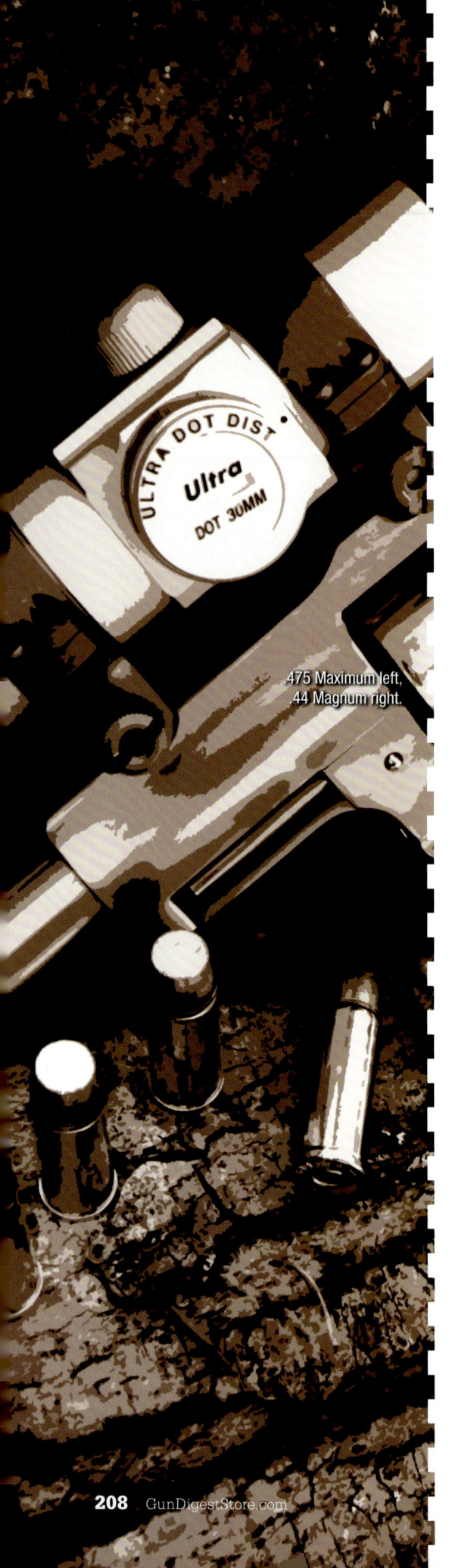

.475 Maximum or Linebaugh Long

The January 1991 issue of *Guns & Ammo* magazine introduced big-bore handgun nuts to the .475 Maximum, and its bigger brother, the .500 Maximum. Ross Seyfried was once again responsible for the exposure, having thoroughly tested the cartridge in a John Linebaugh-built revolver. Also known as the .475 Linebaugh Long, this round is merely a .475 Linebaugh lengthened 0.2 inches to 1.6 inches. The extra length ensured the new round was able to achieve velocities somewhere around 150 fps more than its shorter counterpart while maintaining similar pressures.

The .475 Maximum never really caught on, as the discomfort it created when shooting never outweighed the performance gains that could be realized. Seyfried's penetration testing revealed that little more is gained by running higher velocities, and that those higher velocities may actually compromise the bullet's integrity. That said, if loaded to .475 Linebaugh (the 1.4-inch case) velocity levels, the resulting lower pressures make for a more reliable cartridge in extreme heat — a definite plus when hunting Africa or other hot climes.

Despite all of the above, another .357 Maximum I procured a couple of years ago is being converted to .475 Maximum as this book goes to print. Is the extra horsepower a necessity? Nope, but when does need ever play into custom revolver builds?

A note for reloaders. Brass at one time was produced by Hornady for the .475 Maximum, but this is a used market item now. This is a custom revolver proposition only that requires a longer frame like that of Ruger's only limited-edition .357 Maximum of the early 1980s.

quick facts

BULLET DIAMETER
.476 inches
CASE LENGTH
1.6 inches
OVERALL LENGTH
1.950 inches
MAXIMUM PRESSURE
50,000 psi

1 Rich Pasquarello took this fine trophy mule deer in the Ruby Mountains of Nevada with his well-traveled .480 Ruger Super Redhawk, shooting Hornady 325-grain XTP factory loads. The range was 82 yards. Photo by R. Pasquarello

2 Ashley Emerson, proprietor of Garrett Cartridge, shot this hog with his Bowen Nimrod in .475 Linebaugh, loaded with Buffalo Bore's 420-grain hardcast load. Photo by A. Emerson

3 This trophy American bison was taken by John Taffin with the Freedom Arms .475 Linebaugh. The gun was loaded with Buffalo Bore 420-grain hardcast .480 Ruger ammunition. Photo by J. Taffin

5 James Swidryk used a 112-yard shot to take this red hartebeest using his Freedom Arms .475 Linebaugh loaded with Hornady 400-grain XTPs. Photo by J. Swidryk

6 This monster water buffalo fell to Rich Pasquarello's .480 Super Redhawk while hunting with Caza y Safaris in Argentina. Using Reed's 425-grain hardcast loads, his first shot was 48 yards, the last 15 yards, with three shots in between. Photo by R. Pasquarello

7 Rich Pasquarello's Alaskan black bear taken with a .480 Ruger Super Redhawk. Photo by R. Pasquarello

8 One 420-grain flat-nosed hardcast bullet from the author's custom .475 Linebaugh Super Redhawk caused the demise of this North Carolina wild sow.

9 The author killed this West Virginia buck with one 420-grain hardcast bullet from his custom JRH-built Super Redhawk in .475 Linebaugh.

10 This is a beautiful Corsican ram taken by Craig Copeland II at Wilderness Lodge. He was shooting the Ruger Super Redhawk .480 stoked with the 355-grain WFN projectiles. Range was 50 yards, and the little ram dropped on the spot. Photo by C. Copeland

11 This North Carolina boar dropped to the new Ruger Super Blackhawk in .480 Ruger with one Buffalo Bore reduced-recoil 370-grain LFN load. One bullet was required at 45 yards. Photo by Author

12 The author hammered this boar at Wooley Swamp Farm in Snow Hill, N.C., with a Ruger Super Redhawk in .480 Ruger. Hornady 400-grain XTP ammo did the trick.

Familiarization should not take place shooting from the bench, which is a surefire way of ensuring the new big-bore shooter develops a flinch or simply dreads pulling the trigger. The bench has its place in testing, sighting in and load development, but shooting off of one should be kept to a minimum. Here the author is sighting in a BFR in .500 JRH. Photo by V. Ricardel

CHAPTER 14

the .50s

We handgunners are notorious for arguing the merits of one cartridge's effectiveness over another. But there is little contention when it comes to the .50 cals. — or half-inchers as they are sometimes called — which occupy the top of the big-bore spectrum. I have come to the realization that in order to fully exploit these huge cartridges, you must use them on very large game — right around 1,000 pounds, give or take. I have used smaller calibers on such beasts, and while they work well, nothing quite gets their attention like the .50s. However, on smaller game, .50 cal. advantages become sometimes negligible and are not worth the additional recoil and cost.

Fierce recoil is the norm up here, and loaded properly, the .50-caliber cartridges offer serious medicine for big and dangerous game. They are the no-compromise calibers of the revolver world, and by default they make a big hole. Often considered overkill, I am of the belief that there are no degrees of dead. I have never felt over-gunned when facing a 1,500-pound animal! That said, the big .50s don't need to be loaded hot to be terminally effective. Even at moderate velocities, they work really well even on the toughest game.

.50 AE left,
.44 Magnum right.

.50 Action Express

The .50 Action Express (AE) was actually designed for use in a semi-auto pistol and is not, technically, a revolver round. That said, I would like to point out it was the first commercially available .50-caliber pistol round, one that inevitably ended up in a couple of commercial revolvers. It features a heavily rebated rim, and due to the physical limitations of the auto pistol platform, the round has a relatively short loaded length, which necessitates using light bullets. Heavy bullets must be seated deeply, displacing too much valuable case capacity, something the .50 AE can ill afford. This is a cartridge that is best left to semi-auto pistols. I personally wouldn't waste my time on the .50 AE.

quick facts

BULLET DIAMETER
.500 inches

CASE LENGTH
1.285 inches

OVERALL LENGTH
1.594 inches

MAXIMUM PRESSURE
35,000 psi

214 GunDigestStore.com

.500 Wyoming Express

This proprietary offering from Freedom Arms is a virtual ballistic twin of the .500 JRH, but instead of a traditional rim of a revolver cartridge, Freedom Arms opted to use a belt for head spacing. The end result is a packable .50-caliber revolver, one with power to spare.

Currently, there is only one commercial manufacturer producing ammunition in .500 Wyoming Express (WE), and that is the Grizzly Cartridge Company. Five loads ranging from 370- up to 440-grain hardcast WFNs are offered. Grizzly Cartridge even loads 420-grain Punch bullets if you wish to tackle elephants — or concrete buildings!

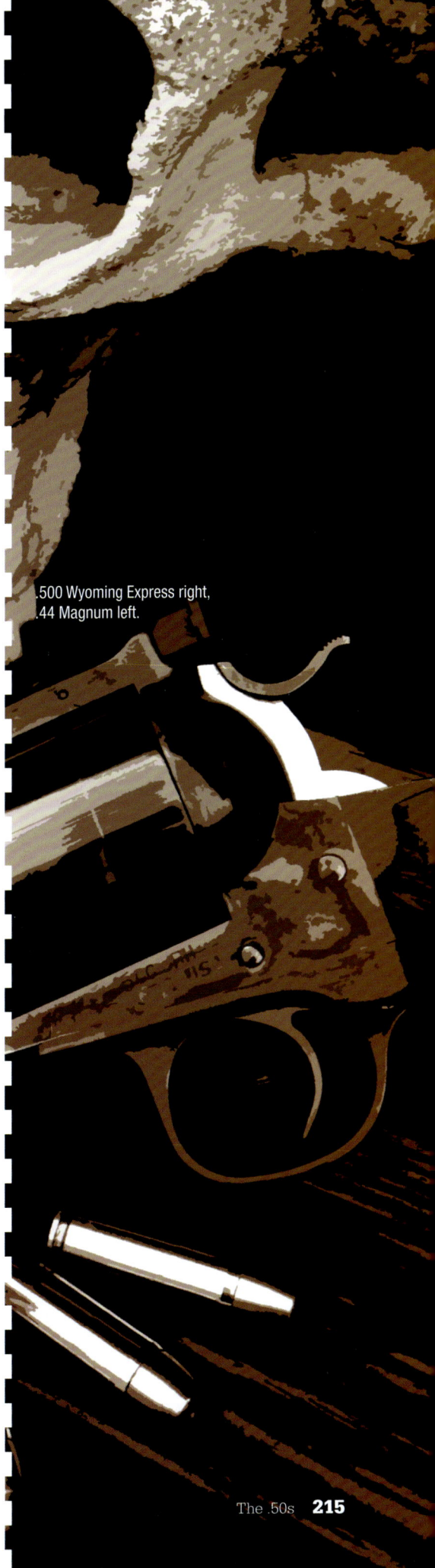

quick facts

BULLET DIAMETER
.500 inches

CASE LENGTH
1.37 inches

OVERALL LENGTH
1.765 inches

MAXIMUM PRESSURE
38,000 psi

.500 Wyoming Express right, .44 Magnum left.

The .50s 215

THE .500 WYOMING EXPRESS
BY KEN O'NEILL

The origin of the Freedom Arms .500 Wyoming Express really began with some perceived shortcomings in the .50 AE cartridge when it was adopted for use in a revolver. The original .50 AE case had been designed for autoloading pistols as a straight-walled case to hold .510-inch bullets. Through a confusion usually reserved for government snafus, IMI and Magnum Research were apparently told that bullets over .500 inches could not legally be used in an autoloading pistol like the Desert Eagle. So, the case was tapered to accept bullets of that diameter. The tapered case worked fine in single-shot pistols and autoloaders. However, when Freedom Arms and a few custom gunsmiths put the new tapered cartridge in a revolver, some problems began to surface.

There are two basic problems for a .50 AE revolver. The first is that the case has no rim, and therefore must headspace on the mouth of the case. Because the case is tapered, however, it can't be satisfactorily taper-crimped enough for heavy loads. Secondly, a roll crimp can't be applied either, or the case may be driven too far into the chamber by the firing pin blow, causing either a misfire or elevated pressures if it should actually fire.

Thus, without a good crimp, really heavy loads can't be practically used without a danger of bullets creeping forward and locking up the gun. Just as bad, even a bullet creep of a few thousandths of an inch can have a negative effect on accuracy. Speer even began to use an adhesive on their factory-loaded bullets to help prevent bullet creep. With this limitation, the .50 AE really wasn't what most people bought a "Fifty" revolver for.

James Swidryk, of New Jersey, took this Cape buffalo with a 6-inch Freedom Arms Model 83 in .500 Wyoming Express, using Grizzly Cartridge's 420-grain Punch load. This is purportedly the first Cape buffalo to fall to the .500 WE. Photo J. Swidryk

I was aware of these potential problems and mostly ignored the .50 AE for the first half-dozen years of its existence until I finally bought one in late 2002. With over 40 years of shooting and reloading experience at that time, I reasoned that surely I could overcome any problems. When I took delivery, I talked with several technical representatives of ammunition producers and did a lot of experimenting with loads over the next month or so. By measuring and tweaking the amount of taper crimp, and by experimenting with powder charges and primers, I was able to develop two pleasingly accurate loads, one with a jacketed 325-grain Speer JHP bullet, and one with a truncated cone cast bullet of the same weight. The load utilizes 21 grains of Alliant 2400 and CCI 350 primers, both of which I found to be essential. These loads shot to the same point of aim and ran a satisfactory velocity of 1,110-1,150 fps from my 6-inch barrel. But, of course, that's not what many people wanted out of their .50, either. It just wasn't the equivalent of a .475 Linebaugh.

Bob Baker, President of Freedom Arms, was well aware of the potential bullet creep problem when we discussed it at the 2003 Safari Club International convention. I had already emailed him a copy of my first .50 AE article prior to its publication in April 2003, and when we talked at the convention, he told me that he'd even had special reloading dies made in an attempt to cure the problem but then set the project aside due to other more pressing demands.

I'll shorten the story here, but at one point in our discussion, Baker asked me, "What would happen if you ran a .50 AE case through a straight-wall sizing die?" He grinned already knowing the obvious answer.

"You'd have a bunch of brass at the base," I said.

"That's right, a belt" he said. I thought I saw a twinkle in his eye.

Of course, the principle was that you could establish headspace on the belt and then roll-crimp the mouth of the case. Jamison International, the brass manufacturer Baker was experimenting with, said they could control the dimensions of the belt when the case was headed better than they could control the rim dimensions, so the experiments continued. Although we discussed the idea of a small rim, Baker became enamored with the idea of the proprietary belted case. Of course, the belt was formed during heading; there was no Rube Goldberg re-sizing process. The resulting Wyoming Express (WE) case was lengthened a bit over the .50 AE length, and the belt diameter was set to not exceed the diameter of the AE case at the base. The straightened walls also allowed for a bit more steel and strength in the cylinder. For all practical purposes, the resulting internal capacity of the two cases is the same, as is gunsmith Jack Huntington's concurrent development, the .500 JRH.

This is Ken O'Neill's wild boar in the mountains of North Carolina, the very first animal taken with the then-new .500 Wyoming Express. The handgun is a Freedom Arms Model 83. Photo by K. O'Neill

Development and testing of the Wyoming Express continued for a number of months, and Baker and I continued to discuss it. In July 2005, Baker invited me to send my Model 83 .50 AE to the factory to have an additional cylinder fitted for the new .500 Wyoming Express cartridge. I received the gun back in late September 2005, and began my own load development. Baker had already done extensive load development and had pressure tested the new cartridge, but I wanted to do some testing on my own. I settled on an extremely accurate recipe of 31 grains of H110, Federal 210 primers and 350-grain Hornady Magnum XTP bullets as a primary load. It ran about 1,350 fps from my gun.

A few days later, I headed for the mountains of North Carolina between Caldwell and Alexander counties and was able to take a very large wild boar, the first animal to be taken with the new cartridge. Since then, I've also used it on other hogs, a couple deer and two bull bison. Loads much heavier than this can be used in the .500 Wyoming Express, but I don't feel the need for 440-grainers at 1,300 fps or 400-grain bullets at over 1,400 fps. My .475 Linebaughs are indeed loaded to that level when I need them, but with the .500 WE, I'm happy where I am.

Interestingly, in my original convertible gun, both of my 325-grain .50 AE jacketed and cast loads shoot to the same point as my heavier 350-grain XTP ones from the .500 WE, out to about 80 yards or so. In fact, the same light powder charges I use in the AE case can be used in the WE case. I do change primers from the CCI 350 to the Federal 210. They shoot to the same point also. I call that versatility.

Headspacing of the Wyoming Express cartridge on its belt has proven 100 percent reliable in my three guns, and case life is excellent, with some of mine loaded over 20 times. I consider the .500 Wyoming Express a nice, elegant thumper. None of mine are for sale.

hunt report

BISON FOR THE FREEZER, COURTESY OF THE .500 WYOMING EXPRESS

As told by Ken O'Neill:

The snow was beginning to blow in a typical Nebraska blizzard as I began hunting bison with friends Wayne and Tim. For this hunt, instead of using one of my well proven .475 Linebaugh revolvers, I was carrying a pair of Freedom Arms revolvers in .500 Wyoming Express: a Premier Grade gun with an octagon barrel and iron sights riding in a belt holster, and my original Field Grade model, scoped with a Leupold 2x and carried in a bandolier-type pouch.

It started snowing the previous night, and now that we were near the Niobrara River, the wind was biting and visibility worsened with heavier snowfall. We unloaded two four-wheelers and started off into the Sandhills prairie area. We saw no bison and no tracks. Wayne and

Who:	Ken O'Neill
What:	American Bison
Where:	Nebraska
Range:	50 yards
Revolver:	Freedom Arms Model 83
Caliber:	.500 WE
Bullet:	350-grain Hornady XTP

Ken O'Neill took this bison in Nebraska with a Freedom Arms Model 83 in .500 WE following an accident riding a four-wheeler — that's determination! Photo by K. O'Neill

I were riding two-up on a four-wheeler as we descended one canyon, crossed a primitive two-board bridge and ascended the other side of the gulch. We then moved around the canyon rim, glassing as we went, but finding nothing. After a while, we decided to go back down into the canyon, and up into the prairie on the other side. Tim would explore a different area.

Midway across the primitive bridge we had crossed earlier, the waterlogged bank on the other side collapsed and fell a couple feet. When it did, the ATV's front end fell through the bridge and rolled over on its left side, trapping Wayne's left foot, ankle and leg under it. I was thrown off the back and through the hole in the bridge into the icy creek below. My left foot, ankle and calf were trapped between the machine, the bridge and Wayne's leg. My head and right shoulder hit at water level on the bank we'd just left. Nearly everything was submerged. Wayne was groaning, we were trapped and that water was cold.

Wayne squirmed and pulled repeatedly, almost to exhaustion. I did the same. The water in that stream was sweeping me downstream a little bit, and I could feel my cognitive senses getting slower from the cold. Finally, I used my elbows and right foot to try to elbow my way back upstream a couple inches at a time, trying to push something — the Kawasaki or the bridge — up with my right leg or foot. Finally, my left leg came free, plopping numb into the water. With me free and out of his way, Wayne was also able to extricate himself and help me out of the stream. I don't know how long we were in this predicament, perhaps 15 to 30 minutes.

We had to leave the ATV for later when we could get some help, because we couldn't lift it. Obviously, the hunting was done for that day, so we headed for the truck and back to Wayne's house so I could get out of the hard frozen clothes and avoid hypothermia. That night, rested and warm in front of the fireplace, I flooded both guns with WD-40, wiping out sand from everywhere. Sand was frozen in the hollow points of the 350-grain XTPs, and I had to tap the frozen sand-encrusted cylinder out of the Premier Grade gun to clean it. A Scotch Brite maroon pad restored it to its previous pristine finish.

The next day, the sun was out and all was well. We found bison, and although they winded us and ran off several times, after multiple abortive stalks I was able to shoot a 4-year-old meat bull through the lungs. That load was one of my favorites — H110 driving a 350-grain Hornady XTP. He stumbled a couple steps, and I shot him again with a 370-grain Cast Performance bullet in the shoulder. He dropped dead at the shot.

By 2011, I was out of bison meat and arranged to hunt with Wayne and Tim again. This time, I was determined to take another bull bison, but with my iron-sighted Premier Grade .500 Wyoming Express. I felt confident that the weather in Nebraska would be better than the last hunt, but as soon as I approached the Nebraska state line from Missouri it began to snow. At Wayne's house we settled in to watch the snow pile up.

The next morning a fresh, white blanket made for beautiful scenery and great stalking with the soft, quiet ground cover. We spent much of the first morning glassing a bit before walking across the open prairie into wood lines, glassing some more, then moving again. Late in the morning we saw some bison moving in a group, not quite in single file, but coming in our general direction. We were in a slight depression and had a good wood line shielding us from them, so we settled in to do some serious glassing. We were confronted with fog and continuing snow, but were comfortably concealed.

The bison continued in our direction, and the lead bull was soon about 125 yards away and moving diagonally toward us. It seemed too good to be true. We watched and waited, remaining well hidden, as several dozen bison fed and drifted past us at varying distances. Then, one stood out.

I couldn't tell the distance, but it looked to be about 50 yards. I had a good rest for my revolver and squeezed the trigger with the sights aligned about a third of the way up behind the bull's shoulder. The bull bucked, ran about 50 yards and dropped dead. When a bison or other type of buffalo is shot, it is common for several others to hang around and push or horn the fallen one, presumably trying to get it on its feet. This time, I counted 32 hanging around, which is the largest number I've seen go through that ritual.

My load for this bison is the same favorite I've used since the .500 WE was introduced: a 350-grain Hornady XTP driven by 31 grains of Hodgdon H110 and Federal 210 primers.

Once again, there was plenty of bison for the freezer!

.500 JRH left,
.44 Magnum right.

.500 JRH

The .500 JRH was the brainchild of renowned California gunsmith, Jack Huntington. Jack wanted a full-power, no-compromise .50-caliber cartridge that would fit in the confines of a revolver such as the Freedom Arms Model 83, having a maximum case length of 1.4 inches. He turned a dummy round in his lathe in 1993, and the .500 JRH became a commercially loaded reality in 2005 when Starline turned the brass and Buffalo Bore produced the first loads. Grizzly Cartridge followed suit and also produces loads in .500 JRH.

The very first revolver to be so chambered in .500 JRH was a Freedom Arms Model 83, providing a workable alternative to the .500 Linebaugh, which features too large a case and rim to fit the rather compact Model 83.

While .500 JRH brass is available from Buffalo Bore (produced by Starline), .500 S&W Magnum brass can easily be cut down for use. The specifications call for turning the rim down, but BFR revolvers in .500 JRH will accept the larger rim of the .500 S&W brass. One ammo manufacturer in an effort to test the upper load limits of the .500 JRH resulted in 1,625 fps with a 440-grain hardcast bullet. The end result was sticky extraction, but the case itself suffered no abnormal wear or damage, and the revolver was unscathed. I don't recommend you attempt to duplicate those load levels, but it is interesting to know where the upper end of its limitations lie.

Loaded ammunition is available from Grizzly Cartridge and Buffalo Bore in a number of different flavors.

quick facts

BULLET DIAMETER
.500 inches

CASE LENGTH
1.4 inches

OVERALL LENGTH
1.90 inches

MAXIMUM PRESSURE
45,000 psi

hunt report

TEXAS BISON

In 2006, the landscape surrounding Hondo, Texas, was suffering the effects of a drought cycle, leaving it dry and open with scattered mesquite scrub. Mike Giboney was armed with a Magnum Research BFR in .500 JRH, testing a new "light" load by Buffalo Bore consisting of a 440-grain flat-nosed hardcast bullet lumbering along at a claimed 950 fps. Giboney was being backed appropriately by the .500 JRH's progenitor, Jack Huntington, carrying a double rifle in 9.3x74. Bison was on the menu for this trek to Hondo with Action Outdoors Adventures.

They were following a small group of bison, but they were having trouble getting a clear shot on the chosen bull as he was staying within the group. Following closely downwind, Giboney finally got his opportunity when his animal cleared the herd and offered him a broadside shot. Giboney stroked the trigger on the BFR, putting a bullet into the bison's left shoulder from about 25 yards. Upon contact, the bison took off, but stopped after a 30-yard sprint.

Giboney, who had given chase, also slid to a stop, dropped to a knee and hammered another 440-grainer into the left shoulder. The bison was not amused and spun around to face the hunter and his BFR. This usually signals trouble, but instead of making a mad dash, the wounded buffalo continued spinning almost in a complete circle before collapsing. Giboney wisely paid the insurance with a bullet in the downed bison's neck, even though the majestic animal was no longer of this world. All of this happened in less than a minute.

Who:	**Mike Giboney**
What:	**American Bison**
Where:	**Hondo, TX**
Range:	**25 yards**
Revolver:	**Magnum Research BFR**
Caliber:	**.500 JRH**
Bullet:	**440-grain Flat-Nosed Hardcast**

One of the bullets shot into the shoulder exited, and the other one did not, though it did make it all the way to the other side of the animal. Pretty impressive for a "light" load by anyone's standards!

Mike Giboney took this bison with a mildly loaded .500 JRH BFR, the Buffalo Bore load pushing a 440-grain hardcast bullet at a subdued 950 fps. Even an animal as large as an American bison is no match for a correctly loaded big-bore revolver in experienced hands. Photo by M. Giboney

.500 S&W Magnum left, .44 Magnum right.

.500 Smith & Wesson Magnum

The biggest of Smith & Wesson's Magnum cartridges, the .500 S&W Magnum was the company's successful attempt at recapturing the crown of most powerful production revolver cartridge. Not only did they seek to create the biggest cartridge in .50 caliber, but also pulled out all the stops by making it one of the highest pressure producers. Smith & Wesson didn't just want to take the top position back — they wanted to put as much distance as possible between the .500 S&W Magnum and the nearest competitor. To that end, Smith & Wesson was able to boast an excess of 2,500 ft-lbs of muzzle energy in some loadings for the new cartridge.

Purportedly based loosely on the old .500 Maximum, or "Linebaugh Long" as it is also known, the .500 S&W Magnum features a case length of 1.6 inches and a diameter of .500 (unlike the Maximum's .510-bore diameter), necessitating a whole new revolver from Smith & Wesson. Enter the X-frame.

Unlike the .500 Maximum, the .500 Smith features a maximum pressure of nearly 62,000 psi, putting it in the company of a small number of revolver cartridges loaded to rifle pressures. Loaded to spec it is capable of impressive velocities even with heavy bullets. When the .500 Smith and the X-frame debuted, CorBon released two loads, a 275-grain hollowpoint and a 440-grain flat-nosed hardcast. Now, a wide range of varying loads are available from the likes of Hornady, CorBon, Grizzly Cartridge, Buffalo Bore and DoubleTap Ammunition with bullet weights ranging from 275 grains on up to 500.

I have to say that I am not enamored with this cartridge when loaded

quick facts

BULLET DIAMETER
.500 inches
CASE LENGTH
1.625 inches
OVERALL LENGTH
2.25 inches
MAXIMUM PRESSURE
61,931 psi

to spec. I don't like the high pressure and the resultant muzzle blast and noise. It can be loaded down, which makes for a more viable cartridge in my estimation; however, if you load it down, you might as well carry a smaller firearm that is capable of the same ballistics. But that's just me.

With the introduction of Smith & Wesson's .500 came a renewed interest in handgun hunting, but this is definitely not a cartridge for the uninitiated. Even when loaded in a heavy revolver such as the X-frame, or even BFR's larger iteration, the .500 Magnum produces significant recoil. You cannot launch bullets this heavy at these speeds and burning this much powder without producing sizeable recoil. This round evokes the term "extreme."

The author likes to place the thumb of his supporting hand over the right hand (just behind the thumb), which strengthens the grip on the revolver and is less likely to break his grip/hold during recoil.

tip from the field

HANG ON TIGHT!

Everyone develops his or her own techniques to handle a big-bore revolver. One method does not fit all. I will offer some techniques that have worked the best for me over the years. Feel free to try them and modify them accordingly. I recommend using a lot of muscle tension, at least initially, until you figure out how much the revolver will move when you touch off a round. This way you are not caught off guard and surprised by getting your forehead creased. Don't laugh, because it happens all the time. I had a two-inch gash opened up in my scalp when I let up just a little bit of muscle tension when firing a custom revolver in .50 Alaskan. A revolver such as this demands your absolute attention and concentration. Getting hit can easily cause a flinch as you anticipate getting hit. Not a good way to start your relationship with your new revolver! The lesson learned? Lots of muscle tension and no distractions to break your concentration.

hunt report

DARREL HARPER AND THE HUNT OF A LIFETIME

As told by Darrell Harper:

I'd been dreaming of taking a brown bear with a handgun for a number of years. After one disappointing attempt a couple of years prior, I was fortunate enough to return to Alaska in 2011 for a second chance at harvesting a big brownie with a handgun. I booked the hunt with Grizzly Skins of Alaska, owned and operated by well-known guide and outdoor writer Phil Shoemaker. Their hunting area is located on the Alaskan Peninsula, which has a history of producing large bears.

Following a debacle where my handguns and gear were diverted to the wrong airport, we eventually ironed things out and made it to base camp with my guns. I went out to the range to check the zero on both of the guns. I wanted to take a bear with my .500 S&W revolver but because this was the hunt of a lifetime, I also brought along my custom XP-100 chambered in .376 Steyr. Even though the gun was capable of longer shots, I placed a 100-yard limit on shots with the .500 S&W revolver. I was comfortable with the .376 Steyr at distances twice that far. I made some slight scope adjustments on both firearms and my guns were ready for hunting.

I was flown to a spike camp that was located about three miles from the nearest salmon stream. I was concerned about being so far away from the river, but Phil assured me that this camp had produced some great bears in the past. I figured that no one knew his hunting area better, so I put 100 percent confidence in his

Who:	**Darrell Harper**
What:	**Brown Bear**
Where:	**Alaska**
Range:	**100 yards**
Revolver:	**Smith & Wesson X-frame**
Caliber:	**.500 Smith & Wesson Magnum**
Bullet:	**375-grain Barnes XPB**

judgment and anxiously waited for opening day of bear season.

Opening morning found our trio of hunter, guide and packer perched on the spotting hill, glassing for bears. Things started off slowly at first. We first spotted some bears fishing in the river, but after a while we began seeing some medium-sized bears roaming the hillsides closer to our position. One was about 800 yards away, and it laid down right on the open tundra and took a two-hour nap. We also spotted several herds of caribou off in the distance.

Around midday, we spotted a big bear that we decided was definitely worth going after. With my guide leading the way, we confined ourselves to the alders as much as possible, moving only when the bear was looking away. When we got within 350 yards of it, we ran out of cover. We began belly crawling, trying to remain out of sight as he continued to amble our way. When the bear was about 200 yards away the guide asked the packer to remain behind in order to minimize movement. I was put up front, and my guide followed along behind as we continued to belly crawl toward the bear. Finally, we came to the edge of a small stream that the bear seemed to be headed toward. I had brought along a rolled-up sleeping bag pad to use as a field rest from the prone position, and I placed it on the ground in front of me.

Darrell thoroughly prepared for his brown bear hunt. He made sure that his revolver, load and shooting ability wouldn't be limiting factors. The .500 S&W revolver is capable of great accuracy out of the box — this three-shot, 100-yard group measures less than 2 inches and was fired from the prone position.

The bear was now only 135 yards away and still heading in our direction. I knew that if he continued on his present course that he would drop out of sight momentarily while he passed through a tiny patch of alders. However, that would allow enough time for me to pop my earplugs in and set up for the shot with the .500 S&W. Once he cleared the alders, he would be standing in an opening that I had ranged at 100 yards, which was inside my comfort zone for the revolver with a steady rest. It was perfect.

After we lost sight of the bear, my guide and I got ready for him to emerge from the alders. Five minutes passed, then ten, then twenty, then thirty — no bear! We finally realized that he had decided to take a nap once he entered the alders. My guide motioned for the packer to join us and he belly crawled up beside me. You can imagine how nerve-wrecking it was to have the bear of a lifetime sleeping in an alder patch, out of sight, only 125 yards away! I prayed that the wind direction would remain constant and that he would continue on his prior course after he awoke from his nap.

Finally, over two hours later, he stood up in the alders and continued in our direction. He stopped once he entered the clearing, but it would have been a steep quartering-to shot. I held my fire, waiting for a broadside shot opportunity. As he reached the top of the creek bank, I hoped that he would continue down to the water's edge, which would have given me a 75-yard shot. Unfortunately, just as my guide had anticipated, he chose the path of least resistance and turned to go downstream in order to find a less-steep bank to descend to the water. Before leaving the clearing, he stopped in a quartering-away position, 100 yards away. I looked over at my guide who was prepared to back me up with a rifle if necessary, and I was given the go ahead to shoot.

I placed the crosshairs of the 2X Leupold just behind the bear's right shoulder and squeezed off the shot. The bear growled and pulled his right shoulder close to his body. He whirled around and began biting the area behind his shoulder. I was able to fire two more shots before the bear retreated into a small patch of alders. My guide and I crossed the creek, circled high above the alder patch where the bear was and descended on the area very cautiously. We spotted a patch of brown fur in the grass beneath the alders, and tensions were high as we approached the downed beast. No movement from the bear indicated that the beast was dead, and after many years of waiting, I had finally fulfilled my handgun quest for brown bear!

Darrel Harper's glorious brown bear taken with his .500 Smith & Wesson revolver.

.500 Linebaugh left,
.44 Magnum right.

.500 Linebaugh

Attention was first drawn to the .500 Linebaugh with the publication of an article by Ross Seyfried in the August 1986 issue of *Guns & Ammo* magazine titled, "The .500 Magnum — The 'Outer Limits' of Handgun Power."

Though not offered in a production revolver, the .500 Linebaugh still boasts a strong following — enough that both Buffalo Bore and Grizzly Cartridge offer a number of production loads for this first .50-plus-caliber handgun cartridge. Brass is available from Starline.

Loaded to potential, the .500 Linebaugh is a true big-game hammer. Based originally on the .348 Winchester case and cut down to a nominal 1.4 inches, the .500 Linebaugh's bore features a .510-inch diameter. Maximum pressures should be kept in the 33,000- to 36,000-psi range, though it will go safely higher.

The beauty of the .500 Linebaugh is that it doesn't need to be pushed hard to work well on large game. In fact, through testing we have found that, with hardcast, wide-meplat bullets in the 500-grain range, even a modest 1,100 fps is more than adequate for even the largest of ungulates. I successfully took an 800-pound moose with a .500 Linebaugh, and the round failed to disappoint. The .500 Linebaugh is a custom proposition only.

quickfacts

BULLET DIAMETER
.511 inches
CASE LENGTH
1.4 inches
OVERALL LENGTH
1.80 inches
MAXIMUM PRESSURE
40,000 psi

hunt report

BROCCOLI BANDITS

In August 2011, I received an opportunity to hunt cow moose in Maine. A number of depredation tags were offered to local outfitters in northern Maine to assist broccoli farmers with protecting their crops from the damage produced by North America's largest ungulate. One-hundred permits were allocated to a drawing similar to the regular moose-tag lottery. The permits were limited to registered guides and broccoli farm owners.

My outfitter was Don Burnett, co-owner of #9 Lake Outfitters of Bridgewater, Maine, who was one of the lucky 10 outfitters picked in the Maine lottery. This is a first-rate outfitting service that not only provides outstanding, tireless and professional guiding, but also comfortable lodging, great company and a mouth-watering menu.

I would be using a custom revolver built by Jack Huntington. The foundation for this custom was a Super Redhawk that I had purchased a decade earlier in .454 Casull. It was a good and accurate revolver, having accounted for the demise of a number of wild hogs, but I decided that it would be sacrificed to the big-bore gods. My intent was to turn this revolver into a back-up piece that could double as a primary hunting gun if need be, so I specified a 5-inch barrel, with a nod toward packability and light weight.

The end result was a revolver that weighs a couple of ounces less than my 6-inch Model 29 Smith & Wesson and, subsequently, kicks like an angry mule on performance-enhancing drugs. It's very hard to shoot due to the debilitating recoil even with the "mild" loads that I had settled on, Grizzly Cartridge's 500-grain LFN hardcast bullets at a leisurely 1,200 fps.

The revolver was put on the back burner of priorities due to a busy editorial schedule. One month prior to the hunt, though, I decided the short Super Redhawk would be my chosen piece. For this hunt, a red-dot sight would ensure good low-light performance while adding a little much needed weight to the unruly little revolver. A used and abused Ultradot 30 was mounted on top. Two sessions with the .500 indicated exceptional accuracy from the little monster, as well as a sore hand. I was ready — at least I convinced myself I was.

We were given permission to hunt on a couple of local farms, and after thoroughly scouting the roads and tree lines surrounding the broccoli fields, we were encour-

Who:	**Max Prasac**
What:	**Canadian Moose**
Where:	**Bridgewater, ME**
Range:	**100-125 yards**
Revolver:	**Ruger Super Redhawk Custom**
Caliber:	**.500 Linebaugh**
Bullet:	**500-grain LFN hardcast**

aged by the fresh and abundant moose sign. We fed the mosquitoes the morning of opening day, but aside from the moose we saw heading into our hunting area an hour before legal shooting light, the morning was uneventful. On our way out we mapped our course of action for the ensuing afternoon hunt in the same field, noting a number of well-traveled game trails leading into the open, through the thick forest.

Above: Ready for Maine moose! The Huntington-built .500 Linebaugh Super Redhawk was sighted in an inch high at 50 yards with Grizzly Cartridge's potent 500-grain LFN loads.

We rested the afternoon following a hearty meal and went back out to the fields. My guide, Mike Hogan and I, set up downwind of two game super highways on one corner of the field, giving us a commanding view of the road that wound its way around the perimeter of the entire clearing. We quietly settled in after positioning my shooting sticks in a spot that offered clear fields of fire in all directions of the treeline.

Throughout the afternoon, we glassed the area and remained optimistic. Roughly 20 minutes before the last legal shooting light, we heard movement in the brush to the rear of our position. The greatest thing about moose is that their size betrays them, they really are incapable of moving through thick brush without making a racket. Expecting moose to emerge to the right, Hogan and I were surprised when a large cow cautiously exited the forest to our left about 15 minutes later. I carefully made my way to my sticks and settled in behind the custom Ruger.

I turned down the Ultradot 30 to its lowest setting, as light was rapidly dwindling. We determined that the moose was indeed a cow and decided that it was a shooter. Not quite sure of the distance, I nonetheless pulled the hammer back and settled the red dot on what I estimated to be the shoulder. I had practiced out to 100 yards and was confident at that range. Once my breathing was under control, I held my breath and slowly squeezed. The Ruger barked, and moments later I heard the telltale "thwack" as lead struck moose flesh. Not waiting to see if my shot was true, I lined the red dot onto the dark blob that was now even farther away and let the next round fly … followed by the next and the next. My final shot resulted in the moose crashing head first into terra firma. I reloaded, grabbed my flashlight and ran down the road toward my moose.

All of my five shots connected, but none were really needed beyond the first shot, which got both lungs. That said, I am of the mindset that if an animal is still standing after the first shot, you should keep shooting until the aforementioned animal is no longer standing. Especially when the animal weighs four times more than a deer and the hunting grounds are surrounded by swamp land. Knowing moose have the propensity to head for water when wounded contributed to my friskiness on the trigger. Though urged to keep shooting by Hogan, I needed no prompting.

After field dressing the moose, we loaded it onto a trailer to get it tagged and weighed. It tortured the scales to the tune of 629 pounds, dressed, meaning the thing weighed more than 700 pounds on the hoof. Do you realize just how many steaks the bride of Bullwinkle yielded? I needed a bigger freezer!

The bride of Bullwinkle meets the .500 Linebaugh. The author's cow moose weighed in at 629 pounds dressed. It was taken with his custom Ruger Super Redhawk in .500 Linebaugh launching 500-grain LFNs from Grizzly Cartridge at 1,200 fps.

.500 Maximum (.500 Linebaugh Long)

Also referred to as the .500 Linebaugh Long, this is the cartridge that the .500 S&W Magnum is purportedly based upon. It's a wildcat that is typically built on Ruger .357 Maximum frames housing custom five-shot cylinders. Recoil at the upper end of the loading spectrum can best be described as very unpleasant to life altering, particularly when loaded to the 50,000-psi range. The .500 Maximum is capable of throwing 525-grain bullets at a blistering 1,500 fps, and some reports indicate even more velocity is possible. While it is not recommended to feed your Maximum a steady diet of such loads, it is fully capable of delivering this level of performance. This cartridge is an exercise in excess.

Dedicated and properly headstamped brass is available occasionally on the used brass market. Hornady actually made a run of the brass, but the perfect parent case is the commercially available .50 Alaskan, which can be easily cut down to 1.6 inches.

In the end, the .500 Maximum is the poster child for "More's Law" being applied to the already potent .500 Linebaugh. Is the added velocity potential and resultant abuse on the shooter necessary? No, but we don't always apply the concept of necessity to our hobby. What fun would that be? However, I will state with certainty that the .500 Maximum, loaded correctly with 525-grain WFNs is a fight stopper. I have shot a number of animals over 1,000 pounds with mine, and its effects are immediate and decisive — more so than any other caliber I have witnessed being used on very large game animals.

I am a glutton for punishment and so enamored with this oversized cartridge that I sacrificed a pristine and collectable Ruger .357 Maximum to build a .500 Maximum, and I would do it again. The .500 Maximum is a custom proposition only on a Ruger Maximum or Seville SuperMag frame.

quick facts

BULLET DIAMETER
.511 inches

CASE LENGTH
1.6 inches

OVERALL LENGTH
2.015 inches

MAXIMUM PRESSURE
50,000 psi

.500 Maximum left, .44 Magnum right.

hunt report

NO QUARTER

In mid-October 2015, I made the trek to Hondo, Texas, to an outfit called Action Outdoors Adventures with a couple of my hunting buddies — Jack Huntington, the JRH in JRH Advanced Gunsmithing, master gunsmith Jason Menefee and handgun-hunter extraordinaire Mike Giboney. Action Outdoor Adventures is the type of operation that is large enough to get lost on, and the hunts are not simply handed to you, forcing you to actually locate, engage and close with your intended quarry.

On day two of our handgun hunting adventure, we got on a small group of water buffalo consisting of a couple of cows, a calf and a large bull. With calf in tow, the group was very skittish, moving every time they got wind of us as we tried to close the distance. By late morning we finally caught a break, managing to get out in front of the advancing bovine unit. We positioned ourselves just ahead of an opening in the thick foliage that we had anticipated would deliver the buffalo to our eager revolvers. Our guess was about to pay off. The first nose that cleared the brush was the cow we had been targeting. She was a large cow by anyone's standards that would weigh in over 1,400 pounds once we got her on the scale.

Who:	Max Prasac
What:	Water Buffalo
Where:	Hondo, TX
Range:	20 yards
Revolver:	Ruger Blackhawk Custom
Caliber:	.500 Maximum
Bullet:	525-grain WFN hardcast

The nose cleared, and then the neck, as the cow steadily advanced. Once its shoulder came into view and into my field of fire, I hammered a 525-grain WFN home from 20 yards. At the shot, the buffalo shuddered as if hit with a 20-pound sledge hammer. I had just enough time to send one more downrange, which also hit home. The cow staggered for a few yards then collapsed face first into the dirt. As is our practice, we paid the insurance by firing a couple more rounds into the prone buffalo.

The necropsy revealed massive internal damage and no recovered bullets as all exited with little resistance. I really like the .500 Maximum!

1. Professional Hunter Bud Rummel with a 371-pound lioness he took in Zimbabwe. Rummel used a .500 Smith & Wesson from the S&W Performance Center and stalked to within 22 yards of the dangerous feline to put a 440-grain flat-nosed hardcast bullet in the animal. Photo by B. Rummel

2. Dur Thomason shot this big sow at 24 yards with a Freedom Arms Model 83 in .500 Wyoming Express. The handgun was topped with a Leupold Delta Point optic and loaded with 350-grain XTPs. Photo by B. Thomason

3. Gunsmith Jason Menefee took a very large water buffalo bull with his BFR in .500 JRH loaded with Buffalo Bore's 440-grain hardcast load.

4 Using his Freedom Arms Model 83 in .500 Wyoming Express, Ken O'Neill took this bison in Nebraska. Photo by K. O'Neill

5 Professional Hunter Bud Rummel killed this big bison at 32 yards in Wyoming with a Smith & Wesson Performance Center .500 S&W Magnum. He used 500-grain Hornady loads. Photo by B. Rummel

6 The author took this North Carolina black bear with a custom JRH-built Super Redhawk in .500 Linebaugh. On top is an Ultradot 30 optic.

7 John Parker shot this enormous bison with his JRH-built .500 Linebaugh shooting Buffalo Bore's 525-grain WFN. Photo by J. Parker

CHAPTER 15

the handgun hunters

I gathered up a number of known — and some not-so-known but very experienced — handgun hunters, and asked them to share their favorite caliber, revolver, bullet and load combinations. I also asked them to explain their reasons for their choices. I weigh in with my own top picks as well, but I hedged my bets by choosing more than one favorite. Why? Well, because some game calls for a different caliber/bullet combination in my humble opinion, and some calibers I simply prefer over others. I will explain fully.

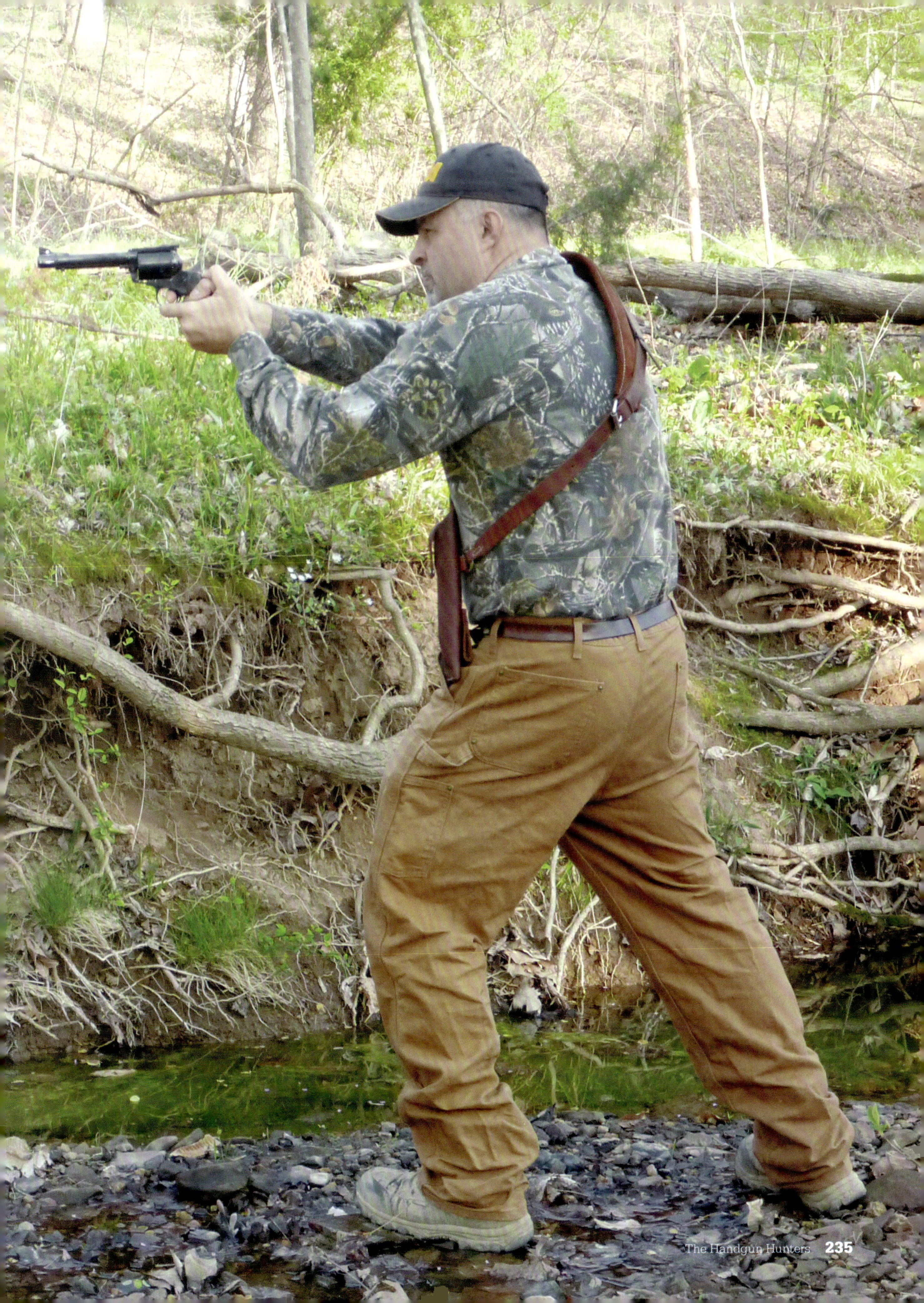

JOHN TAFFIN
THE SIXGUN GODFATHER

As told by John Taffin:

When Max Prasac asked me to select my favorite sixgun for hunting, my immediate reaction was, that is just about like trying to pick one of my 12 grandkids as a favorite! I could easily pick a favorite wife and a favorite pickup since I only have one of each, but trying to pick one favorite sixgun? Absolutely impossible. The best I can do is pick just a few from a long list of favorites. I've been blessed to be able to do a lot of hunting, and any revolver that performed well was immediately moved to my list of favorites. So here are a few specially selected sixguns for hunting.

I grew up reading Elmer Keith, and I graduated from high school the same year the .44 Magnum showed up. So, naturally, the .44 Special and .44 Magnum have been a great part of my shooting and hunting life. My most used hunting .44 Special is a cherished 7.5-inch West Texas Flat-Top Target from Texas Longhorn Arms. This beautiful example of the sixgunsmith's art came from my dear friend, the late Bill Grover, who, for the short time he was in business, put out some of the nicest single-actions to ever come from the mind of man.

This particular .44 has four cylinders: .44 Magnum, .44 Special, .44-40 and .44 Russian. The first three have all been used for hunting, and my favorite combination is the .44 Special using Keith's bullet hollow-pointed and his favorite #2400 load. One memorable day I took two huge feral pigs, the smallest of which tipped the scales at 500 pounds and the bigger one going over 650 pounds, both put down within two minutes of each other using this .44 Special. The bullet totally penetrated the smaller pig, in one side and out the other, while the bullet was found perfectly mushroomed under the hide on the opposite side of the larger pig — perfect performance for this old but classic cartridge.

John Taffin took this meat bison with his Ruger Super Redhawk in .454 Casull. Photo by J. Taffin

When it comes to the .44 Magnum, my most used sixgun is the Freedom Arms Model 83. The 7.5-inch version has taken 24 straight one-shot whitetails while the 6-inch sixgun was used on the hardest hunt I ever accomplished, a mountain lion straight up a hill in deep snow. In all cases my load of choice has been the Black Hills 240-grain JHP, which is loaded with the Hornady XTP-JHP. This is not a particularly hot load, but it performs perfectly on whitetails and has also been used on Catalina goats. If I had to pick my favorite big game hunting, it would be sitting on a productive deer stand in Texas on the Penn Baggett Ranch with my Freedom Arms .44 Magnum.

Ashley Emerson shot this wild hog with a Freedom Arms Model 83 in .454 Casull. The revolver was loaded with Hornady 300-grain XTPs. Photo by A. Emerson

My last hunting trip was for elk and meat bison on the Rocky Mountain Elk Ranch in southeastern Idaho. This was a special hunt put together for me by many of my friends in the industry. For this particular hunt, I chose the Ruger Super Redhawk 9.5-inch .454 loaded with Garrett Cartridges 365-grain hardcast bullet, rated at 1,350 fps. This load performed perfectly, and the 7x7 bull elk I shot with it never took a step. I have also used the 7.5-inch Freedom Arms .454 loaded with 300-grain bullets on both feral pigs and warthogs in Africa. The largest game I have ever taken was a huge American bison using the Freedom Arms Model 83 4.75-inch .475 Linebaugh, loaded with Buffalo Bore's .480 Ruger loading consisting of a 410-grain hardcast bullet at just under 1,200 fps. At 40 yards the bullet penetrated completely from side to side, and that big bull never took a step.

– *John Taffin, Boise, Idaho*

John Taffin and an African warthog taken with his Freedom Arms Model 83 in .454. Photo by J. Taffin

ASHLEY EMERSON
Proprietor of Garrett Cartridge Company

As told by Ashley Emerson:

If we are to talk about what I shoot in the centerfire world, then the majority will be .44 and .45 revolvers, usually custom guns and loads on the strong side.

Understand up front that I am an old-school gun nut and play with every kind of handgun I can get my hands on. Because of unlimited numbers and no closed season, wild hogs have been the most common critter pursued for testing in meat and bone. I have shot and killed deer and hogs with calibers from .22 to .75, velocities from about 600 fps to 3,800 fps and bullets from 40 grains to around 560 grains. These projectiles have been of every construction and shape from dead, soft lead to solid brass and shapes that run on and on — RN, FN, LFN, WFN, HH, JSP, JHP, SWC, WC, K, etc.

At the end of my fourteenth year, I had to have a .44 Super Blackhawk. At that time, the .44 Magnum was my favorite, and the load was usually a 240-grain JHP bullet seated over a full dose of 2400. When I was 17 years old, I had a friend whose father introduced me to the world of the warmed-up .45 Colt in a Ruger Blackhawk. Keep in mind that my hunting back then was limited to a few whitetail and endless jackrabbits, even though I was pretty hard on cottontails, too. A few years later, I was getting into rural law enforcement, and a .44 seemed like the right answer.

In the early 1980s I got my first Redhawk, and with the need to arm myself for my duties, I was also introduced to N-frame Smith & Wessons. Once again, I chose the .44 over the .45 simply because I had .44 stuff. Working as a deputy sheriff in Co-

The Handgun Hunters 237

manche County, Texas, I carried a 7.5-inch Redhawk in a Bianchi No. 111 cross-draw holster and for main backup a 4-inch M29 in a small of the back custom holster. I went to work in Somervell County, Texas, the next year. When the chief deputy, a 400-pound guy that went by "Tiny," told me he didn't want me carrying "the big silver pistol," I showed him one of my 4-inch M29s and he said it looked fine, though he also issued me a M58 S&W. So I carried a 4-inch M29 in a Bianchi high-ride, strong-side holster, and my main backup was a twin 4-inch M29. The full-power .44 Mag with a 240-grain JHP or JSP was still my "do all" load. For a short while I played with 180s, but they didn't have the same authority on deer as the 240s, so I went back.

Shortly after, I finished my Criminal Justice degree and got out of law enforcement and fell back in to the automotive machine/general machine shop world. I still shot quite a bit, but my favorite hunting load remained the jacketed 240 from a .44. This lasted until I got my first taste of hunting wild hogs and fell into the gun-sight business. I could justify more hunting than any gainfully employed human and had access to a 200-square-mile cattle ranch overrun with volunteer test hogs. It took a couple years to catch on, but I suffered the results of "failure to penetrate" on many occasions. Not just with jacketed .44s, but also with high-powered rifles shooting "deer" bullets.

One hunting episode with my wife convinced me for good against using soft handgun bullets on hogs. One early morning, she had a shot on a real trophy, a toothy 300-pound-plus mature boar. Not knowing any

This porcine "volunteer" fell to Emerson's .45 Colt Redhawk. Photo by A. Emerson

better, I whispered to her to shoot for the front near leg. I was watching with binos at 40 yards as she shot her 16-inch Marlin loaded with 240-grain JHPs as I'd instructed. The boar took off and survived just fine.

Six months later, a friend I was guiding had another crack at the same boar with a .284 Winchester. He hit it once in the chest at about 150 yards, and it took off. As it ran up a steep hill, he spine shot it at 170-180 yards. Examination of the wounds showed that the boar had been getting by fine with its front right leg not working. The .44 from my wife's gun had gone through the shield only to stop after going into but not through the leg bone — she had placed it exactly where told. The 240 JHP had penetrated 2 or 3 inches max.

This and many more experiences showed me that what is great for a broadside deer will cause heartache on a big boar. In my quest for something that worked better, I tried heavier jacketed projectiles because early attempts at shooting cast bullets had been plagued with leading issues, so I shied away. As I learned more about cast bullets and started re-reading the exploits of my old friend J.D. Jones and others, I started using 300-plus-grain quality hardcast bullets with gas checks. Failure to at least go deep enough was not a problem, and with two holes, bleeding was more probable but not something to count on. Big hogs don't always bleed much on the ground because their hair soaks it up more than most critters.

As for the heavy .44 hunting revolvers such as the Ruger Redhawk, my favorite load was one with quality hardcast flat-nosed bullets like those found in Garrett's 330-grain +P .44 Mag Hammerhead. This load never failed to get 'er done, and while I was a handloader, I could not load ammo that ever demonstrated a better balance of wound channel and penetration. However, in the lighter weight Smith & Wesson M29 gun, I preferred the Garrett 310HH load. Randy Garrett specifically designed the 310HH for the ultimate performance in a "N" frame Smith & Wesson — it is full-power but not +P, with the bullet set out in the cylinder to take advantage of the M29 cylinder length — to maximize powder capacity for increased power while staying inside SAAMI pressure specs.

All through the trials and experiences, the Garrett .44 Mag 330+P load was what all handguns and rifles were compared to. It was my standard. I often bugged Randy Garrett about how Hammerhead loads optimized for the Blackhawk, the Redhawk and the Freedom Arms 83 would be really useful in .45 Colt and .454 Casull. I envisioned the gas-checked 330/.44 bullet grown up to .45 caliber and begged him for it. Randy's answer: "When you own and run Garrett, knock yourself out!"

Now that I actually own Garrett Cartridge, my first order of business was to focus all I had learned to build the ultimate Hammerheads for three classes of .45 Colt and two levels of .454 Casull. For a modern Colt single action and clones, as well as the M29 series Smith & Wesson (great in Marlins too, though not by design), there is now a 265 HH at 1,000 fps (7.5-inch barrel) and less than 23,000 psi. For the full-sized Blackhawk-based guns, we offer a 365-grain LFR load, 365HH at 1,250 fps (7.5-inch barrel) under 35,000 psi (1.735 o.a.l., won't fit in a Colt or S&W). For the .45 Colt-chambered Redhawk, to take full advantage of its heavy, long cylinder and its 1:16 rate of twist, I've developed the 405 RHO (Redhawk Only) load consisting of a 405HH at 1,250 fps (7.5-inch barrel) at 45,000 psi, (1.785 o.a.l., won't fit in Colt, S&W or large frame Blackhawk). The .454 has two loads, both featuring 365HH bullets, and they are safe in any factory chambered .454. The .454 Hammerheads go 1,350 fps from my 7.5-inch Freedom Arms 83 while the H454 loads go 1,500 fps.

I've got new favorites! In the .45 Colt, it is the 365LFR load. This bullet is a copy of the 330-grain 44 Hammerhead to the last detail, including the bore riding nose and super hard and tough alloy, with the crimp groove set for the longest possible o.a.l. in a Blackhawk or Bisley. This frees up case capacity and keeps them out of the vast majority of lesser guns. This load optimizes the factory .45 Colt Blackhawk/Bisley for killing potential. I believe it to be the equal of the +P 330-grain Hammerhead load for the .44 Redhawk in killing power, and it is easier to shoot because of noticeably less blast. It is particularly easy to shoot from a Bisley, but it is also what I carry in my .45 Colt-chambered 5.5-inch Bowen/Rowen Redhawk.

Why not the 405RHO load? It is a great load, and if I am packing my 4-inch Bowen/Rowen Redhawk in big bear country or just because I'm in the mood, it is what I will have in that gun. However, in only a 4-inch gun this load surpasses the killing potential of the original Springfield carbine load for the .45-70 Government. Like the .475 and .500 Linebaugh cartridges, unless loaded down they are a bit rough on the shooter for daily play. I will shoot a couple hundred rounds at rocks, cans, grasshoppers and steel targets for each round I send through a critter. The .45 LFR, with its optimized Hammerhead design and super hard/tough alloy at 1,250 fps from my 7.5-inch Bisley and 1,180 fps out of my favorite custom 5.5-inch Redhawk, is my new favorite and likely to be for a long time. In fact, my only .454, a Freedom Arms Model 83, is sighted in for the 1,350 fps load for a reason. With thousands of pounds of lead through my guns and decades of intense and compounding experience, I designed this .45 LFR load to offer the most killing potential from the packable six-shot Blackhawk Bisley. That was the design goal, and I am thrilled with the results. I hand cast and hand load every one of them. – *Ashley Emerson*

GARY SMITH

As told by Gary Smith:

I often get asked about my favorite handgun; mostly by people who have but a few, which is a desperate situation I cannot condone. I see hunting handguns as specialized for the task at hand. I would not take a .44 Magnum on a Wyoming pronghorn hunt unless I made the conscious decision to only take shots out to the effective range of that cartridge and gun combination. At that, it would be a long-barreled revolver with a relatively high-powered scope. If you've ever hunted pronghorn in Wyoming, 150 yards is close!

If you choose to classify a favorite as the gun that has seen the most use, then it would be my 10-inch Freedom Arms Model 83 chambered in .454 Casull. It was my first Freedom Arms gun, and it was expensive even used. I found it nonchalantly hanging on a peg on the back wall of a large gun shop in Virginia with a T-SOB mount in which rode a Leupold 2.5x8 scope. I had to put it on layaway. Up to that point, I had owned just about every mainstream .44 Mag-

Gary Smith considers the 10-inch-barreled Freedom Arms in .454 Casull to be possibly the best all-around big-bore hunting revolver. With a scope and the right bullet, it meets all of his criteria for accuracy and terminal effectiveness. Photo by G. Smith

num in the book — Smith's, Dan Wesson's, Ruger's, both single and double action, even a Colt. Out of all of those, I had settled on Ruger as my preferred brand and it's still a favorite.

I missed out on the first run of Super Blackhawk Hunter's, but when they re-introduced them I jumped on the wagon and owned them in .41 and .44 Magnums and the .45 Long Colt. All three served me well, but in the end I only have the .44 Magnum left in the Hunter configuration. The Ruger Super Blackhawk has accompanied me on many hunts, including my first trip to Africa where I used it to take several animals. I have used bullets ranging from 180-grain jacketed hollow points up to 310-grain hardcast on game up to about

AT THIS POINT IN MY HUNTING ENDEAVORS, I ALMOST EXCLUSIVELY HUNT WITH REVOLVERS AND HAVE COME TO PREFER THE SINGLE-ACTION PLATFORM. THIS IS NOT DUE TO SOME COWBOY MENTALITY OR OTHER ESOTERIC HISTORICAL NOTION; I JUST LIKE THE WAY THEY FEEL IN MY HAND AND THE WAY THEY SHOOT. — GARY SMITH

600 pounds. Effectiveness has never been an issue.

I have also been fortunate enough to pick up a couple of other Rugers that are iconic in their own rite. Back in the 1970s, when I first became interested in hunting with a handgun, I was reading about some guy named Larry Kelly who was killing everything on the planet with his custom Ruger Super Blackhawks, specifically the Predator and the Stalker. I think that photo of Larry with his Stalker and a large brown bear is permanently burned into my retinas. They have been favorites of mine for over 35 years, even though I've only owned them for a short time. They have not disappointed in any way.

At this point in my hunting endeavors, I almost exclusively hunt with revolvers and have come to prefer the single-action platform. This is not due to some cowboy mentality or other esoteric historical notion; I just like the way they feel in my hand and the way they shoot. If you want to perform some customizations there are a number of good options from cosmetic to full-on rebuild and caliber change. And if your preference or budget don't warrant any fancy stuff just yet, an off-the-shelf Ruger will do anything you ask within your own limitations. With that said, I personally think the Freedom Arms is the best revolver money can buy. You only occasionally see one that has been modified beyond the factory offerings with the exception of grips and, even then, most I've seen have factory grips, too. I think the reason for this is because they are nearly perfect as they come. I certainly own more Freedom Arms guns than I need but not as many as I want. However, I do have short- and long-barrel versions in .22 L.R., .44, .454 and .475. I have the same setup with my Predator and Stalker packages, too.

You may wonder why both short- and long-barrel guns? I like them both for different reasons, and I usually carry both whenever I'm hunting. The short gun is handy and always on my belt, while the other one is there for longer shots and when game is hard to separate from cover, which would make an open-sighted shot unwise. I also enjoy shooting the shorter-barrel guns more than shooting the long-barrel scoped revolvers at the range. Why? It is simply more of a challenge, which is why we hunt with handguns in the first place.

When it comes to sights there are three basic choices: irons, a red-dot and a scope. Red-dot sights are certainly well liked and offer a benefit over irons in most circumstances. They eliminate parallax issues that are of some minor concern, and they can be quicker than iron sights to align on the target once you've become accustomed to them. Most issues relating to alignment of the target with a red dot or a scope are caused by insufficient practice and a lack of proper muscle memory to quickly acquire the sight picture. Iron sights are harder to align for proper shot placement, but the perception is they are faster because you can see them. When a scope or red dot is misaligned you may struggle to find the sight picture. My eyes are not great, but I have not gotten to the point where I feel like a red dot is required or preferred over open sights.

I find a certain utility with open sights. I also think they can very much be a limitation on longer shots or where the target is in heavy cover. Not that iron sights are inferior, but in these situations, a scope is the only way to go. Take my experiences hunting lions, for example. The cats would be in heavy cover and often shaded. A red dot is a poor choice here as are iron sights. There simply isn't any ability to accurately place a shot when you can't distinguish the target from the background.

Favorite guns? Yes, perhaps I'm guilty of favorites, perhaps not, but I know what has worked for me for a long time and know what I like. Some factors in my choices are due to aesthetics, and some are for other reasons. At the end of the day, I like single-action big-bore revolvers. If it's a Ruger, great. If it's a Freedom Arms, even better — and I'm not ill equipped with either. Scope, iron sights or red dot, long barrel or short — it doesn't matter as long as you accept the limitations and aesthetic differences of each.

If I had to pick one gun, though, it would be my 10-inch Freedom Arms chambered in .454 Casull with a Leupold 2.5x8 scope and Mag-na-ported. After all, it's the perfect hunting revolver whether you're chasing 100-pound blackbuck or one-ton Cape buffalo. – *Gary Smith*

Photo by B. Towsley

BRYCE TOWSLEY

As told by Bryce Towsley:
What's my favorite hunting handgun?
Hard to say, as I am a fickle fellow when it comes to that topic. I never met a gun I didn't like, and I think I have owned, shot and hunted with just about all the popular cartridges and handguns. I have made meat with handguns as diverse as the .22 Short through the .375 JDJ, and at one point or another they were all my favorite.

One that is a longtime favorite is a Smith & Wesson Model 19 in .357 Magnum that has taken every critter legal to shoot in my home state of Vermont, except a black bear and a bobcat. Squirrels, grouse, deer, woodchucks, coyotes, rabbits and even muskrats; the list is long and as diverse as it gets.

I have an old and worn Ruger Single Six in .22 LR/.22 Mag that I carried on a trap line back in another life. It's accounted for a train-car load of small game and at least one whitetail deer. That gun will always be a favorite.

I have a TC Contender in .45 Colt/.410. I've lost count of the grouse, rabbits and pheasants that gun steered to my crockpot. Needless to say, it's a favorite.

I suppose, at heart, I feel most pure when I am hunting big game with a revolver, and by rights my favorite should be the .44 Magnum. It's the cartridge I have shot the most game with over the years. Deer, bear, hogs and even turkeys, the .44 Mag has put them in my freezer. It's the gun that launched my handgun hunting career. Much of my generation will agree that it's all Dirty Harry's fault. That flick came out in 1971, a long time ago, but I'll bet everybody reading this knows the scene.

That movie did more to promote the Smith & Wesson Model 29 .44 Magnum revolver than all the ads and all the articles featuring the gun combined. By the time I decided to buy one in 1973, the waiting list was a mile long and just as wide. The black market was bumping the price to double or triple the suggested retail price, and to be honest Smith & Wesson was cranking them out so fast that most were not up to their usual high-quality standards. But, with a loan from my sister and some insider help from a buddy in a gun shop, I finally got my hands on a 6.5-inch Model 29. It was for many years my gun of choice for hunting and wilderness rambling. I used to tell my wife that if there was ever a house fire she was to get the kids, dog and my Model 29 out of danger. The cat was on his own.

I have shot it to shambles and had Smith & Wesson rebuild it twice, so yeah, that Model 29 is a favorite. I don't know how many .44 Magnums I own today, but it's enough to keep Obama awake nights and staring at the ceiling.

One Ruger Super Blackhawk that I won years ago in an IHMSA match collected my first handgun whitetail. It wasn't much of a deer, but that Ruger is a perpetual favorite.

As you can see, "my favorite hunting handgun" is a very long list, and I gotta say asking a gun guy to pick a favorite is like asking a mom to pick a favorite child. It's not fair, it's not right and, in truth, it changes day by day anyway.

I must admit that one lingering favorite has always been the Freedom Arms .454 Casull. I believe the cartridge provides the best balance of power and shootability in a handgun. The .454 Casull has whack enough for anything in North America, yet my Freedom Arms handguns are easy to carry in a holster.

This is a cartridge that can stop a grizzly with anger issues, but it is not out of place shooting whitetails or hogs. Indeed, the Freedom Arms revolvers are made with precision that have Swiss watchmakers crying in shame.

The cartridge dates back to 1957 when it was developed by Dick Casull and Jack Fulmer. The public first took notice when P.O. Ackley published an article about the .454 Casull in the November 1959 issue of *Guns & Ammo* magazine. Back then they used .45 Colt cases and a tri-plex charge with three different powders. The only guns were custom made. The cartridge lingered as an interesting novelty until Freedom Arms started making handguns in 1983, along with factory-loaded ammo, and then the world of the .454 Casull changed dramatically.

The .454 Casull operates at a SAAMI-approved Mean Average Pressure of 65,000 psi, the same pressure as the most powerful magnum rifle cartridges. When you consider that the "hot" .44 Magnum operates at 36,000 psi, the truly radical nature of the Casull comes into sharp focus. The .454 Casull can drive a 300-grain bullet out the muzzle of a handgun at more than 1,750 fps, and that's edging into the territory of serious handgun power.

I got my first one, a Freedom Arms Model 83 Field Model with a 7.5-inch barrel, in 1988. It has a Leupold

Towsley's Freedom Arms Model 83 in .454 Casull was massaged by Mag-na-port International. When it comes to protection against the biggest predators in the wilderness, size matters. Photo by B. Towsley

2X scope in a SSK T-SOB scope mount and Pachmayr rubber grips. It quickly became my hunting handgun of choice. Over the years, I have shot black bear, wild hog and lots of deer with the gun. The best testament to it was after I shot a bear while hunting with hounds when one of the guides blurted out, "That's the deadest damn bear I have ever seen!"

A few years back, I sent another Freedom Arms Model 83 in .454 Casull to Ken Kelly at Mag-na-port Arms to work his magic.

For those who don't know, Ken Kelly runs Mag-na-port International, a company his Dad, the legendary handgunner Larry Kelly, started in 1972. Ken Kelly is a "boots on concrete" guy and one of the top handgun gunsmiths in the world.

I wanted the gun to be easy to carry in a holster in bear country. If a gun is too heavy and too big, you will find an excuse to leave it in camp. But trouble is not something you can schedule. For example, I once rode up on a sow grizzly with two big cubs while they were feeding on a dead moose. My panicked horse swapped ends and took off without me. As I hit the ground, I had two thoughts running though my mind. First was that my rifle was in the scabbard on the horse, and second, if I survived this, I was going to gut-shoot that damn horse. The truth is, I would have traded my kingdom for a pistol in a holster at that moment.

Now, the Mag-na-ported Freedom Arms revolver is my current favorite hunting handgun. I had Ken shorten the barrel to 5.5 inches and then work his magic on the rest of the gun. Of course, he added their trademark Mag-na-port trapezoid recoil-reducing ports at the muzzle. The trigger now breaks at a crisp and perfect 2.75 pounds, while the action is smoother than a newborn's bottom.

The gun is finished in Mag-na-port's Velvet Hone bead-blast finish with polished highlights and polished pin-striping on the muzzle, as well as both the front and rear of the cylinder. The hammer and trigger are jeweled. The trigger guard's left-front has a scooped-out section on which to rest my trigger finger while waiting for the shot. Ken engraved my name on the backstrap, which, of course, means I can never sell the gun. (Like I ever would!)

High-visibility sights were installed by Ken with a green ramp on the front. These adjustable sights allow me to fine-tune the zero for any ammo I am using. My favorite load is with a 300-grain bullet I cast from linotype. I use 32 grains of WW296 powder to push them out the barrel at 1,614 fps. This is a bear-stopper load if I need it, but it also works well on big game such as elk or moose and even deer. Though for deer and hogs, I prefer an expanding bullet. Barnes has a factory load with a 250-grain XPB that will hit 1,700 fps and expands to almost an inch in diameter. It simply stomps deer into submission.

The main idea was for a carry gun in bear country, but this is also the ultimate, iron-sighted hunting revolver. I have used it for hunts as diverse as chasing black bear with dogs in Vermont to hunting nilgai in South Texas, with lots of deer and hog hunts mixed in between. It's been with me on many backcountry trips, and I used it just last fall while hunting grizzlies in Alaska. I'll admit I had a rifle along for the hunt, but the pistol was my constant companion in my tent as well as when I was fishing and packing game. Weighing in at exactly 3 pounds, I have carried it all day — many days — and hardly noticed it was there.

The .454 Casull and the Freedom Arms Model 83 revolver are a well-balanced match. Like those old couples who have been married for 50 years, they complete each other. The gun is very controllable to shoot, but it is still small and light enough to carry on your belt, the way handguns were meant to be carried. Yet, the cartridge is more than powerful enough for anything that walks the earth.

If I gotta pick a favorite right now, yeah, it's that gun. – *Bryce Towsley*

Towsley took this black bear in Maine in the mid-80s. It was his first bear, and he used a Ruger Super Blackhawk with an Aimpoint sight. He used a handload with a 320-grain JDJ hardcast bullet, and the bear was shot at 20 yards from a treestand.
Photo by B. Towsley

Jim Tertin shot this Corsican ram with a BFR in .30-30 loaded with Federal Fusion 170-grain ammo at the YO Ranch. Photo by J. Tertin

JIM TERTIN

Imagineer of Magnum Research
As told by Jim Tertin:

I'm an avid revolver shooter and handgun hunter. In 2000, I designed the current BFR five-shot revolver that Magnum Research currently markets globally. It's designed and built as a super-strong single-action hunting/shooting gun that is capable of uncanny accuracy. When Jack Huntington called me and talked about his new .500 JRH Cartridge, I became very excited and had to try it.

I built a "one off" BFR in .500 JRH with a 6.5-inch barrel. It had a Badger Cut barrel with a fairly quick 1:15 twist. It immediately became apparent that the .500 JRH was tailor made for the BFR. Everything fit perfectly, and overall length of the loaded rounds, even with 440-grain bullets, fit the cylinder with no horsing around on seating depth of the bullets. The .500 JRH immediately became my favorite big-game handgun cartridge. It's easy to load, easy to make brass if needed and can be loaded with everything from 350 hollow-point bullets to 500-grain soft points at any recoil level you want.

Initially, I loaded the .500 with Hornady 350-grain XTP HP bullets, and performance was fabulous. I loaded 32 grains of H110 with a CCI Mag Pistol primer and crimped bullets solidly in the cannelure. I was able to use .500 S&W Hornady dies with no modification, which also drew me to the cartridge. Since then, I have tried numerous bullets up to a 500-grain soft point.

In the last few years, I've settled in on the Oregon Trails 370-grain TrueShot cast flat-point bullet with a gas check. It does everything I ask of it with mild recoil and no leading. It's super accurate and my go-to load for big-game hunting. I never have recovered one to date, as even on shoulder hits they penetrate through a whitetail. For this bullet I use cut-down .500 S&W brass, as my original lot of Jack's .500 JRH brass has been depleted. Under the 370-grain GC Oregon Trails bullet, I put 31 grains of H110, a CCI large pistol magnum primer and a very stout crimp in the provided groove. This combo gives me an overall length of 1.771 inches and runs at 1,410 FPS from my 6.5-inch BFR. It is manageable to shoot, even for extended range sessions, and is deadly on big game.

A few years back, I took a running shot with this load on a whitetail that flushed out of a swamp. That shot was angling away from me at full tilt. The bullet broke both front and rear left legs, as well as raked along the rib cage taking out several ribs. I considered that excellent performance on a less than perfect shot.

One activity we engage in during the long Minnesota winters is harvesting porcupines. The local Native Americans love the quills for earrings and beadwork. The BFR/.500 JRH combo is superlative medicine for this sport. It is hands down the best. Not that we need as much horsepower as this cartridge affords, but rather the accuracy to hit them out of a tree swaying in high winds. This cartridge will definitely do it. *– Jim Tertin*

questions | answers

MIKE RINTOUL
Proprietor of Grizzly Cartridge Company

I caught up with Mike Rintoul recently to ask him a few questions pertaining to his preferences for handgun hunting.

Q: When did you start handgun hunting and why?
A: About 30 years ago I took up handgun hunting as I thought it would be more challenging. I've been hooked since. I started Grizzly Cartridge back in 2000 and sold my first box of ammo in 2003. At that time, we offered only handgun ammo from .38 Special on up to .500 Linebaugh.

Q: What is your favorite big-game hunting handgun?
A: Hands down, my custom Hamilton Bowen-built Redhawk in .500 Linebaugh, sporting a 5.5-inch barrel. It balances well and has been my go-to revolver for years. As far as loads are concerned, my favorite is one that I produce featuring a 525-grain bullet traveling right around 1,200 fps. It's a really effective load on big animals.

Q: What is your favorite big game to hunt?
A: I enjoy really big game, and bison would be at the top of my list.

Q: What big game is at the top of your bucket list?
A: Most definitely hippo.

KEN O'NEILL

Ken O'Neill bought his first handgun, a government surplus 1911 in .45 ACP, in 1960. He began hunting with handguns in his home state of Pennsylvania in 1963, focusing on small game at first, using a Ruger Single Six .22 revolver that he had traded from a fellow Marine. Before long, his interest expanded to hunting larger game, mostly using a Ruger Super Blackhawk .44 Magnum.

In 1969, Ken and his young family relocated to North Carolina. When handgun metallic silhouette shooting was introduced in the Southwestern United States and those matches began to catch on in the East, he became a very active participant, serving as a match director in two North Carolina clubs and finally as the North Carolina state director of the International Handgun Metallic Silhouette Association (IHMSA). Over this period, he won one South Carolina and 13 North Carolina NRA and IHMSA state championships, as well as numerous club matches in various states. He feels that the intense level of concentration required in that competition was helpful in refining his hunting marksmanship.

In 1990 he took his first African safari in Zimbabwe, where he used two Ruger Redhawks in .44 Magnum and a Thompson/Center Contender with a custom SSK barrel in .375 JDJ. The following year, he hunted in Argentina using that same .375 JDJ Contender, and was then off to Australia, followed by the Asian side of Turkey, and back to Africa. Sometime during this period, he set a goal of hunting broadly on all six continents. Since that time, he has been able to meet his goal, returning to hunt multiple times in several African countries, as well as Australia and Argentina. His travels have also taken him on six hunts in four European countries, the Asian side of Russia, and twice each to New Zealand and Canada. He continues to hunt throughout the United States and says he particularly enjoys hunting in several western states and Alaska.

Here is his response when asked to name a favorite revolver for hunting:

"I don't really have one favorite; it depends upon the type of game being hunted. When hunting medium-size game like white-tailed deer, wild pigs of various types, smaller sheep, antelope and goat, as well as mountain lion and varmint, I like to use a .44 Magnum. I've used Ruger Super Blackhawks, Redhawks and Super Redhawks, as well as Freedom Arms' outstanding Model 83. All of these have been excellent. I have probably taken more game, though, with a Smith & Wesson Model 629 than any of my other .44s. Two of my most cherished hunting memories are those for mountain lions in Utah and Idaho. They were as grueling and exciting as any hunts I've ever taken … or probably will take. I used that 629 on both of those hunts."

As told by Ken O'Neill:

I have used 200- to 300-grain bullets in .44 Magnum, both cast and jacketed, but generally prefer the Sierra 240-grain JHC bullet for game of this size.

I've also used a Freedom Arms .454 Casull quite a bit, mostly for African game, including lion, and have taken deer in the U.S. with it as well. I've used the very hard Freedom Arms 260-grain bullet, the Hornady 300-grain XTP and Magnum XTP, and the 300-grain Sierra. For all-around use in the .454 Casull, though, the 300-grain Magnum XTP is my choice.

Frankly, as good as the .454 Casull is, I prefer the .475 Linebaugh for larger animals and most dangerous game. For animals such as this, I have used the Hornady 400-grain Magnum XTP and 420-grain WFN hardcast bullets, and both have performed very satisfactorily for me on bull elk, large bears and hogs, as well as North American bison and South American water buffalo. I have also used the Speer 400-grain jacketed soft-nose bullet, but only on wild boar, where it has also performed well.

I have experience hunting with the .475 Linebaugh in each of my three Freedom Arms revolvers with barrel lengths of 6, 7.5 and a special build 9 inch. Velocities of those bullets have ranged from 1,200 fps to 1,400 fps, well within good performance parameters for the bullets and game being hunted. Between the XTP and the hardcast WFN, I wouldn't argue much over a choice, but I slightly prefer the XTP. I have recovered expanded XTPs from buffalo retaining more than 90 percent of their weight and expanded to ragged diameters ranging from .640 to 800 inches. On the other hand, I once recovered a .475 420-grain WFN after it had penetrated the length of an Argentine buffalo to his hip, then turned and went halfway down the leg. It could be resized, reloaded and shot again. It's the only hardcast .475 bullet I've ever recovered.

Obviously the recoil and power of the full-charge .475 Linebaugh revolver is more than necessary for the hunting of deer- and hog-size animals. Nevertheless, it remains my choice for hunting large, dangerous game, or for hunting in situations like the pursuit of African plains game where the big stuff may also be encountered and legally taken.

I will admit to having a sentimental favorite the last 10 years or so. Not because it has any magic powers; I just like it. I load it lighter than my .475 Linebaughs, yet

A Ken O'Neill favorite is this specially built Freedom Arms Model 83 in .475 Linebaugh with a 4x Leupold. Photo by K. O'Neill

it has killed everything I've shot with it, up through bison, and done it handily. That favorite is the Freedom Arms .500 Wyoming Express.

I admit to having a great passion for handgun hunting bears, buffalo and the great cats. However, I've also spent many a day in my life hunting another favorite game animal, the squirrel. I own a pair of scoped Freedom Arms revolvers for this pastime, but I think my sentimental favorite here is a stainless 9.5-inch Ruger Single Six that I've owned for more than 40 years, campaigned hard in Silhouette matches, and then had my old friend Gordon Logan gussie up with a series of his aesthetic touches. After all, good looks don't hurt. – Ken O'Neill

DR. MARK KEY

As told by Dr. Mark Key:

Having hunted with a handgun for just over 20 years now, I've had the privilege to use nearly every reasonably common revolver caliber in existence.

Dr. Key took this mountain lion with one 15-yard shot from his 6-inch Freedom Arms 83 .454 loaded with Barnes Vortex ammo, pushing 260-grain XPBs at 1,640 fps. Photo by M. Key

The .500 Maximum and .475 Maximums are two notable exceptions, along with the Dan Wesson Supermags. In my mind there's big bore, then what I've always termed the "mega mags" and then the lightweights. In the lightweights I would place the .357, the .41 Mag and heretically to some, the .44 Mag (many feel it should be in the big-bore category as I define it).

The big bores start for me at the .45s on up to the smaller .500s. The mega-mags are creatures like the .460 and .500 Smith and Wesson, along with the maximum cartridges, the .45-70 and .450 Marlin from

Magnum Research. With this many excellent revolver hunting choices out there, how do I pick my favorite? This is my line of thinking and how I come to a conclusion.

As far as the lightweights go, my favorite is the .41 Mag. I feel it does everything the .44 Mag does and a lot more than the .357 ever could. It does it with great accuracy and very, very low recoil. Shooting it out of a Freedom Arms Model 83 I can load it to a level above that of a Smith and Wesson Model 29 in .44 mag. However, it provides low-level loads very capable of hunting deer and black bear with less recoil out of the full-size Model 83 than a .357 from a Ruger GP100 platform.

In what I term the big-bore class, my favorite is the .454 Casull. I have used both the .475 and .500 Linebaughs and currently shoot a .500 JRH. There's a lot to love about these calibers. If you just shoot cast bullets, you do not have to look any further. The .454 is, and has been for many years now, my go-to caliber. I have .454 loads with heavy hardcast bullets that put it in the league of the .475 Linebaugh. I also have loads with some premium expandables that I've found to kill as efficiently as any cartridge I've ever used.

The .454's high-pressure loads have caused some concern to some. I feel this has been an inadvertent advantage. Most expandables, and in particular the premium expandables, have to be made with thick jackets to withstand the pressure, and this has allowed for bullets that hold together well and offer excellent penetration, but with expanded diameters from .65 inches up to 1 inch.

As a side note, I do not have bullet-pull problems with the .454 Casull. I use an RCBS sizing die which provides more case tension than other .454 dies. I also have a crimp procedure that I use, which is to start the crimp slightly while seating the bullet. Then I put a heavy crimp on with a Lee Precision factory crimp die. I routinely run 340-grain Beartooth hardcast bullets over 1,700 fps with no bullet pull out of a Freedom Arms 4.75-inch barrel.

As far as the mega-mags go, picking a favorite is a little bit tougher. I love the .460 and the .500 Smith & Wessons. One is bigger, and one is faster. A 325-grain A-frame at 1,950 fps will expand and penetrate extremely well, but the .500 will push a large 400-plus-grain slug easily over 1,600 fps. Both have loads that will kill anything that walks. I give the edge to the .500 due to one platform, and that is X-frame with the 6.5-inch half under-lug barrel. It is similar in dimension

This Cape buffalo was shot by Dr. Mark Key in South Africa with a 6-inch Freedom Arms Model 83 in .454 Casull stoked with 325-grain Swift A-frames at 1,550 fps. The revolver is topped with an Ultradot.

and a touch heavier than a Ruger Super Redhawk. To me, it is not unwieldy, not "clunky" and brings as much firepower as one can find in a revolver that can be toted through the mountains.

So how do I size these guns up and pick just one as my favorite? I factor in a given cartridge's ability to kill anything that walks. I take into account the number of available platforms. I also consider the availability of bullets both in gun stores and online, but also in gun stores around the globe where I have hunted. I also factor in how many roles a given cartridge can fill. In that vein, I pick the .454 Casull as my favorite big-bore revolver hunting round. It offers the widest variety of loads. There's .44 Mag- and .45 Colt-level loads available. I have the ability with the Freedom Arms to have .45 ACP and .45 Colt cylinders, and I do have them for most of my Freedom Arms revolvers. There are very flat, fast 240-grain loads available, along with the industry standard 300-grain expandables at 1,650 fps. There are hardcast loads available from 265 grains up to 400 grains. There are also Punch bullet loads offered from Grizzly Cartridge. I have found .454 loads in gun stores and hardware stores in Alaska. I've also found them in Vryburg, South Africa, in a gun store, though only the .44 Mag and .454 Casull were available. My favorite factory load would be Federal or CorBon's 300-grain A-frame at 1,650 fps (despite federal listing at as a much lower 1,530 fps, which it outperforms through the chrony by over 100 fps).

My favorite handload is the 325-grain A-frame running right at 1,550 fps. This was the load I used to take my Cape buffalo. It took one shot to get the buff on the ground, and due to self-preservation I put another in him ... then another to prove a point to an old chap that had claimed over and over publicly that a .454 Casull wouldn't penetrate the boss on a Cape buffalo. It did, as well as the whole head of the animal. I guess some rifle hunters never learn.

Would a .475 Linebaugh, .500 Smith & Wesson or a .500 JRH have done the same? Sure, but none offer a nice, light 265-grain hardcast load at 1,200 fps for my daughter to shoot or deer hunt with. None of them offer factory loads for under $30 a box. None of those will ever be on the shelf in South Africa or Alaska. Brass cannot be bought at Cabela's regularly. The .454 runs the gamut if you reload and offers an excellent choice of bullets from monometals, Barnes Busters, hardcasts to premium expandables. This is why it's my all-around favorite. – *Dr. Mark Key*

LARRY WEISHUHN

As told by Larry Weishuhn:

Favorite hunting handgun: Ruger Super Blackhawk Hunter in .44 Magnum, topped with a Zeiss prototype variable, long eye relief or LER scope, which has to date not gone to market. I primarily use Hornady 240-grain XTP ammo.

I started shooting this handgun a short time after it was introduced, while I was the hunting editor for *Handgunning* and also serving on staff with *Shooting Times*. I've used it to shoot some terribly big-bodied elk, as well as black bears, mule deer, many whitetails (including some weighing over 300 pounds live weight), numerous "exotic" deer and antelope, and plains game in South Africa. If I had to get rid of all my other pistols, heaven forbid, this would be the one I'd keep! At the FTW Ranch ranges, I've shot it out to 400 yards and can consistently hit a 12-inch gong at that distance when I'm really shooting a fair amount.

If I need a larger caliber, then it would be the .480 Ruger. I've shot a few things with it, including a zebra in South Texas at what the ranch owner ranged at well over 700 yards. Don't ask me where I held — it was a fluke. We'd chased this zebra for days trying to kill it. It would never offer a reasonable shot. Last afternoon of my stay it stopped at just short of 800 yards. Several of those with me goaded me saying my bullet wouldn't even reach that far if indeed I did shoot. I smiled, turned back toward the zebra, raised the gun high and pulled the trigger on the Ruger Super Redhawk.

It seemed to take forever, but the zebra simply dropped in its tracks. On close inspection, I had hit the thing right behind its ear, severing the spine. It was a lucky shot, with no forethought or range estimation, nor drop or windage adjustments — other than a good high sight hold. Just my day and not the zebra's! – *Larry Weishuhn*

One of Larry's favorites is this Ruger Super Blackhawk Hunter in 44 Magnum, topped with a Zeiss Conquest scope. Photo by L. Weishuhn

BUD RUMMEL

In Bud Rummel's words:

It never fails. Every time I get into a discussion about handgun hunting, I am always asked what my favorite revolver hunting cartridge is, and I have to reply by asking, "To hunt what?" It's very hard for me to pick only one cartridge, as I hunt so many different animals in remote parts of the world in varied types of terrain. Thus, making one, and only one choice, is nearly impossible for me. I can, however, narrow it down to three.

Let me start with whitetail deer in the eastern side of the lower 48 states, where most of the hunting is in thick cover with shots under 75 yards. In this case, my choice is the .44 Magnum. I like this in any style or make revolver as long as it is accurate and able to thread a needle, as a lot of the shots presented are small windows through hardwoods or thick brush.

I like either a single action with a good 1-4x variable-power or a fixed 2x scope. I don't feel I need more magnification for thick cover and short-range hunting. If I am using a double-action revolver, then I like to use a red dot of some kind or one of the scopes mentioned above.

I have a couple of .44 Mag. revolvers right now. Both are by the Smith & Wesson Performance Center, sporting 7.5-inch barrels. On one is a 1-4x Burris posi-lock scope, the other an Aimpoint red dot. I use the Burris scoped model on late-afternoon hunts and the Aimpoint red dot for morning sits. With my aging eyes, I have some difficulty seeing game in low light with the red-dot scopes. I have accepted the fact that I need two rigs set up in two different ways. With both .44s, I use 240-grain cast bullets, giving me sub-MOA accuracy.

If I happen to be hunting over an open field, then I like my .460 S&W Performance Center revolver with a 7.5-inch barrel. It sports a 2-7x power Burris posi-lock scope. This revolver loves Hornady 200-grain FTX ammo, but it also likes Hornady 200-grain SST rounds. I like the performance that I get out of hardcast bullets on thick-boned animals.

My third-favorite revolver cartridge is the .500 S&W Magnum, a round that I have had a lot of experience with. I like this round so much that I have two Smith & Wesson Performance Center revolvers chambered in it. Like before, I have one set up with an Aimpoint red dot and the other with a 4x Leupold scope. Once again, I use the red dot in the morning and the 4x gun in the late afternoon.

The first animal that I took with this round was an American bison. At that time, ammo was very hard to come by and there were not a lot of choices. I chose a 500-grain jacketed factory load. It shot well in this revolver, but I wasn't happy with the results. After a good stalk, I was 33 yards from the huge bull, broadside. I dropped the hammer and, at the shot, the bull hunched up a bit, with not much more reaction than being stung by a bee. The bull turned to his left, taking three steps only to turn and face me.

He put his head down and tried to rake the ground with his right front foot, but couldn't. He then tried to stomp the ground with his left leg but couldn't hold the weight. He was about to try and charge me when a cow walked in front of him, at which time he then turned to his left to follow her, took one step and fell over dead.

Yes, the bullet did the job, but not in a very spectacular fashion. The bull — which stood less than 40 yards from me — could have easily caused some problems. The bullet only penetrated about 12 inches, but did take a good size chunk of the leg and shoulder bone out, retaining 491 grains of weight.

This set me on a mission to find something suitable for the cartridge and bullet for big animals, as I was about to leave for Africa for six months, working the hunting season as a PH (Professional Hunter). My plans were to use this revolver as much as I could on that trip.

I watched a program on TV where an employee of Smith & Wesson was hunting an Alaskan brown bear with the .500 Smith & Wesson. I saw this gentleman at the SHOT show and asked him what he used on his bear. His reply was CorBon's 440-grain hardcast. I was very fortunate to find that my .500 with the red dot loved this ammo, putting three shots in a group consistently under an inch at 100 yards off sand bags. I used this combo in Africa on several species of plains game, plus Cape buffalo and an African lioness. I had great results on my buffalo with this ammo, taking a shot at 44 yards, dropping him in his tracks. With the buff at a slight angle, the bullet went in behind the left front shoulder, passing through to hit the right front shoulder blade, deflecting forward and lodging under the skin on the right side of its chest.

I shot the lioness behind its left front shoulder. At the shot, the big cat jumped straight up in the air, walked three steps forward, then turned, took three more steps, turned again and took three more steps. She then stretched out down on the ground as gingerly as could be, then expired. The 440 hardcast bullet had taken the top of her heart completely off.

To review all of this, my favorite cartridge for Africa and Alaska would be the .500 Smith and Wesson, for longer-range hunting the .460 S&W, and with any hunting at 75 yards or less for 150-pound animals and under, the old faithful .44 Magnum. – *Bud Rummel*

DAVID BRADSHAW

As told by David Bradshaw:

Twenty years after Remington introduced the .44 Remington Magnum — and Smith & Wesson the revolver chambered for the new cartridge — handgun silhouette competition came along and imposed discipline on magnum handgunning. Low-powered or inaccurate revolvers were out.

It seems the .45 Colt cannot be discussed without reference to the .44 Magnum, the big .45 touted as doing everything better than the .44. The truth is, the .44 Mag. does not need to be compared with any other cartridge. It stands on its own merits, despite the fact that its grandfather was the .45 Colt and the early .44 Magnums were made by stretching .44 Special brass to .45 Colt length.

The .44 Magnum has high intrinsic accuracy and gives up nothing to the .44 Special. It boosts velocity and flattens trajectory. It's very accurate and isn't load-sensitive which, in this shooter's experience, cannot be said of the .45 Colt. A top revolver is capable of five-shots in 2 inches at 100 yards. A scope helps prove this. Such a revolver is good for 5 inches at 200 meters (219 yards) and can play the silhouette game to the highest level.

You owe it to the game animal to know the accuracy of your revolver, and the only way to learn that is to practice like you mean business. Range must be learned beyond comfortable distances at which game is expected to be engaged.

My first buck and many thereafter were taken with a Smith & Wesson M29 with a 6.5-inch barrel and factory red ramp front and square-notch rear sights. I swaged a pure lead core into a copper half-jacket to form a semi-wadcutter. The bearing surface was half copper, half soft lead, and would start to lead the bore at 1,100 fps. No matter. Deep-seating the bullet over 17 grains of Hercules 2400, to crimp .030 to .060 inches above the bearing surface and using a CCI 350 primer averaged 1,060 fps. The effect on a lung-shot whitetail was nearly immediate, with the animal folding at 20 to 50 yards, sometimes sooner, seldom more. Neither Special nor Magnum, I call it a mid-magnum, suitable for indefinite consumption in the Model 29.

A feature of tracking a deer in the snowy mountains, you cannot forever be downwind of it. Wind swirls. Once you jump a deer and pick up the pace, the animal's in possession of some personal data. Your scent, your sound, your appearance —intimate details of the pursuing predator dance in its brain, just as thermals swirl the mountain. A bullet with forgiveness belongs in your revolver. That forgiveness is not there to forgive sloppy shooting. It is there to override the will to live in a supreme athlete.

I prefer a bullet that expands — or acts like it — to spread a shock wave. JHPs of 180 and 200 grains do this, but penetration on an angle shot or large deer predictably suffers. A good 240-grain JHP launched at 1,300-1,400 fps works better. For heavier deer there is nothing wrong with a 300 JHP built on a soft core and pushed with Win 296/H110 (both are 296). Of late, heavier cast bullets that are powder coated then baked at 400 degrees for 20 minutes demonstrate an aptitude for blunting into a headed wadcutter. Plastic deformation results from baking and consequent annealing. "PC" cast bullets are not greased and do not lead the bore.

Were a .44 Magnum to pick up a magazine today, surrounded by huge revolver rounds, it might feel put out to pasture. But the .44 doesn't care to read. All it knows is honest work. – *David Bradshaw*

JAMES SWIDRYK

Unlike most, James actually started hunting with handguns initially, and it wasn't until much later that he even considered using a rifle. He'd bought his first firearm in 1973, a Colt Government Model 1911, and was hooked from the start. Eight years later, in the early '80s, he participated in his first handgun hunt after being invited by his foreman to pursue deer in Pennsylvania. James didn't own a rifle, but discovered it was legal to hunt with a revolver. From that point on, he took 13 deer in succession before his first with a rifle.

Then there was a seismic event that rocked him to his very core. James was on a hunt on the YO Ranch in Texas, and was by chance paired up with a certain Bill Grover — the Bill Grover, of Texas Longhorn Arms fame. James, young and impressionable and not yet the confident hunter he is today, was more than a little nervous to be in the company of such greatness. He was particularly intimidated when he witnessed Bill hop out of the hunting vehicle, take a knee, steady his revolver, squeeze and drop a deer in its tracks, all in one smooth motion. The shot was measured at 165 yards and delivered with open iron sights! This one event steeled James' resolve to be all that he could be with a sixgun in his hand.

He had the good fortune of handgun hunting Africa on a number of occasions, as well as Alaska. Now that he is retired, he has even more free time on his hands and even more hunts on the docket. I asked James what his favorite revolver, caliber, bullet and load were, as well as his favorite game animal to hunt.

In James' own words:

"As much as I enjoy hunting wild boar I would have to say that my favorite big-game animal to hunt is brown bear. To be stalking through the alders of southern Alaska is a thrill in and of itself. The .454 Casull has taken most of the game I`ve shot. A 300-grain Swift A-frame over 30.5 grains of H110 is a sure killer when placed in the right spot. However, the more I use the .500 Wyoming Express, the more I like it. Being the first handgun hunter to take a Cape buffalo with this cartridge is an honor I will always hold dear. I used Grizzly Cartridge's 420-grain Punch bullet to take the buff, but closer to home I load a 325-grain A-frame over 30.0 grains of LilGun to make half-inch holes in whatever I shoot."

James shot this kudu at 50 yards with a Freedom Arms 83 in .454 Casull. The big gun was loaded with CorBon 320 grain Penetrator ammo. One shot was all that was necessary.

questions | answers

LYNN THOMPSON
Proprietor of Cold Steel

I recently caught up with Lynn Thompson of Cold Steel to ask him a few questions pertaining to his preferences for handgun hunting.

Q: When did you start handgun hunting and why?

A: There was this article I read in *Guns & Ammo* magazine sometime around the mid-'80s by Ross Seyfried where he took a custom-built .45 Colt revolver to Africa on a Cape buffalo hunt — without backup. When I read that, I really wanted to see if I could do it myself. Living in a country that is losing its machismo, I thought hunting with a handgun was a celebration of machismo.

In '86 I attended the Safari Club International show, and I talked to a vendor and expressed that I wanted to shoot Cape buffalo with a handgun. He laughed at me. The next year I brought pictures from my successful handgun safari to the show, and I found that particular outfitter. I showed him my pictures, and he was not only dumbfounded, but also embarrassed, as he should have been.

Q: What is your favorite big-game hunting handgun?

A: Without a doubt, my Freedom Arms 83 in .454 Casull. Not only is the accuracy superior, you cannot hurt it! It will digest full-power .454 Casull loads for breakfast, lunch and dinner and come back for

When Lynn Thompson's Freedom Arms .454 Casull barks, large animals fall, as is evidenced by this white rhinoceros. Photo by L. Thompson

more. My favorite load is an off-the-shelf one by Hornady, featuring a 300-grain XTP at something over 1,600 fps. It penetrates really well.

Q: What is your favorite big game to hunt?

A: Cape buffalo is right up near the top, along with elephant and hippo. I like hunting the big cats, too, but they are hard to stop when things go wrong. They present a small, fast target when they come for you.

Q: What was your most memorable handgun hunt to date?

A: There have been many, but my bull elephant in '92 stands out the most for me — and my wife who was filming. It didn't help that I had a premonition I would get killed. We got so close — less than 20 yards — and we didn't have adequate backup. It took four CorBon 360-grain Penetrators, but it worked out. I'm happy to say my premonition didn't come true!

Q: Any last thoughts to impart to the neophyte handgun hunter?

A: Practice, practice, practice and then practice some more. If you don't practice, don't bother wasting your time. You should be able to hit a 12-inch circle at 100 meters with open sights. You need trigger time to build muscle reflex so that your body acts without the mind intervening. You need to have confidence in your sight alignment and trigger squeeze, and you get that confidence through practice.

One more thing for the doubters out there. Don't judge me by your incompetence. In other words, don't impose your limitations on others. Just because you can't shoot a handgun well doesn't mean I can't. I practice eight hours a week to get good and to stay good. If you really want to handgun hunt, you need to fully dedicate yourself to it.

Another outstanding trophy, an enormous hippopotamus, taken by Lynn Thompson and his Freedom Arms 83 in .454 Casull. Photo by L. Thompson

The Handgun Hunters

MAX PRASAC

Choosing a favorite with so many great options is a difficult task. So, I took the easy way out and chose several. Hey, it's my book, and I can do what I want — at least here!

First up and all-around favorite is the .45 Colt. If ever there was a versatile big-game chambering, the modern .45 Colt is it. Even in its black-powder days it was a force to be reckoned with. Ironically, cowboy-action-type loads don't meet the black-powder loads of the Old West. We've discussed this elsewhere in this book, but the .45 Colt is held to a 14,000-psi maximum to make it safe for use in the many old .45 Colt revolvers in circulation that cannot withstand high pressure levels. That said, chamber a Ruger in .45 Colt, and the old warhorse caliber is a different animal. I am not advocating turning the .45 Colt into a .454 Casull, but turning up the wick to the 30,000-psi level makes for one mean hunting round. More and more ammunition manufacturers are producing +P-type loads in .45 Colt that have firmly moved the .45 Colt into the modern world.

I normally use two bullet weights in my .45 Colts, a 335-grain WFN and a 360-grain WFN. I push the 335s up over 1,300 fps and limit the 360s to the 1,200 fps range. Both are tremendously accurate, and put a real hurt on large game. My hammer of choice is Ruger's 5.5-inch stainless steel Bisley available through Williams Shooter Supply. The barrel length balances well, and the accuracy has been excellent. I recently had the opportunity to use a real heavyweight loading by Garrett Cartridges of Texas in .45 Colt on a water buffalo that went 2,000-pounds. The 405-grain bullets performed admirably.

My next favorite is the .480 Ruger. This is arguably one of the top all-around big-game cartridges available commercially. It can be loaded with light bullets to high velocities for use on small and thin-skinned game, or you can load it heavy for pachyderm and everything in between. Even when loaded hot, 425s at 1,200 fps for example, this cartridge offers minimal abuse to the shooter. Yes, I use the term "minimal" rather loosely. When chambered in the Super Redhawk (the first revolver ever to be chambered in this cartridge), abuse is further minimized as there is sufficient weight in that revolver, and the double-action design sends the recoil straight back into the web of your hand, making for easy control. 2015 was the year Ruger finally gave us a single-action .480 Ruger. My two favorite firearms in .480 Ruger are my 7.5-inch Super Redhawk and my newer Super Blackhawk with a 6.5-inch barrel. One of my favorite loads is a factory offering by Buffalo Bore consisting of a 410-grain WFN running around 1,200 fps. This load is serious big-game medicine.

The author took this large water buffalo in Argentina with a Super Redhawk in .480 Ruger at about 30 yards.

Left: This spike buck was taken in West Virginia with the author's custom .475 Linebaugh Super Redhawk.

Below: The author considers this custom JRH-built .500 Maximum to be one of his all-time favorite hunting revolvers, loaded with a 525-grain WFN from Cast Performance. Photo by V. Ricardel

My last favorite in this triumvirate is the .500 JRH. I was divided between the .500 Linebaugh and the .500 JRH, and the JRH won by a very narrow margin and boiled down to bullet availability. Let's face it: there are many more bullets available in .500-inch diameter than .511-inch diameter. I have had a number of revolvers chambered in this cartridge but have since narrowed my collection down to two, a factory BFR with a 5.5-inch barrel and a custom Ruger Bisley by JRH Advanced Gunsmithing, also equipped with a 5.5-inch barrel. The BFR has an Ultradot L/T reflexive red-dot sight on top of the factory scope base; the Bisley is running open iron sights. My favorite load for everything consists of a 440-grain flat-nosed hardcast bullet over a stiff charge of 296. It clocks right around 1,350 fps and is deadly accurate and incredibly proficient at dispatching game.

Addendum

I have owned a custom JRH-built .500 Maximum for a number of years now. The recoil is heavy, burning 38 grains of 1680 under a 525-grain WFN bullet, but the gun is accurate. And despite the additional length of the Maximum frame, it handles really well. It sports a Bisley grip frame adorned with beautiful custom English walnut grips and a 6.5-inch barrel with a barrel band.

I've shot a couple head of game with it, including a wild hog and a large black bear. Shortly thereafter, it found a place in my safe, the novelty wearing off with other revolvers taking up positions of importance ahead of the Maximum. That said, I dusted it off last October, located some handloads I had stashed on a shelf (525 grain WFNs over the aforementioned 38 grains of 1680), and dragged it the 1,500 miles to Hondo, Texas, to use on water buffalo. I killed a large cow with it and stopped a wounded Watusi with bad intent on its mind, the Maximum putting both animals down with decisiveness.

I can't with good conscience put together my favorites list without including the brutally effective .500 Maximum. It's an extreme caliber for extreme cases where compromise is unacceptable.

IT'S BACK!

From the publisher of *Gun Digest*, the "World's Greatest Gun Book," returns the "World's Greatest Handloading Book." That's right – the *Handloader's Digest* 19th edition is back and it's better than ever with more in-depth features, industry resources and eye-catching photos. Whether it's information on this year's new ammunition reloading equipment or detailed articles on obscure wildcat cartridges, you're certain to find what you're looking for in this authoritative resource.

- Learn how to reload ammo
- Search for new techniques and equipment
- Expand your understanding of ammunition and ballistics

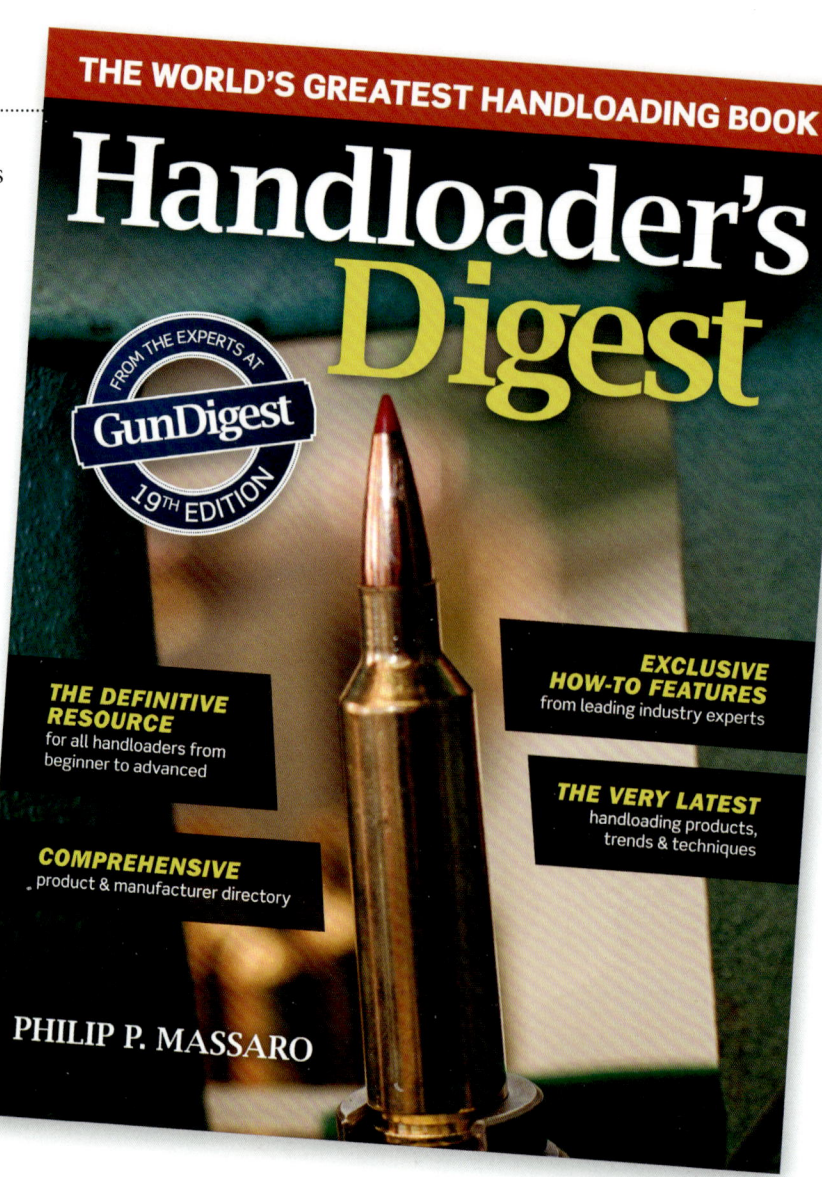

THE WORLD'S GREATEST HANDLOADING BOOK

Handloader's Digest

FROM THE EXPERTS AT GunDigest — 19TH EDITION

THE DEFINITIVE RESOURCE for all handloaders from beginner to advanced

COMPREHENSIVE product & manufacturer directory

EXCLUSIVE HOW-TO FEATURES from leading industry experts

THE VERY LATEST handloading products, trends & techniques

PHILIP P. MASSARO

Visit **GunDigestStore.com**
or 855-840-5120